THE WORLD OF THE

GLADIATOR

THE WORLD OF THE GLADIATOR

SUSANNA SHADRAKE

TEMPUS

FOR MY FATHER, GEORGE ALBERT MOORE
INVICTUS

All illustrations are the work of Dan Shadrake unless otherwise indicated

First published 2005

Tempus Publishing Limited
The Mill, Brimscombe Port,
Stroud, Gloucestershire, GL5 2QG
www.tempus-publishing.com

British Library Cataloguing in Publication Data.
A catalogue record for this book is available from the British Library.

ISBN 0 7524 3442 X

Typesetting and origination by Tempus Publishing Limited
Printed in Great Britain

CONTENTS

I

RITUAL COMBAT: THE EVOLUTION OF THE GLADIATOR

And human blood would be an enjoyable sight.
(Seneca, *De Tranquillitate Animi*)

To us, the gladiator has become a metaphor for Rome, a kind of shorthand way of saying what is generally perceived as the Roman attitude to life and death. The image of the gladiator conveys the whole sweep of casual cruelty; the cheapness of life, the sheer incomprehensibility of a civilisation apparently built on blood and suffering (*1*). In looking at all of this, we must be careful of imposing our own values on Rome; they do not necessarily reflect what actually goes on in our own society, and certainly have no place in one born nine centuries before Christ.

Nowadays, the idea of two armed men fighting each other to the death as an entertainment and a spectacle for a cheering crowd is held up as an affront to the civilised mind. For a couple of seconds we can sign up to that belief, before the modern equivalents to gladiatorial combat start to occur to us. Hypocrisy is an ancient vice still practised today. Living as we do in a society where the most popular forms of mass entertainment use increasingly graphic images of bloody violence and pointless cruelty, we are in no position to assert our moral superiority. So perhaps the history of gladiators, and especially their origins, can provide relevant and useful insights towards that most modern of preoccupations – the quest to 'know ourselves'. Many writers through the centuries, even to the present day, have felt drawn to speculate on the meaning of the brutality played out on the sand of the arena, and especially what it reveals of human nature.

The pathology and practice of ritualised and institutionalised violence within an organised society deserve closer scrutiny, not least because of what they tell us about the extraordinary human ability to transform something 'bad' like violent death into something 'good' such as public reassurance in time of crisis. The truth is that we are just as fascinated by the prospect of two men locked in a life

1 Third-century AD tombstone depicting *retiarius* type of gladiator, showing several of his victories. *Museo Nuovo Capitolino*

and death struggle as our ancient Roman counterparts in the Colosseum were; the insatiable public appetite for celluloid gore, celebrity mayhem and graphic newsreel footage bears witness to that. The modern excuse that we are too civilised to make people fight to the death makes it sound as if there would be no spectators if such a match were actually staged, when in fact common sense tells us that tickets would fly out of the touts' hands. In fact, the very word 'fascinate', coming as it does from the Latin verb *fascino*, meaning 'to bewitch, enchant', and additionally, with *fascinum* being a phallus-shaped amulet to ward off the evil eye, as well as slang for the male member itself, gives ample indication of the kind of influence such a spectacle, whether real or simulated, has on the spectators, whatever century they happen to find themselves in. It must be better to look steadily into the face of the monster than to turn away and deny its existence.

After all, the Romans, in several hundred years and body counts running into many hundreds of thousands, had the business of bloodshed as performance down to a fine art. That cannot be airbrushed out of the picture if there is to be any sincere attempt to grasp the total reality of Rome. Political correctness has no place in the ancient world; indeed, the phrase would have made no sense to a Roman, to whom politics were not chopped up and kept in a separate box from the rest of life. To understand the gladiatorial phenomenon, we must put aside our modern perspective and sensitivities, or we will miss the whole point of all that spilt blood.

Despite our tendency to interpret the past by using the present as a template, the gladiators and their world seem to exert as strong a pull now as they did then. For a start, the audience's appetite for endless reruns of *Spartacus* and, more recently, *Gladiator*, has not abated. They supply us, however historically flawed they may be, with our own sanitised version of the heroes of the arena. However, it would be a mistake to think, just because we share a predilection for bloody spectacle, that our cultures are the same and that the parallels are obvious, although it is tempting to think that the Romans would enjoy the celluloid cruelty regularly served up to us. Over several centuries, the Western European mindset has developed into a highly analytical, demarcating tradition, where every aspect of life is identified, labelled, categorised. It is important to remember that the Romans would not understand or recognise our insistence on separating the private and public aspects of life, such as religion, politics, social interaction, emotions. For them, daily life was a complex interweaving of all of those influences and more besides, in a way that seems utterly alien to us now. The interaction of social, political and religious spheres made public life in Rome a subtle balancing act.

Gladiators were just one of many cultural expressions that Romans had at their disposal, quite a few of which we would find hard to stomach, such as sacrificing puppies to avert mould growth on garden plants. This should be kept in mind whenever we feel the urge to make any moral judgments on the bloody business of the arena.

It would be satisfying to be able to follow the trail right back through the centuries to its source, to point at one thing and say with confidence, 'yes, this is definitely how gladiators began', in order to understand what gave rise to the phenomenon of the *munus gladiatorum*, the gladiatorial combat, in the first place. However, the sum total of all the evidence, when drawn from the literary, iconographic and archaeological fields, unfortunately fails to point in any one particular direction. No matter how much we may long to solve the mystery with a convenient and tidy explanation, we may have to accept that the gladiator's origins can never be pinpointed with absolute certainty, unless or until some fresh discovery is made.

In addition, we may be guilty of a failure of imagination in assuming that the development of the gladiatorial games, the *munera*, can be attributed to a single cause or easily explained by one set of circumstances in the first place. Very few forms of entertainment or sport owe their birth to a specific and singular event. Why should gladiators be any different? They arose out of a very specific set of conditions, a combination of history and circumstance. The background for gladiatorial combat is Rome itself.

ROME'S FIRST GLADIATORS

Down by the Tiber, where the river bends round the Tiberine Island, the Palatine hill overlooks the *Forum Boarium*, the old cattle market of Rome (*2*). It is a public space now, smaller than the *Forum Romanum*, but big enough for the modest combats about to take place. Today human livestock may be slaughtered here, as three pairs of gladiators prepare to fight in honour of one of Rome's important public figures, the recently deceased ex-consul Junius Brutus Pera. His sons, Decimus and Marcus have put on these combats as part of the funeral games, as a duty and an obligation they owe to the *manes*, the shade or spirit of their dead father. The men who are to fight aren't even called *gladiatores* in the earliest sources; instead, they are known as *bustuarii*, from the Latin for a tomb or a funeral pyre, *bustum*. Not that they are necessarily going to fight by the side of the tomb or the pyre, though they often did; their name derives from their association with the funeral rites, whenever and wherever they were conducted.

It is 264 BC. This is the accepted date for the earliest record of gladiatorial combat, the *munus gladiatorum*, at Rome itself. Whether there were crowds of onlookers, in the manner of a public event, or just mourning family and friends,

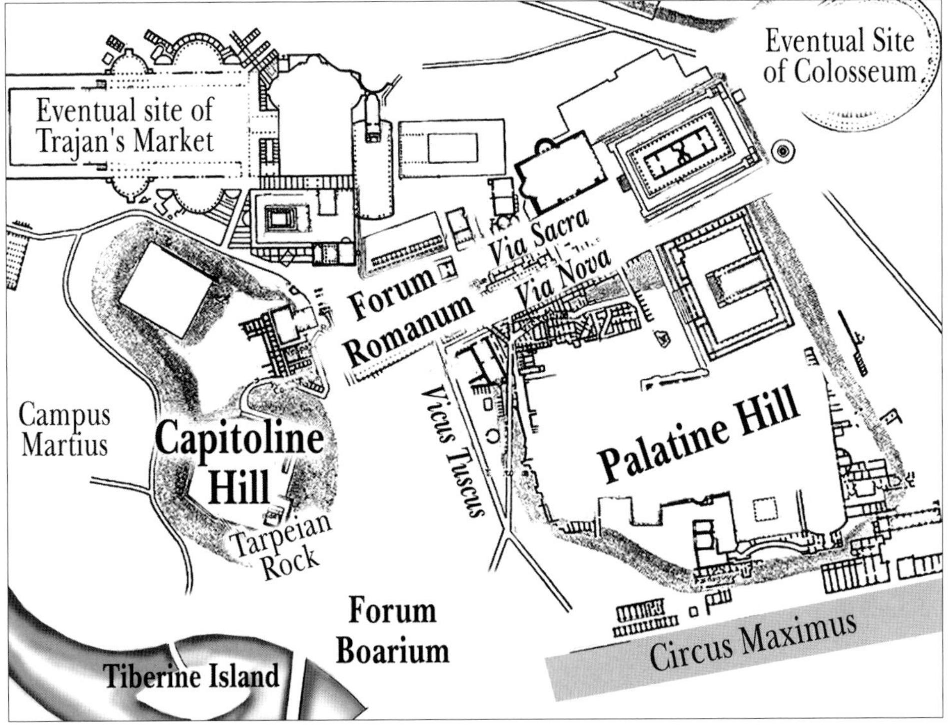

2 Map of early central Rome BC, showing the location of the first gladiator contests at the *Forum Boarium*

is not recorded. Whether they sat on hastily erected bleachers, or just stood in the ancient windswept forum to witness the performance of a rite that would spill blood to purify the pollution of death and propitiate the dead man's spirit, it is impossible to say.

In fact, even the identity of the deceased is a mystery. Some writers have called him Junius Brutus Pera, but it is possible that he was another illustrious Roman by the name of Decimus Junius Brutus Scaeva, who, as consul in 292 BC, had defeated the northern Faliscan tribes; alternatively, he was father to the Decimus Junius Pera who, as consul in 266 BC, had military success against Italic tribes. All three possibilities have their supporters, but the confusion serves as a reminder that certainty on this subject as with so much else in the world of the gladiator is elusive. It is interesting that in all three cases the potential honoree had connections to the consulship, and recent military success.

What is beyond doubt is that this duty to the dead, usually performed at the end of full mourning, at least nine days later, was an expensive business. It would not have formed part of the average funeral, as the cost of using several captives or slaves to fight in the *munus* would have been unaffordable for all but the very rich. From its inception, the *munus* was the prerogative of the elite, the wealthy, the bluebloods, and as such, it was always about much more than an obligation to the dead.

It has been suggested that Rome developed these violent contests spontaneously from within its own culture. There has been a tendency, both in modern times and by the Romans themselves, to attribute gladiatorial combats to outside influence, typically Etruscan or Campanian, but the truth could be even simpler than that; perhaps the *munus* did in fact emerge from within Roman society, firstly, as an expression of its piety and religiosity, but then becoming an end in itself, satisfying the crowd's naked love of spectacle. It is yet another theory to add to the list of potential explanations.

What we do know is that in 264 BC, which just happens to be the year that Rome first picked a fight with mighty Carthage, the occurrence of gladiators at the funeral games for one of Rome's illustrious dead is considered worthy of inclusion in the historical record (*3*).

To put it into the historical context, the record shows that, at a time of great uncertainty for Rome in the very year that saw the start of the First Punic War, gladiators had fought at the *ludi funebres*, the funeral games of a high status Roman, who had either been consul himself, or whose son had held that office; is it possible that those gladiators were prisoners of war from an earlier conflict, who were then put on show for a demonstrably morale-boosting performance of Rome versus the rest of the world?

There is strong evidence, however, for rites of execution and even human sacrifice being performed in Rome long before gladiators appear in the historical record; the common theme is all of these activities involve the shedding of blood, and therefore they were all in some sense propitiary offerings, intended to ward

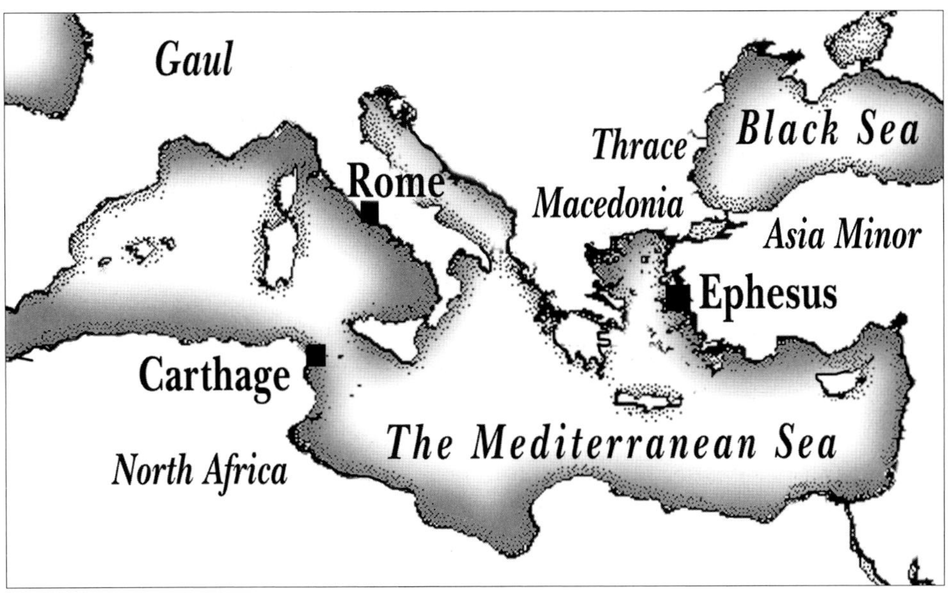

3 Western Mediterranean, showing Rome in relation to Carthage

off the gods' displeasure at the commission of a capital offence, avert disaster in time of crisis, or pay tribute to the shade of a dead relative. The Romans were familiar with bloodshed of all kinds. As Bauman put it, there were no bleeding hearts in ancient Rome; *misericordia*, the emotion of pity, was thought unmanly compared to its rational cousin, *clementia*, clemency, which was essentially prompted by reason rather than emotion.

The Christian author, Tertullian, certainly seemed to have believed that there was an element of human sacrifice in the *munera*, replacing a more barbaric, archaic form:

> The ancients thought that by this sort of spectacle they rendered a service to the dead, after they had tempered it with a more cultured form of cruelty. For of old, in the belief that the souls of the dead are propitiated with human blood, they used at funerals to sacrifice captives or slaves of poor quality whom they bought. Afterwards it seemed good to obscure their impiety by making it a pleasure. So after the persons procured had been trained in such arms as they had and as best they might – their training was to learn to be killed! – they did them to death on the appointed day at the tombs. So they found comfort for death in murder.
> (Tertullian, *De Spectaculis* 12.2-3)

The danger here, of course, is in taking Tertullian at face value. As a Christian apologist of the second century AD and a vociferous critic of pagan Roman *mores*, his explanation of how the ancient custom of human sacrifice was superseded by the slightly less impious one of death by gladiator combat could be regarded as a partisan construction. However, he was from North Africa; Carthage had a centuries-old tradition of human sacrifice to Baal-Hammon and Tanit, of which he was intensely aware. It is at least worth considering that he might be writing from local knowledge rather than outright bias.

The combats at the *Forum Boarium*, modest though they were in comparison to the lavish shows that evolved from them, had to have had some special significance to be deemed worthy of inclusion in the public records. Why mention them otherwise? Nevertheless, they were a world away from the organised spectacles so beloved of the Roman mobs in later centuries.

AB URBE CONDITA

There are two ways of looking at Roman history. One is how the Romans saw it; the other, what we have pieced together from the archaeology, the written sources, together with the pictorial, iconographic and historiographical evidence. The history of the gladiatorial games is buried within that larger history of Rome. With few exceptions, of which Livy was the most notable, Roman historians tended to be senators or men of high rank. The aim of the Roman historian was primarily to chronicle Roman matters, to preserve the memory of Rome itself and to record and pass on to future generations of Roman citizens the words, deeds and characters of her famous men. The history of Rome was not purely secular, either; it was concerned with how the gods interacted with Rome, and so a good historian of public affairs would ideally have participated in the conduct of religious and ceremonial practices that were felt to be so important to the safety and prosperity of Rome, practices that included gladiatorial games. Rome's historians tried to record not only what happened in their lifetimes, but also to reconstruct Rome's past with whatever material they could find.

Their conclusions tended not to be challenged, and in due course became accepted history. By appreciating their methods, we can see why the origins of gladiators, as with so much else of Rome's history, were gradually obscured as the annals and chronicles of public life assimilated errors, conjecture and personal interpretation as if they were facts.

For our purposes, an understanding of the history of Rome is vital as it provides the impetus, as well as the backdrop, for the cultural phenomenon of gladiator combats. That history falls neatly into three periods, identifiable by the type of government in each: the monarchy, or 'the rule of seven kings', the republic, and the empire.

Romulus, the legendary founder of Rome in 753 BC, was the first of these kings. Their rule covers two and a half centuries from 753 to 510 BC, which stretches them rather thinly over that timespan.

We should remember also that these were not kings in the modern sense; rather, they were like clan-chieftains, overlords who headed their family groups, and were recognised as leaders of their communities. Kingship was not necessarily hereditary; each new king had to get himself elected by the assembly of 30 clans, the *comitia curia*. Once he was acclaimed as king, he could exercise his power in political, military and religious matters. The Romans called this concept *imperium*; anyone invested with this divine authority had the right to give orders to those of lower status, and to expect obedience to those orders. It was a vague, all-encompassing power that gave its holder the right to impose their authority by force of arms, not just within the community, but also on any neighbouring peoples who were deemed to have challenged it. It incorporated conquest into the Roman psyche. *Imperium* was the word they came to use to describe their domination of the world.

The symbol of *imperium* was the *fasces*, a bundle of rods bound round an axe, which was carried by officials known as *lictores* in front of the ruler (*4*). The *fasces* may well have been an Etruscan symbol, representing the sacred right of the king to punish and execute anyone opposing his authority. The Greek historian Strabo records that Rome had inherited other symbols of political status whilst under the Etruscan hegemony:

> It is said that the triumphal garb and that of the consuls and basically that of any magistrate was brought there from Tarquinia, as were the *fasces*, trumpets, sacrificial rituals, divination

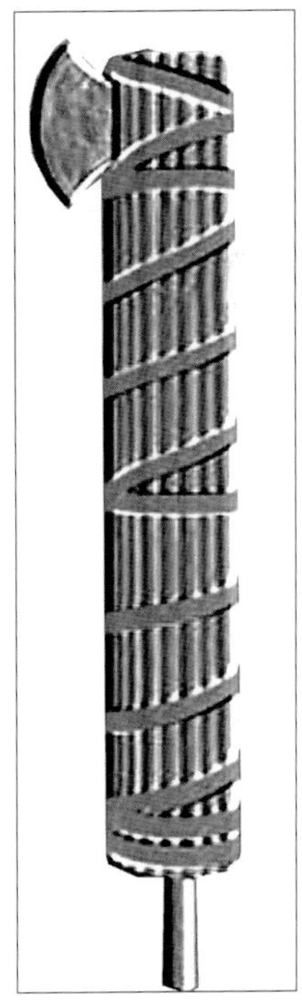

4 *Fasces*, the symbol of *imperium*, a bundle of rods tied around an axe used in state ceremony

> and music, as they are used publicly by the Romans.
> (Strabo, *Geographica*)

If some Romans believed that their symbols of state were Etruscan in origin, this says as much about their ambivalent attitude to the power of the state as it does about the historical truth of Strabo's suggestion. By the same argument, their attribution of elements of gladiatorial combat to an Etruscan source is possibly indicative of a Roman desire to keep the events of the *munera* from polluting their native traditions.

Nothing certain is known about the first four legendary kings, but the historicity of the last three is not in doubt. Etruscan expansion in 616 BC brought Tarquinius Priscus, the first of Rome's Etruscan kings, and it is during his reign that the major civic building works began. When he was murdered in 578 BC, his successor, Servius Tullius, who was a Latin, not an Etruscan, seized power by force in a popular uprising. His main contribution to Rome was to create the first citizen army, the first legion, with a reported 4000 infantry and 600 cavalry.

The last king of Rome, Tarquinius Superbus, was again an Etruscan, but he behaved so tyrannically that the outraged aristocracy expelled him, after a sexual scandal involving his son, who had raped a Latin woman called Lucretia. There followed a power struggle; it was not that the aristocracy were anti-Etruscan, but they declared themselves to be against all forms of tyranny, and set themselves up as Rome's protectors.

A new form of government was devised; they created the Senate, a body that could bestow the *imperium* by election on two magistrates, later known as the consuls, whose rule would last only for a year. Each had the right to check the other's actions. The republic (509–31 BC) was established.

Although Etruscan rule had ended with the ejection of Tarquin the Proud, the Etruscans had overseen the creation of a programme of civic works and urban development that would be carried on by the Romans for the next thousand years. They had bequeathed to Rome the idea of the city-state. They left behind other helpful items, such as their alphabet, (though not their mysterious language, being neither Greek nor Latin, and which is unlike the other Indo-European based languages of the peoples of the Italic peninsula), their Greek-influenced art and culture, religious rituals and ceremonies, mythology, methods of civil administration, their calendar, sophisticated agricultural methods, a love of chariot-racing, and a number of feats of construction, notably the main sewer draining into the Tiber, the Cloaca Maxima, the Circus Maximus, for the aforementioned races, a number of impressive temples and the Forum Romanum. Because of this legacy, Rome went from being an insignificant trading settlement to a burgeoning city, inhabited by Latins, but underwritten by Etruscan culture.

Despite the headstart this inheritance had given them, the Romans always remained ambivalent about the Etruscans. The historian Herodotus

(490-420 BC) thought that the Etruscans were not an indigenous people of Italy, and that they were in some way 'oriental', coming from Lydia (now Turkey) in Asia Minor. The Lydian link proved fictitious. Instead, it is believed that the eastern influences so marked in the Etruscan culture came to them by way of the Syrian and Asian products traded by the Greeks in the Campanian markets and colonies.

Modern archaeology has established beyond doubt that the Etruscans were an indigenous people of the Bronze Age Villanovan culture: their civilisation originated within Italy itself, not some mysterious part of Asia Minor: they just happened to speak a language unlike the other tongues of the Italic tribes, and to have developed a culture heavy with eastern ornament (5). This always marked them out as exotic and alien.

After breaking free of the Etruscan yoke in around 510 BC, Rome spent the next 250 years in an almost constant state of warfare as it struggled to dominate its many rival city-states and the assorted tribes of the Italian peninsula (*6*). Finally, in 290 BC, Rome subjugated its most formidable enemies, the Samnites, an organised and powerful people from the mountainous interior of Italy. By 272 BC, the entire peninsula was under Roman control, and prisoners of war were so plentiful that the terms 'Samnite' and 'gladiator' were practically synonymous.

5 Etruscan warriors and a woman of rank, possibly a priestess. Bronze statuettes from around 590 BC. *Photograph: courtesy of Misha Nedeljkovich, College of Journalism and Mass Communication, University of Oklahoma USA*

6 Tribes of the Italian peninsular 1000–500 BC

MYTH AS HISTORY

Roman historians did not have, and would probably not have welcomed, the modern benefit of archaeology to help them piece together their past. Alongside their prosaic, if incomplete, history of dates and places, they used a variety of legends from both Greek and Roman sources to fill in the gaps, rather as we do with King Arthur, and to create their own interpretations of the foundation of Rome; over time, just two versions began to dominate these accounts.

The first of these told of Aeneas, the Trojan prince who escaped from the city of Troy after the Trojan War. To put that event on some sort of historical footing, there is evidence that Bronze Age Troy was indeed destroyed towards the end of the thirteenth century BC, some 500 years before the *Iliad* was composed. Aeneas was a favourite hero of the Etruscans, whose cultural seedcorn was sown deep in the Roman psyche.

In this story, Aeneas and his companions landed on the shores of Italy, settled in Latium and founded the city of Lavinium, while his son, Iulus, founded the first Latin city of Alba Longa. So Aeneas became the father of the Roman people, by establishing a line of kings who conveniently bridged the gap until the birth of Romulus and Remus, and following that, the foundation of Rome.

The Aeneas story was already circulating in Etruria in the sixth century BC; his flight from Troy is depicted on a number of Athenian black-figure vases found there, and the same theme crops up on Etruscan gems and votive statuettes found at the Etruscan town of Veii. It found its ultimate expression in the Augustan epic poem by Virgil, the *Aeneid*.

The second version is the story of Romulus and Remus. At first, some early Roman historians said they were the sons, or grandsons, of Aeneas. Then they started doing the calculations, using 1184 BC, the date of the fall of Troy as fixed by Eratosthenes of Cyrene (275-194 BC) in his *Chronographia*; they realised that from Aeneas to Romulus and Remus was far more than two generations, hence the creative use of a line of Alban kings descended from Aeneas. Some even managed to join the two legends by making Romulus and Remus the product of the rape of the king's daughter, Rhea Silvia, who was a Vestal Virgin, by Mars, god of war. Her offspring were thrown into the river Tiber on the orders of her father, the ruthless king, but ended up on the bank of the river where a she-wolf found them and suckled them. Then a shepherd found them and took them home; when they grew up, they overthrew the tyrant who had tried to do away with them. Because the city of Alba was getting overpopulated, they decided to found a new city. As they quarrelled over who should be the one to give his name to the fledgling city, a fight broke out in which Romulus slew his brother. Another, more common, story has Remus mocking his brother by jumping over the partially-built walls; angered, Romulus kills him, with the prophetic words, 'So perish anyone else who shall jump over my walls.'

The new city would be called Rome, after Romulus. The date the Romans eventually settled on for the foundation is traditionally recorded as 21 April, 753 BC.

Buried deep in these stories, and in their multifarious and inventive offshoots, are grains of truth about Rome's ancient beginnings. The city of Rome is always the focus of the story. The Aeneas legend joins it to the Greek civilization and culture so admired by Rome, and thus to the Etruscans, who had always been susceptible to the charms of Greek culture, and who regarded Aeneas as their hero. The foundation story of the birth of Rome pivots on a rape and a murder, and a fratricide at that. It hints at human sacrifice (the shedding of Remus' blood as a foundation offering, vital for the city's protection and future prosperity), traditions of duelling champions in the heroic manner of the *Iliad*, and roots in migrations of peoples long since grown over (*colour plate 1*). The Greek and Etruscan elements within them are important because they demonstrate the effect of other cultures on the Romans, and that is no less true in the case of the evolution of gladiators.

HISTORY AS MYTH

A clue to the way the Roman mind runs is found in the tradition of voluntary self-sacrifice noted even at this early point in Rome's history. Romans had a taste for the grand sacrificial gesture, the difference that one man could make if he dedicated his life to the gods in return for the good of the nation, and this was reflected in their foundation myths as much as in their actual recorded history.

A famous example occurred during the Samnite Wars, when the beleaguered Roman general Publius Decius Mus gave himself as a voluntary sacrifice at the hands of Rome's enemies in an act of *devotio*, to secure a Roman victory. By dedicating his life to the gods of the underworld (*dii inferi*), he was making a deal to trade his own life together with the lives of the slain Samnites, in return for success in battle. As Livy said, he gave himself and the legions of the enemy to the Earth and the infernal gods to be slaughtered.

Once having made this bargain with the gods, he became an unstoppably fierce fighter; his death was already a foregone conclusion, so he plunged into the enemy ranks without fear, knowing that his demise would be the completion of the contract. As a result, he utterly terrified the Samnites. Cicero said that he looked for death more ardently than Epicurus thought pleasure should be pursued. His was the *amor mortis* of the gladiator. He went down under a rain of spears and lances, and his self-sacrifice inspired the Roman soldiers to renew their attack on the Samnites.

The *devotio* and the oath of the gladiator, the *sacramentum*, share the common element of voluntary dedication of a life honourably discharged by death in battle or in the arena. It might be argued that gladiators were not always volunteers; this is true, as the gladiator, once having been acquired for the arena, by whatever means, had no choice but to make his oath; thereafter he was bound by something more important than mere compulsion. This had the effect of freeing him, within the confines of the combat. Provided that he held nothing back, and fought with the same contempt for his life that Decius Mus had done, he would have the glory, whether or not he survived. He had the chance to regain lost dignity, to redeem his place in society, but to gain it he had to be prepared to let go of hope and fear, and fight with the rage of the truly desperate.

FERIAE, LUDI

The enactment of bloody games, by the first century AD, had become one of the defining characteristics of what it meant to be Roman, and the gladiator show is still one of the first images to come to our minds when we think of Rome. Because of this stereotyping, there is great potential for confusion over the different types of event loosely described as 'games', and in order to draw any useful conclusions about the origin of gladiator combats, it is important to make distinctions between them. All too easily, the modern mind is lured into thinking that the term, 'gladiators' is synonymous with 'games'. The main difference to keep in mind is that the *ludi* were state-funded public celebrations involving processions, theatrical shows and circus-games, such as chariot-races, whereas the gladiator fights were *munera*, privately-funded ceremonial obligations owed to deceased men of standing in the community, the purpose of which was to create publicity for them, enhancing their status, and, by association, their family.

Gladiators were part of Rome's repertoire of entertainment, a separate strand that joined the mainstream just as the Republic was giving way to the Caesars and empire. It is important to examine the other elements, as they were all designed for the same purpose, gladiators included – to hold the attention of the public.

From Rome's earliest days, it celebrated religious festivals and holidays known as *feriae*. Rome was at heart a society based on agriculture; its foundation stories were full of farmers and shepherds. The *feriae* originated in the need to honour, placate and enlist the support of the gods associated with fertility of crops, livestock, weather, good health, and the myriad concerns of the rustic life. Some of Rome's most ancient festivals were related to the yearly cycle of the land, and the effect of the seasons. These festivals, dedicated to particular divinities, were spread over the months of the year; despite the plural noun, *feriae* could be single-day festivals The ceremonies invariably included sacrifice, a word we tend to associate with ritual killing, but which encompasses the performance of any sacred action, which is the literal meaning of *sacrificium*.

Various offerings were common, such as wine, oil, cakes, grain, honey, milk, and incense, as well as blood offerings in the form of the slaughter of domestic animals, reflecting the ancient human appreciation of the mechanism of giving up something valuable in order to obtain an even greater benefit (7). In this respect, death and blood were the ultimate gifts available to secure life and prosperity, regeneration and fertility from the gods. The most acceptable sacrifice was one in which the beast, by appearing to offer its neck to the priest's knife, indicated its

7 Relief on column base in the *Forum Romanum*, showing ritual sacrifice. *Photograph: author*

willingness. This is strongly reminiscent of the position of the defeated gladiator who, according to Cicero, unflinchingly faces death:

> Just look at the gladiators, either debased men or foreigners, and consider the blows they endure! Consider how they who have been well disciplined prefer to accept a blow than ignominiously avoid it! How often it is made clear that they consider nothing other than the satisfaction of their master or the people! Even when they are covered with wounds they send a messenger to their master to enquire his will. If they have given satisfaction to their masters, they are pleased to fall. What even mediocre gladiator ever groans, ever alters the expression on his face? Which one of them acts shamefully either standing or falling? And which of them, even when he does succumb, ever contracts his neck when ordered to receive the blow? (Cicero, *Tusculanae Disputationes* 2.17.41)

In the same way that the animal going compliantly to slaughter was seen as a good sign, so too was it considered admirable when a vanquished gladiator offered his neck for the *coup de grâce* (*8* and *9*). The Romans expected the same quality of willingness in the gladiator as in the sacrificial beast, in that the latter was led to slaughter by a slack rope, without a struggle; if the animal resisted, the offering might not be pleasing to the gods. Another example of this parallel is from Seneca, from his *De Tranquillitate* (11.5), when he casts the goddess Fortuna (equated to Nemesis, and like her, a goddess associated with the amphitheatre)

8 Re-enactment of a vanquished gladiator offering his neck for the killing blow. *Photograph courtesy of Graham Ashford*, Ludus Gladiatorius

9 Oil lamp from the first or second century AD, depicting a gladiator kneeling in defeat and awaiting the deathblow. *From the Guttman Collection, reproduced with kind permission of Christies Images Ltd*

as the *editor* of the games: 'Why should I save you,' she said, 'weak and quivering beast? All the more will you be mangled and stabbed because you do not know how to offer your throat.' What Fortuna, and by implication, the Roman audience, is angry about, is the gladiator who doesn't go bravely to his death, who doesn't co-operate in his own slaughter. They are filled with disgust; they feel insulted.

Similar audience reactions can be seen today at any stadium, football pitch, tennis court, sports hall or even bullring, in fact anywhere that sporting prowess is called for, anywhere that the contestant fails to demonstrate the required amount of 'grit'; it is as if he, as the representative of all their aspirations, stands in for them; he becomes the offering to whatever deity is running the luck that day, and then, by falling short, whether of expected courage or skill, embarrasses and humiliates both himself and them. At that point, the crowd gets derisive, and angry, cheated out of the exemplary behaviour they came to witness.

The gladiator must be seen against that cultural backdrop, in the context of a society to whom sacrifice and substitution were fully functioning parts of the Roman psyche. The Roman year was heavy with holidays, festivals and games, all with special significance and responsibilities for the people. This was a complicated business; some days were lucky; others best avoided. Romans thought odd numbered days were good, and that even dates were therefore unlucky, so the *feriae* took place on the odd days spread over the year.

In fact, Trimalchio, in Petronius' *Satyricon*, had two boards put up on either side of his door to keep track of his dinner engagements and the special days of the year, which was a good idea, because on public holidays, all legal and political work halted, to avoid polluting the sacred day. For Romans, it was important to be aware of the dates of the festivals and holidays because of the effect they had on everyday life. Not that all work ceased; some was permitted by the priests. Certainly, the city did not grind to a halt; the shops were probably open, and people had the choice of treating the holiday piously, perhaps by visiting temples, or just enjoying the opportunity for relaxation and festivities, or as Pliny called it, harmless relaxation, *innoxia remissio*.

Although the *feriae* were essentially religious occasions, Roman citizens were not compelled to treat them as such, by performing acts of worship, provided they observed the rules about working. In any case, by the end of the Republic, it is doubtful whether the average Roman citizen attached any real religious significance to any of the festivals. Centuries of ritual had eroded the meaning of the acts performed; the origin of the beliefs had slowly bled away, leaving a hollow body of tradition.

However, some celebrations did hold a powerful significance for the Romans; chief amongst these were the *feriae Latinae* (festival of all the Latin peoples) at the end of April and the *ludi Romani* (also known as the *ludi magni*) in September, which marked the start and finish of Rome's traditional summer war months, when farmers would have been free to join military campaigns, in order to enrich the state by raids on neighbours, and to defend it, a peculiar admixture of good husbandry and martial vigour, two things of which the Romans were very proud.

So ancient were some of the festivals that time had clouded their beginnings, and yet it is clear that they were all in some way related to the rustic life of Rome's forefathers. The *Equirria*, a horseracing festival held on 27 February was supposedly set up by Romulus in honour of Rome's first god, Mars. The *Parilia* was also associated with Romulus, being concerned with the purification of sheep and shepherds; it fell on the supposed date of the anniversary of Rome's foundation, in April. Another, the *equus October*, sacrifice of the October horse, was a chariot race held on the Ides of October, in which the near-side horse of the winning team was sacrificed to Mars; its severed head was garlanded with loaves of bread and nailed to one of Rome's most sacred buildings, the *regia*. *Lupercalia* was held on 15 February, and involved rites of purification and fertility, drunkenness and animal sacrifice, when two teams of youths dressed in the bloody skins of slaughtered goats ran through the streets striking people with strips of goatskin called *februa*, thereby bestowing fecundity. *Consualia* honoured Consus, god of the granary, whose festivals in August and December celebrated harvest and autumn crop sowing with burnt sacrifices, chariot- and horse races in the Circus Maximus. The religious year ended with possibly the most popular holiday of all, *Saturnalia*, the feast of the winter solstice on 17 December, which honoured ancient Saturn from the Golden Age (the good old days), as a god of seed-sowing and prosperity. It was a time when shops and businesses were shut, school was out, and a public feast, open to all, was held; everyone wore their comfortable holiday clothes, master and slave changed places, friends exchanged candles, children got presents of little dolls, and the streets were full of happy, noisy crowds.

The Roman calendar had many such festivals; most were state events, administered by priests and officials of the magistracy, usually the *aediles* and *praetores*. Attached to the religious festivals were the public games, *ludi publici*, which, as time went by, became more important for their entertainment value than for any sacred aspect. The oldest and greatest of these were the *ludi Romani*; these originated as votive games in honour of Jupiter Optimus Maximus, dating from at least 366 BC, and supposedly instituted even earlier by the kings of Rome. They were the first and only annual games until around 220 BC, when the *ludi plebeii*, also in honour of Jupiter, were established.

In fact, from the third century BC onwards, there was a steady increase in the number of festivals and games, whilst the existing *feriae* and *ludi* were extended to occupy more days. The marked growth of Rome's entertainment calendar reflected its new, improved status in the Italian peninsula and the Mediterranean world. The last serious wars fought by Rome against coalitions of its enemies in Italy, the Samnite wars, had been won by 295 BC, ensuring plentiful supplies of prisoners of war, and by 264 BC Roman domination of most of the Italian peninsula was complete, at which point Rome turned to challenge Carthage, its only real rival for supremacy in the Mediterranean. After three Punic Wars, and despite suffering heavy losses, Rome wiped Carthage from the face of the earth in 146 BC, and emerged as the undisputed new superpower of the western world.

As a direct consequence of so much military success, the wealth of the Mediterranean started to pour into Rome's coffers; not only monies exacted from defeated enemies, but also booty, treasure, artefacts and slave labour provided by prisoners of war. This vast influx of new money stimulated grand new building projects, as temples, aqueducts, monuments, sprang up throughout Italy, not just at Rome; much of the money was used by the elite to buy up vast tracts of land in central Italy for farming enterprises run on slave labour, such as vineyards, olive groves, market gardens, sheep farming.

This was the dynamic economic and political climate in which all of Rome's instruments of celebration – the festivals, the games, the triumphs and even the gladiators – began to proliferate. The Roman people's desire to enjoy this newly acquired importance and dominance expressed itself in their appetite for display of all kinds.

As each fresh victory was enjoyed, Rome had more reason to give thanks to the gods and more wealth to show off; and so, by the foundation of new games and festivals, both needs were satisfied.

Between 212 and 173 BC, four more sets of games were instituted, in addition to the *ludi Romani* (5–19 September), and the *ludi plebeii* (4–17 November): the *ludi apollinares* (6–13 July), the *ludi megalenses* (4–10 April), the *ludi ceriales* (12–19 April), and the *ludi florales* (28 April–3 May). During the Republic, the games were specifically devoted to theatre shows (*ludi scaenici*) or to chariot-races (*ludi circenses*). At this stage, the gladiatorial contests had not yet joined the *ludi* as public games; nor had beast spectacles, *venationes*, been incorporated as regular features of public entertainment.

VENATIONES

It was not until 186 BC that M. Fulvius Nobilior, in fulfilment of a vow after his victories in Greece, presented a hunt of lions and panthers (leopards) as part of votive games, *ludi votivi*, in the Circus Maximus during the *magni ludi* for Jupiter Optimus Maximus (*10*). Before Nobilior's *venatio*, no substantial evidence of animals in spectacles or hunts in the circus is available to build a picture of its use as a widespread practice.

10 Roman mosaic of a leopard; many such exotic beasts were imported into Rome and other major cities for the games. *Musei Capitolini. Photograph: author*

However, even as a side-product of religious ceremonies, we should not ignore rituals like the releasing of foxes with burning torches tied to their tails on the last day of the festival of *Cerialia*, or the hunting of hares and deer in the circus games at the *ludi florales* at the end of the festival of the goddess Flora. In these, the victims are nothing like the large fighting animals such as the lions and tigers; the role of small wild herbivores relates more to their association with goddesses like Flora, whose purlieu was the domesticated landscape, the gardens and cultivated fields, and Ceres, the goddess of cereal crops and regenerative nature. They are akin to blood sacrifices with a ritual activity preceding the offering, presumably to increase its efficacy.

These kinds of customs, whose origins were long forgotten, in which Romans tormented, abused, hunted and killed small wild animals, from hares and foxes to goats, deer and wild boar, not forgetting the domestic animals often used in sacrifice, were already well-established long before the exotic beasts started to make appearances in the votive games and triumphs. As a rule, the bigger the animal, the more likely it was to be killed for a show. This was especially so under the empire, when the most popular beasts were big and dangerous ones like bears, lions, tigers, leopards, bulls and elephants, all preferably taken from the wild rather than captive-bred or tamed. In 26 hunts put on by Augustus, he boasted in his *Res gestae* that 3,500 beasts had been slaughtered. By AD 80, Titus had 9,000 animals killed in the dedicatory games for the Colosseum, and 30 years later, Trajan's games used 11,000 beasts. In the arena holocaust, the numbers of animals killed far exceeded the human deathcount.

If the hunts that were staged in the circus were rituals subliminally underlining territorial hunting rights and the power of Rome over the realm of nature itself, then the wild beast shows were over-the-top extensions of this principle. The big cats, elephants and giraffes and all the rare and strange creatures that Rome's resources could track down and transport back to the arena, were like prisoners of war, exhibited as proof of Rome's dominion over foreign lands. An account of games in AD 248 in the reign of Gordian lists 32 elephants, 10 elk, 10 tigers, 60 tame lions, 30 tame leopards, 10 hyena, 2,000 gladiators, 6 hippos, one rhino, 10 wild lions, 10 giraffes, 20 wild asses, and 40 wild horses.

Plenty of evidence exists for the practical methods by which these animals were hunted, trapped and transported back to Rome, from mosaics to Cicero's letters, but Petronius sums it up nicely:

> The wild beast is searched out in the woods at a great price, and men trouble Hammon (*as in Baal-Hammon, the god*) deep in Africa to supply the beast whose teeth make him precious for slaying men; strange ravening creatures freight the fleets, and the padding tiger is wheeled in a gilded palace to drink the blood of men while the crowd applauds. (Petronius, *Satyricon* 119.14-18)

Roman attitudes to the displays of animal cruelty and death need some explanation to put the beast spectacles in perspective. Again, there is no point in condemning the apparently callous disregard for suffering. How they regarded *venationes* would have been similar to their perception of the moral value of gladiatorial combat and bloodshed; beneficial effects to the individual and to the state were taken as read. In a society based on farming, hunting and military virtues, the regular exposure to human and non-human sacrifice and other rituals, like beast hunts, *venationes* and combats, *munera*, in which blood was spilt, all demonstrated for the people's benefit the proper relationships between man, nature and state. It also had the effect of training out any response of squeamishness in the face of death, whether animal or human.

From childhood onwards, Romans, in common with most ancient societies, were quickly habituated to regular killing: small creatures and domestic beasts were sacrificed, larger animals were hunted; decimation arbitrarily punished the innocent soldier alongside the guilty, men of status were executed in the Forum by the sword, *ad gladium*, and criminals by less straightforward, but more inventive, means (*11*). Turning away from the sight of men being executed was thought to be puerile, something to grow out of, though the emperor Caracalla as a boy was praised for this supposed weakness:

> ... if he ever saw condemned men thrown to the wild beasts he wept or turned away his eyes; and this was more than pleasing to the people. (*Scriptores Historiae Augustae, Caracalla* 1-5)

Obviously, if the *Augustan Histories* are to be believed, (many historians feel they have limited credibility), he overcame his childish sympathies; once he was emperor, again in the words of the *Historiae Augustae*, 'thereafter there was slaughter everywhere'. Punishment by flogging was also carried out in the Forum, in the ancient fashion, *more maiorum*. In particular, the unusual punishments, such as that

11 Roman beast hunt relief in marble. *Musei Capitolini. Photograph: author*

of the *poena cullei*, the ritual penalty for the parricide (or murderer of any close relative), who could expect to be tied in a leather sack with a dog, a monkey, a snake and a cock, which was then thrown in the river Tiber, were intended to be seen, in order to assure society that the polluting presence of the killer had been fully expunged. This was the purpose of the unfortunate animals; as they struggled and attacked the victim in the sack, it was thought that the miasma of the foul deed would be cancelled out, leaving no trace of the evil behind. Denied the dignity of burial in earth, the evildoer and the wickedness of his deed would literally be washed out of the city, and into Hades. This was exceptional, however; the Forum was the normal venue for corporal and capital penalties, until gradually, the arena, with its convenient viewing, replaced the Forum as the most practical and popular site of public punishments and executions.

By adulthood, most Romans would have witnessed a great deal of physical punishment. It is not surprising, therefore, that attitudes to it would have been completely shaped by these experiences. This must be remembered when we start to wonder how people can comfortably watch thousands of frightened, crazed animals being despatched, let alone the gladiatorial fights. However, as with bullfights, it is likely that the key to their popularity was not the bloodshed itself, as the appetite for it must undoubtedly have become jaded with time, but how it was achieved; the sheer level of showmanship is what elevated the *venationes* from mere slaughterhouse spectacle. Once people had become hardened to the actual sight of death in the arena, they were able to focus on the different forms that killing took, rather as spectators at a bullfight may learn to recognise the various death-strokes, once they have overcome their squeamishness and sensitivities.

As for the beginnings of the *venatio* itself, it is true that much earlier than 186 BC four elephants were brought to Rome in triumph, in 275 BC, by M. Curius Dentatus, as part of the war booty from his victory against the Greek king, Pyrrhus. They were probably Indian elephants, exhibited as spoils of war rather than used in games. This attitude would especially apply to any animals being seen for the first time. Because of their novelty, the likelihood is that they would be put on show, as in a zoo or menagerie, rather than be hunted and killed. A similar approach was taken with ostriches when they first appeared at the Circus in 197 BC.

Although the Romans had great enthusiasm for all kinds of wild beasts, there was no zoo in Rome: Ptolemy II had set one up at Alexandria, but strangely, the Romans never tried to copy it. However, they did have game reserves and menageries for exotic birds and beasts, and later, there was even an imperial herd of elephants kept outside Rome, according to the second century rhetorician, Aelius Aristides.

A much more lavish display, with 142 elephants, had been put on in 252 BC by L. Caecilius Metellus. Then, in 186 BC, came Nobilior's lion hunt, which was the first recorded instance of a true *venatio* in which the animals were actually killed. After that, in 169 BC, in a jump from triumphal or votive games, a *venatio* was given as part of the regular *ludi circenses*, within the Roman religious calendar, when Scipio Nasica and Cornelius Lentulus exhibited 63 big cats, and 40 elephants and bears (*10*). These are just the cases we know about; it is probable that somewhere between 275 and 186 BC, animal spectacles were incorporated into the state games.

Having been incorporated, they proved an economical part of the programme, as it was always going to be cheaper to put on beasts than men, despite the expense of shipping and housing. However, one thing is clear: by 169 BC, the animal spectacles were very definitely an official part of the state festivals, with the big animals, the carnivores, bulls and bears being the most popular. According to Cassius Dio and other literary sources, carnivores like the big cats were often known as *africanae* and *libycae*, after their places of origin.

The first crocodiles and hippos were seen at the games of Aemilius Scaurus in 58 BC; Pompey's games were the first to show the rhinoceros ('Ethiopian bulls' as the Greek writer Pausanias later called them), and Caesar was first to put on a giraffe in his magnificent games of 46 BC. The same competitive escalation occurred with animal exhibitions as was happening in the *munera*.

This pressure to find new and exciting animals is perfectly illustrated by Cicero's experience when he was governor of Cilicia (southern Turkey) around 51/50 BC, and was being harassed by letter about getting hold of some panthers (leopards) to send to Rome. His friend Marcus Caelius Rufus had been elected *aedile*, and he was putting pressure on Cicero in his post as provincial governor to supply as many panthers as possible, to use in the shows he would be organising later that year:

> Dear Caelius,
>
> About the panthers! The matter is being handled with diligence and according to my orders by men who are skilful hunters. But there is a remarkable scarcity of panthers. And they tell me that the few panthers left are complaining bitterly that they are the only animals in my province for whom traps are set. And therefore they have decided, or so the rumour goes, to leave my province and move to Caria. But the matter is receiving careful attention, especially from Patiscus. Any animal found will be yours. But whether any will be found, we really don't know... (Cicero, *Epistulae* 2.11.2)

This letter speaks volumes about the voracious Roman appetite for animal shows, and from the difficulties Cicero was having in finding some panthers, it sounds like the Roman hunters, in responding to the excessive demands for wild beasts, may very well have hunted the big cats in Cilicia to near extinction. This is what is thought to have happened to the desert lions of Namibia, perhaps helped on their way by Pompey's games of 55 BC, when 600 lions and 400 leopards were slaughtered. In environmental terms, the effect of Rome's inexhaustible appetite for beast shows was disastrous for the animal kingdom, particularly in North Africa.

AD BESTIAS

We can see the very beginnings of the public method of execution known as *damnatio ad bestias*, which would later become such a notorious part of the activities in the arena, at some triumphal games held at Amphipolis in 167 BC, when, so Valerius Maximus tells us, Aemilius Paullus had army deserters publicly trampled to death by elephants. Although the process by which the elephants were made to crush the condemned men underfoot is not recorded, this ancient punishment has a parallel in India. It may have taken place as late as the times of the British Raj; provided the following method is not simply anecdotal, the victim was staked to the ground, while an elephant, tethered by a long line to the same stake, was encouraged to walk in ever-decreasing circles until the inevitable occurred. Whatever variant of this method the Romans practised, it must have been both cruelly compelling and exemplary. Other accounts tell of herds of elephants intoxicated by myrrh and incense being encouraged to rampage around the arena, trampling human victims at random.

Harsh and spectacular acts of capital punishment involving wild beasts became increasingly common; Valerius thought they were conducive to greater discipline amongst the men, because of the fear engendered at the prospect of such a humiliating public death. Furthermore, the deserters were foreign auxiliaries, not standard Roman soldiers, and might have been thought to deserve a fate more appropriate to their lower, non-Roman status and exotic origins. In addition, they might have acted as substitute Carthaginians, scapegoats in effect, in a very public act of delayed revenge.

In 146 BC, following in his adoptive father's footsteps, Scipio Aemilianus, as well as beheading Latin deserters and crucifying Roman ones in Carthage itself, had foreign auxiliary deserters thrown to wild beasts, probably in the Circus, as part of his triumphal games to celebrate victory over Carthage. Significantly, he reserved crucifixion, the normal form of execution for criminal slaves, and therefore the most humiliating, for the Roman deserters, as they had fallen the furthest from their duty to Rome. Their lingering deaths, far from home, would have had a salutary effect on those soldiers whose job it was to crucify them.

Wild beasts were used in the arena, sometimes as an exhibition in themselves, but mostly in shows where they were 'hunted', pitched against other beasts, or used to mutilate and kill condemned criminals. Tied to stakes or wheeled into the arena by handlers on little carts to which they were bound, the naked or barely covered *noxii* were exposed to the attacks of wild animals, as vividly depicted in the mosaics of Zliten, Lepcis Magna and El Djem, Tunisia. One piece of North African souvenir terracotta shows a condemned female, hands bound, tied onto a bull and being savaged by a leopard; this neatly illustrates the robust Roman attitude to the aggravated execution of criminals. No skill or sport was being glorified in this punishment: it was purely the ritual disposal of enemies of society. Christian *noxii* were a common sight in the arena. Sometimes the beasts had to be provoked into aggression; their instinct, in the alien landscape of the amphitheatre, was not always to attack, and often their condition, by the time they entered the arena, had deteriorated, despite the best efforts of the beast handlers. All in all, the scene could be described as a sorry spectacle, in which both human and animal participants were pathetic victims of the penal system.

ANNONA ET SPECTACULIS

Whatever the occasion for celebration, but particularly in the case of festivals, it was imperative to do it properly, with priests to conduct the rituals, prayers and sacrifices; failure to render the god his (or her) due could be disastrous, for the individual and for the state. From the time of the kings to the end of the Republic, there were about 58 special days in the religious calendar, supposedly established by the second of Rome's kings, Numa Pompilius, and this list of days remained unaltered throughout that period.

Even in the Republican era, so plentiful were the *feriae*, that there was never too much of a gap between one holiday and another. But with the coming of Caesar and the imperial era that followed him, the number of games and festivals mushroomed as the Senate's sycophantic tendencies found new expression in voting for the commemoration of the emperor's military victories, accessions, consecrations, birthdays, and even, where applicable, his deification. By the time of Claudius, the total had risen to 159, of which 93 were specifically devoted to *ludi*, games paid for out of the public purse.

By the second century AD, festival days had multiplied to such an extent that the emperor Marcus Aurelius decreed they should be restricted to 135 a year. To put it in perspective, however, the Romans didn't split the year into weeks and weekends in the modern sense; therefore, the customary two days off out of every seven which most of us enjoy was unavailable to them, although Jews with a regular Sabbath each week would observe that day, and not the festivals. Instead, although what might look to us like a large number of working days were lost through festivals and games, the loss was in fact comparable to that of the average working man nowadays with 52 weekends, three weeks annual leave and seven days of bank holidays per year. We should therefore take care to adjust our preconceptions of the feckless Roman underclass with nothing to do but sit on its collective backside, watching games for half the year and waiting for the monthly grain handout (the *panem* or 'bread' of Juvenal's ascerbic verse).

Marcus Aurelius' tutor, the rhetorician Marcus Cornelius Fronto, writing 40 years after Juvenal's over-used comment about '*panem et circenses*', observed of the Roman people that the emperor (Trajan) knew they were held in control principally by two things – free grain and shows, *annona et spectaculis*.

Between them, Juvenal and Fronto have managed to create a memorably vivid image of Roman degeneracy, which, by virtue of its simplistic stance, casts a shadow over the true picture. For example, in Augustan Rome, out of 77 days of public games, only 17 were taken up with chariot-races in the circus, even less with gladiator shows—the rest were shows in the theatre, which might be pantomime, farce, comedy, tragedy, or even striptease by prostitutes, a regular feature of the *Floralia* (*12*). In fact, actresses themselves were classed as prostitutes, and the common opinion of actors in general was that they were degraded, indecent, and licentious.

LUDI SCAENICI, LUDI CIRCENSES

It was a social stigma to be an actor, as it was to be a gladiator; no decent person would wish to perform in public, whether in the *scaena*, or the arena, as it would expose them to contempt and derision. Strangely, the charioteer was exempted from this social leprosy. For this reason, most performers in Rome were outsiders, foreigners, or slaves; anything but Roman citizens. As Tacitus put it: *nec quemquam Romae honesto loco ortum ad theatrales artes degeneravisse* – no decent Roman had lowered himself to going on the stage in the last 200 years. Rome liked to spectate; it was just not done to participate.

One thing is clear from Rome's many social commentators: in the reverse hierarchy of infamy, the gladiator is lower than the actor, yet the performance in

12 Roman theatre at Ostia; this well preserved theatre with marble seats was constructed in the first century BC and renovated between the second and fourth centuries AD. Seating capacity has been estimated at 3-4000. *Photograph*: *author*

the arena has more value than anything taking place on the stage. This is because the arena performances demonstrated *virtus*, the highest Roman moral quality, without which Rome itself would not have existed, so they had great usefulness, and were uplifting and educational; the theatre was associated with its opposite, *vitium*, vice, and *voluptas*, pleasure for its own sake, which threatened to drag Rome down by corrupting and softening its citizens.

The arena exerted a form of social control; the spectators knew their place, and played their part, but in the theatre, audiences were unpredictable, unruly; the social order on which Rome was built was noticeably absent. Valerius Maximus, like Suetonius and Tacitus, felt that theatres were dangerous, rowdy places, where fighting could, and often did, break out, akin to the military barracks in town, *urbana castra*, 'where what was originally meant to be a pleasure for man and a tribute to the gods had often been stained by the blood of citizens, much to the shame of peace'. No wonder, then, that during the first century AD, every now and then acting would be banned, and actors were expelled; several emperors, including Tiberius, Nero, Domitian and Trajan felt it was a necessary step for the good of public order and morals, though it was inevitably thwarted by the sheer persistence of actors who found ways round the ban.

Like chariot-races in the circus, traditionally the original 'true' entertainment of the Romans, theatre had already had a long history in Rome by the time gladiatorial combats started to gather popular momentum. Livy records that in 364 BC a terrible plague was ravaging Rome; the Romans decided to placate the gods by promising to introduce theatrical festivals to supplement the existing circus games.

From Valerius Maximus we learn that they called in *histriones*, professional Etruscan actors (*histrio*, the Latin word for actor, has an Etruscan root) to help them fulfil their vow. The Etruscan approach to theatre was very hellenized, due to their close contact with the Greek cities of southern Italy, and it is likely that they were dancers in the traditional Greek form of pantomime (like ballet) that was prevalent at the time, rather than actors portraying scripted drama. Nevertheless, it was the start of theatre in Rome, and led to *histrionalis favor*, a craze for actors, that came to be viewed by the starchy intellectual elite as one of Rome's greatest defects, together with its obsession for horses and gladiators.

Over the next two centuries, this new brand of entertainment took on other influences; it was 240 BC when the Greek author and actor-producer Livius Andronicus, who had been brought to Rome as a prisoner of war from the Greek city of Tarentum in southern Italy, introduced, at the Senate's command, Greek plays in Latin to Rome. Thereafter, Roman theatre, with its Etruscan, Latin and Greek elements, performed a variety of styles: tragedy, comedy, rustic farce, historical and pantomime, which we would think of as ballet, or perhaps a musical. However, as time went on, it became clear that the Roman taste was for the comedies, the coarse and popular mimes and especially the Atellan farces, which were a home-produced form of entertainment, from Atella, outside

13 Marble relief of Graeco-Roman theatre masks. *Photograph: author*

Naples. They were originally put on after tragedies for light relief, and had a range of easily recognised masked characters, lots of gesticulating, *doubles entendres* and political wisecracks (*13*). The common folk loved them, whilst higher up the social scale they were thought unbearably vulgar.

The Roman attitude to actors was that they were disreputable, as with gladiators, and any Roman who trod the boards was officially stigmatised as *infamis*, disgraced, and was disqualified from appearing on the property-owning list, taking a post in local government, or being called up for military service.

Romans made an equally unsympathetic, if interactive, audience, who were rowdy, easily bored, and liable to heckle and jeer: as the poet Horace records, in the middle of performances they would shout: 'We want boxers!' and 'We want bears!'. Horace expressed the opinion that the behaviour of the audience was more extraordinary than anything happening on the stage. Riots regularly broke out. The playwright Terence, in the prologue to the third performance of his play, *Hecyra*, (The Mother-in-Law), gives an account of how the two previous attempts to stage it had failed; it speaks volumes about the trying conditions he had to contend with:

> The first time I began to perform this play, there was talk of a boxing-match, and there were also rumours that a tight-rope walker was going to perform. Slaves were arriving, there was a din, women were shouting; and the result was that I had to give up before the end.... I put it on again: the first act went down well, but then word got around that a gladiatorial show was going to be given. People flew together, there was an uproar, they were shouting and fighting for somewhere to sit. It was impossible for me to hold my own against that.

As late as 59 BC, Rome, unlike its more cultured neighbours at Capua and the southern Greek cities, had no permanent stone theatre; one had been proposed almost a century before Pompey's was built. However, work on it was halted when the Senate was persuaded that it would be harmful to public morals if people were able to sit and listen as they did in the dangerously unregulated Greek cities, where the theatres were actually used for public assemblies and meetings. Pompey's stone theatre, situated in the Campus Martius where he owned much of the land, was built in the face of criticism and prejudice based on the fear that Roman tradition would be at risk if people could sit and hold meetings, rather than stand at elections and public assemblies in the time-honoured Roman fashion. It was completed in 52 BC, and it was not until the time of Augustus that two more theatres, of Balbus and Marcellus, were built.

Prior to the permanent stone theatres' construction, people had always sat on wooden bleachers to watch plays being performed on temporary wooden staging, just as the first gladiator combats were put on in the forum. The concept of purpose-built structures for entertainment had not arisen.

As with the circus, and later on the amphitheatre, the theatre was an ideal place for airing social protest, and for public figures to gauge their popularity by the volume of applause they got when they entered, although then as now the dirty tricks of political opponents would extend to rent-a-mob tactics at public meetings, with heckling, disturbances, coached retorts and rigged applause from hired gangs of agitators.

An instance of the theatre acting as a barometer of public opinion is the occasion at the *ludi apollinares* when Caesar, during his first consulship in 59 BC, had such a low popularity rating that no-one cheered when he arrived at the theatre, although his friend and rival Curio got roars of acclaim. It is revealing that his reception shows he was not always the darling of the people that we now think him.

The theatre was never officially censored. It is not surprising, however, that the ruling class kept a close watch on what went on in the theatre, both on the stage where important figures were lampooned and insulted in the mimes and farces, and in the audience, where grievances about food shortages, injustices, and character flaws in their leaders were regularly and loudly voiced. It became a sounding board for political viewpoints. As Cicero said in 56 BC, 'There are three places where popular feeling finds expression, at public meetings, at public assemblies, and at the games and fights'. As the Roman Empire superseded the republic, those meetings and assemblies became redundant, but the circus and the arena, by virtue of the people's attachment to their entertainments, remained places where popular feeling always found expression.

By the time gladiatorial combats first appeared, the people had been enjoying chariot races, *ludi circenses*, and theatrical performances, *ludi scaenici*, for centuries, and it was believed that they were somehow purer, more traditional Roman forms of entertainment than the *munus,* which was a comparative newcomer.

According to legend, the introduction of chariot and horse races was credited to Romulus when he arranged a festival in honour of Consus, an ancient god of the granary who was also associated with horses, like Neptune and the Greek equivalent, Poseidon (*14*). An alternative belief was that Tarquinius Priscus, Rome's first Etruscan king, laid out the Circus Maximus at the same time he created the Roman Forum, and thus brought the sport of chariot races so beloved of the Etruscans to the Romans. Either way, the circus games were already established in the public's affection long centuries before gladiatorial displays started to make an impact.

The public games, whether they took place in the circus or the theatre, were known as *ludi*, having the meaning of 'games, exercise, sport', although by transference it could also mean 'training'; hence, the term *ludus* for the gladiator school, or training camp. These games were state occasions, paid for out of the

14 Detail of first- or second-century AD marble relief of a chariot race; the imperial enclosure is depicted at the top left. *Musei Vaticani. Photograph: author*

state treasury, organised by magistrates. The *ludi* arose out of a different context from that of the festivals, although they were often attached to them. They started when Rome's generals vowed to dedicate triumphal games to Jupiter Optimus Maximus in return for victory in battle.

TRIUMPHI INTO *LUDI ROMANI*

To qualify for the highest honour that Rome could bestow on its military commanders, at least 5000 enemy deaths were supposedly required. This honour, the *triumphus*, was a parade of booty and prisoners of war that started at the Campus Martius, then round the Palatine, along the Via Sacra up to the Capitoline Hill (*2*). The victorious general, known as the *triumphator*, was lavishly dressed as Jupiter in purple and gold, with a crown of laurel on his head and precious metal bracelets on his arms; having handed out gifts, booty and military decorations, and speeches of praise to the soldiers serving under him, he mounted an ornately decorated tower-shaped chariot. Thus began the *pompa*, the victory procession.

With him, he took his children and young relatives; older male relatives rode horses as out-riders in a guard of honour. Behind the general, a slave held above his head a jewel-encrusted gold crown, whispering in his ear that he was mortal, and warning him to look back: the Romans believed that your future crept up on you from behind, catching you unawares.

At the head of the *pompa* were the trophies and spoils, including important prisoners of war, who were dragged in chains, mocked and spat at by the crowds (*15*); then there were parades of signs and placards with representations of all the captured cities, forts and territories; then came the soldiers who had fought to gain the victory; finally, at the end of the procession, rode the general, loudly greeted as *imperator* by his men, and by the cheering crowds. No detail of the victory was omitted. As a representation, it had all the properties of an epic as we would understand it today, a blockbuster production designed to elicit awe and admiration from a vast audience.

When the entire procession reached the end of the route, the general was escorted into the Roman Forum, where, at his order, the enemy leader was publicly killed, clearly demonstrating how Rome had disposed of the threat to its security. Another aspect of triumphs was the military execution of non-Roman condemned men, like deserters, usually in the games that followed, in an eye-catching way designed to provide a powerful object lesson for anyone foolish enough to consider rebellion against Rome's authority.

As Rome's reach extended with each new campaign, foreign and exotic beasts were added to the display, symbolising the territorial gains, just as great numbers of human captives were paraded and killed outright in Rome itself. The magnificence of the spectacle grew with each fresh conquest. After the end of the Punic Wars, with the defeat of Hannibal and Carthage, the flow of

15 Condemned men (*damnati ad bestias*) led to their deaths with ropes around their necks. Third-century AD relief carving. *Illustration of upper detail from an original relief in the Ashmolean Museum, Oxford*

wild animals from North Africa into Rome greatly increased, the big cats being the most popular. Similarly, after Rome's links with Egypt were consolidated, crocodiles, hippos and giraffes started to appear on display in Rome.

When a triumphal parade had ended, triumphal games would start, enhancing the glorious victory. Such games were paid for by the general out of his share of the spoils of war, in fulfilment of his vow to a god, like Jupiter, before the campaign. Over time, these triumphal games, because they happened only occasionally, split away from the triumph, and became a permanent annual fixture in the festival calendar in their own right.

This was how the *ludi Romani*, or *ludi magni*, *votivi*, the first and most ancient games, originated. Instituted in 366 BC, as votive games to Jupiter, but possibly going back to the times of the kings, they were the only annual games until about 220 BC, when the next most important games, the *ludi plebeii*, were established. The *ludi Romani* started as a single day, on 13 September, but gradually increased to 15 days by the time of Julius Caesar. A solemn procession to the Circus Maximus was followed by sacrifice, then circus-games, including chariot-races, and theatrical performances.

At this stage, gladiator shows were not included in the *ludi*; they remained a separate entity, privately funded rather than state-sponsored. The public games were free to all who wanted to spectate – easier to do at either of Rome's circuses, the Circus Maximus, holding 250,000, or the smaller Circus Flaminius. There was really no practical method of restricting the access to either of the circuses, and no allocation of seats, unlike the amphitheatres; it was just a case of turning up.

THE ETRUSCAN CONNECTION

The case for gladiators originating in Etruscan culture rests on flimsy proof which nevertheless stubbornly lingers on, despite growing evidence to the contrary. It derives mainly from literary sources, the strongest of which is provided by Nicolaus of Damascus, writing in the late first century BC, as quoted by Athenaeus in a description of gladiator contests, *monomachias*, at banquets:

> The Romans staged spectacles of fighting gladiators not merely at their festivals and in their theatres, borrowing the custom from the Etruscans, but also at their banquets ... some would invite their friends to dinner ... that they might witness two or three pairs of contestants in gladiatorial combat ... when sated with dining and drink, they called in the gladiators. No sooner did one have his throat cut than the masters applauded with delight at this feat...

If nothing else, this is an indication that the Romans themselves had a tradition of belief in the *munera* as Etruscan in origin. Much has been made of another tenuous link between *munera* and Etruria, in the explanation offered by Isidorus of Seville, the seventh-century AD compiler of an etymological dictionary, that the Latin word for a gladiator trainer, *lanista*, has an Etruscan origin. Further linguistic analysis has upheld that supposition, relying on the – a suffix to *lanista*, and the proper name 'Lani' in Etruscan sources. The words *laniare* (to mutilate, tear to pieces), and *lanius* (butcher, executioner), apparently come from the same root word. However, the further proposition that gladiators emanated from Etruria just because the word for a trainer of gladiators may have been Etruscan, is an unstable one. Proof of trade in gladiators is not necessarily proof of origin.

The Romans themselves did wonder about the paradox of the gladiator, a creature hardly human that they both despised and admired. Scholars down the centuries tried to explain how the gladiator came to be held in such contempt that he was literally outside decent society, *infamis*, a man without worth or dignity, a social pariah.

In 1845, W. Henzen suggested a solution in response to the conundrum: the first gladiators were not Roman at all, but an Etruscan invention. He based this solution mainly on the statement by Nicolaus of Damascus, with support from the etymological evidence by Isidorus.

The final pieces of literary evidence come from Tertullian, the Christian apologist. To call them evidence is perhaps charitable; at best, they are interesting comments on the proceedings of *spectacula*.

Tertullian was born in the Roman province of North Africa in AD 160 and he spent most of his life there, dying in AD 230. He was trained as a lawyer, and converted to Christianity; he wrote many works about the history and character of the church, and famously composed the *Apologeticum*, in which he rebutted the accusations made against Christians. Living in Carthage, he had plenty of opportunities to observe the workings of the amphitheatre there; he was a contemporary of Perpetua, the third century martyr; indeed, she received written guidance from him.

Perpetua was a young Roman matron of respectable family, who converted to Christianity, insisted on proclaiming her beliefs, and refused to make any sacrifices to the emperor. This led to her arrest and imprisonment; eventually, she was tried and sentenced *ad bestias*; and she ended her life in the amphitheatre at Carthage (now Tunisia). Remarkably, she kept a diary, not just of her experiences leading up to her appearance in the arena, but also as an eyewitness account of the last days of the other martyrs with her.

The importance of this association is that the practices she reports and the comments of Tertullian can be weighed up and put into the bigger picture of Carthage's amphitheatre; consequently, when Tertullian discusses various aspects of the *spectacula*, we can have some confidence that he is writing from a degree of personal knowledge. Yes, it is true that his Christian beliefs led him to write critically about the events in the arena, but this should not entirely discredit the information he supplies. Because of his predisposition to home in on what he saw as idolatry and and religious malpractice, he has often been regarded as a less than reliable commentator. However, as long as caution is exercised, he is a valuable source of detail on the practices of the *spectacula*. With that in mind, he gives useful details about the arena personnel who stood in for underworld deities or demons. The suggestion that the Etruscan death-demon Charun was involved in the business of attending to the dead gladiators comes from Tertullian by a tortuous route (*16*). These are the references responsible for this attribution:

> But you really are still more religious in the amphitheatre, where over human blood, over the dirt of pollution of capital punishment, your gods dance, supplying plots and themes for the guilty – unless it is that often the guilty play the parts of gods. (Tertullian, *Apologeticum*, 15.4)

By this, Tertullian means the representation of deities by men in masks, taking part in ritual activities in the arena. He goes on to clarify this:

> We have laughed, amid the noon's blend of cruelty and absurdity, at Mercury using his burning iron to see who was dead. We have seen Jove's brother, too, conducting out the corpses of gladiators, hammer in hand. (Tertullian, *Apologeticum*, 15.5)

16 The Underworld demon *Charun* with hammer. Fresco from fourth-century BC Etruscan tomb. The plaster walls have suffered considerable damage but Charun's blue-tinted skin and off-white tunic with deep red flame pattern around the hem can be clearly seen. *Illustration based on images kindly supplied by Misha Nedeljkovich*

Tertullian is talking here about executions of *noxii*, condemned criminals in the *meridianum spectaculum*, when the *noxii* (if there were any) would be killed in the arena in the break between the morning *venatio* and the afternoon's main event, the *munera*, the gladiatorial combats. Although he uses the term 'gladiator' in this and other references, he gives it a loose meaning; as far as he is concerned, the victims are either Christian martyrs or heathen fighters. He makes no distinction between professional gladiators and the untrained, doomed criminals who enter the arena under a definite death sentence. Perpetua fell into the *noxii* category, by virtue of her refusal to deny her new beliefs.

By Jove's brother, he means the god of the dead and ruler of the underworld, *Dis Pater*, *Dis* being a contracted form of *Dives*, 'rich', thus this deity is 'father of riches', perhaps indicating the mineral wealth of the land beneath the feet. *Dis Pater* is equated with Hades and Pluto. The two activities described in this passage are the testing of corpses (for positive proof of death) with a heated iron by a figure dressed in winged cap as the god Mercury or Hermes, and the carting out of gladiators' corpses by the god of the dead. This is supported by a further comment about these arena officials: *Ditis pater, Iovis frater, gladiatorum exsequias cum malleo deducit* (Tertullian, *Ad Nationes* 1.10.47). This also tells of *Dis Pater* with his hammer leading the funeral procession. Nowhere does Tertullian refer to Charun or even Charon. This association has been made solely on the basis of the hammer or mallet carried by the major Roman deity Dis Pater, and the depictions of the Etruscan death-demon Charun, not a deity in the same sense, who also wielded a hammer. That they both had mallets or hammers, and both had a connection with the recently dead, is the extent of the reason for the assertion that *Dis Pater* and Charun were interchangeable.

Mercury's identification with *Hermes Psychopompus* as conductor of souls is widely accepted as an authentic presence in the arena, though not until the close of the first century AD, but Charun, who was later transformed into the Greek Charon, Stygian ferryman of the dead, is harder to justify. Tertullian was a well-educated man, and it seems unlikely he was mistaken in his selection of Mercury and *Dis Pater*. As a piece of evidence, the Charun theory is tenuous to say the least. It seems to have no reasonable starting point.

Although it was not a comprehensive justification, the Etruscan origin for gladiators rested largely on the foregoing literary scraps. This explanation was widely accepted, especially when it was seen in conjunction with the evidence from the strange paintings on Etruscan tombs. It found favour with classical scholars in the late nineteenth and early twentieth centuries because it was a neat way of squaring the strongly held view of classical Rome as a cradle of civilisation with the perceived contradictory barbarism of the arena.

The thinking went that the Romans could be excused if their objectionable tradition of gladiatorial combat, and all the violent and cruel excesses that accompanied it, could be blamed on the Etruscans, a mysterious and 'oriental' people, who, according to Herodotus, had fled famine in Lydia in Asia Minor (modern Turkey), and had fetched up on the shores of northern Italy.

After decades of research into the original location of the Etruscans, current thinking has cast doubt on Herodotus' claim; they are to be seen more as an indigenous people of the Italic peninsula, who led the transition from the Villanovan Bronze Age culture to a dominant Iron Age society which first thrived in Etruria. They appeared as alien to the Romans as they did to the scholars of the last two centuries, mainly because their language and customs seemed impenetrable and unconnected to that of the Latins around them; they had a reputation for moral laxness and decadence, in part due to the higher status of women in their society, if classical sources were to be believed. The Etruscan kingdom on Rome's doorstep came to represent 'otherness' in a stylised, non-historical way, to the modern scholars who wanted to use them as scapegoats for Roman immorality as much as to the Romans themselves.

As an illustration of what can go wrong when assumption supersedes analysis, it was this scholarly apprehension of 'otherness' and of oriental decadence in the Etruscans that led to the ridiculous Nazi 'explanation' of the Roman adoption of Catholic Christianity in Italy as a direct result of the decadent influence of Etruscan 'priestcraft'. The crudely composed and utterly skewed Nazi logic classed the Romans as superior Indo-Europeans, who had been corrupted by the morally inferior (and racially different) Etruscans. We now know that the Etruscans were an indigenous people, although distinct from the Latins with whom they shared the Italic peninsula.

The Romans had a very complicated attitude towards their erstwhile rulers; to claim Etruscan ancestry gave a connection to an aristocracy of honourable antiquity, and in the late republic and early empire it had a certain cachet. Ambitious local politicians might well have found it useful when seeking office, as it implied an ancient and respected lineage. The emperor Claudius, for example, would boast of his wife's Etruscan blood and the poet Ovid, not that he advertised it, had Etruscan ancestry, as did Virgil. Nevertheless, by the late empire, names of Etruscan origin had all but disappeared from the lists of the ruling elite, indicating the final absorption of Etruria's aristocracy into that of Rome.

By contrast, during the first few centuries of Rome's existence, it was dominated by the Etruscans, and then ruled by an Etruscan king, though to clarify Rome's true position at that time, it remained a state of Latin-speaking people ruled by an Etruscan elite, with imported customs and social history. There is no doubt that it inherited key aspects of Etruscan culture; certainly in the matters of religion, art, architecture, culture and civil administration, there is plenty of archaeological, epigraphic and iconographic evidence showing how pervasive the Etruscan influence was throughout the fabric of everyday life in Rome.

Branching off from the main theory of gladiatorial combats originating in Etruria is the alternative proposal that the Etruscans themselves, reaching out from the north of the Italic peninsula during their campaigns of expansion, borrowed the idea of the gladiatorial spectacle from the southern tribes of Italy, principally the Samnites occupying the hill pastures above Campania. The Etruscan overlords then supposedly passed the habit of funeral games involving armed combat to the then much smaller city-state of Rome. So, to summarise the controversy, the scholarly debate has boiled down to whether gladiators originated in Etruria or Campania, or a combination of both, with varying degrees of influence from north and south being cited to prove the argument either way.

In defence of the direct Etruscan origin for gladiators, there are other reasons for connecting them to the use of ritual in killing, and to carry that one step further, for the link between that ritual and funeral rites. The ancient Mediterranean was full of stories of the sacrifice of prisoners at the funeral pyre or tomb of a dead warrior, especially if that warrior had been killed in battle. The classic example of this practice has its highest expression in the *Iliad*, book 23, at the funeral of Patroklos:

> Achilleus cut the throats of … twelve noble sons of the great-hearted Trojans, slaughtering them with the bronze for the grim purpose he had for them: and he set the iron strength of fire at work, to feed on them. Then he groaned out loud and called by name on his dear companion: 'Fare you well, Patroklos, even in the house of Hades. See, I am fulfilling now all that I promised you before. There are twelve noble sons of the great-hearted Trojans with you in the fire ….

In typical Greek fashion, Achilles' vow to honour his dead friend took the form of human sacrifice by the side of Patroklos' pyre.

To judge from the prominence of various depictions of the above scene on the walls of tombs in Etruria, this dramatic moment in the *Iliad* had great significance for the Etruscans. As a people, they had been exposed to many hellenizing influences, and the tradition of sacrificing captives to appease and honour the shades of dead warriors seems to have persisted in their own culture.

One of the best examples of the enduring Etruscan interest in the sacrificial themes of the *Iliad* is on the fresco from the Francois tomb at Vulci, in Etruria. It depicts Achilles in the act of cutting the throat of one of his Trojan captives (*colour plate 1*). Also shown is the Greek hero Ajax, very popular with the Etruscans, and the figures of Charun, a gatekeeper of the underworld (not to be confused with the Greek Charon, the ferryman over the river Styx) and his female counterpart, Vanth, a winged servant of the dead, often shown as a torch-bearer. Charun is depicted prominently; he is central to the action, watching the prisoner's execution. In this picture, as in most representations of Charun, he has blueish skin, a hooked nose, a strange unkempt tunic, and most importantly, a great mallet. He looks like the demon he is. It has been suggested that the mallet is for banging on the doors of Hades, or knocking the crossbar of the gates into place, thus sealing the fate of the deceased. Other depictions of Charun show him with rather incongruous little wings, though in the Francois fresco he has no apparent wings at all. At the Anina tomb, Charun and Vanth have been painted as fresco figures appropriately sited on either side of the tomb entrance, as guardians of the Underworld. Charun and Vanth are both official guides and protectors of that infernal region; however, only Charun may have made the transition into the Roman gladiatorial arena, if indeed that is a safe identification of the personification of the deity responsible for escorting the dead out of the arena. Thought to have been yet another introduction of the emperor Augustus, these Charun figures dressed as the hammer-wielding demon acted as an escort for the bodies of dead gladiators.

There is a suggestion that this character might have actually struck the fallen gladiators on the head with the mallet or hammer, in order to claim them for Hades. In view of the carnage and killing that went on, the arena might well have been thought of as a threshold of the Underworld, necessitating the presence of these chthonic figures to claim the dead and confirm the sacred nature of the executions, however pitiful, squalid and devoid of skill they may have actually appeared.

In an echo of this ritual, it had long been the practice of the Vatican officials, in the event of a Pope's death, to tap three times on the forehead of the dead Pontiff with a silver hammer, and to call out the baptismal name three times. This last act of *conclamatio* is said to be a rite that the Roman Catholic Church inherited from the ancient Roman funeral. The *conclamatio* may in turn have its roots in a custom mentioned in the *Odyssey*:

> No ship made sail next day until some shipmate had raised a cry, three times, for each poor ghost unfleshed .... (Book IX, 65)

In the case of gladiators, the hammer or mallet blow may have had the extra function of checking they were in fact dead, and perhaps finishing them off if they weren't. Indeed, Lactantius, the fourth-century Christian apologist, mentions this very concern in his *Human and Divine Institutions* when he says that spectators demanded that the bodies of gladiators who had killed in the arena be mutilated (*dissipari*) to make sure they were not feigning death.

By the fourth century AD, other Christian writers such as Prudentius were still finding plenty to criticise in the amphitheatre, and the reliability of their reports on what actually went on must be tempered by their partiality creating a tendency to generalise about the pagan atrocities they were so vociferously condemning:

> Look at the crime – stained offerings to frightful Dis, to whom is sacrificed the gladiator laid low on the ill-starred arena, a victim offered to Phlegethon in misconceived expiation for Rome .... Why, Charon by the murder of these poor wretches receives offerings that pay for his services as guide, and is propitiated by a crime in the name of religion. Such are the delights of the Jupiter of the dead...Is it not shameful that a strong imperial nation thinks it needful to offer such sacrifices for its country's welfare? .... With blood, alas, it calls up the minister of death from his dark abode to present him with a splendid offering of dead men...human blood is shed at the Latin god's festival and the assembled onlookers there pay savage offerings at the altar of their own Pluto.
> (Prudentius, *C. Symm.* 1.379-398)

Here, Charun has become Charon, Stygian ferryman and conductor of souls, and from the tone of the passage, Prudentius appears to think that the criminals were ritually offered as a matter of course to the infernal gods. Thus, what started in the republic as the disposal of *noxii* by aggravated penalties of execution conveniently combined with a public show, becomes, in his eyes, human sacrifice for the good of Rome. The appearance of Charun/Charon as an arena official, if ever that could be established as fact, would be a small further hint at Etruscan connection with the *munera*, but it is hardly conclusive.

Another example of this preoccupation with the myths of the Greek heroes is to be found on the 'priest' sarcophagus of Laris Partenu, dated to around 340 BC, and made from fine Greek Parian marble. Although the sarcophagus itself has Carthaginian elements on it, the sides have painted figures of warring Greeks and Amazons, and again the famous scene from the *Iliad* showing Achilles sacrificing Trojan prisoners at the funeral of Patroklos, complete with Etruscan Underworld figures in attendance.

So many of the tombs at these Etruscan cities of the dead are decorated with Greek myths that it is tempting to think that the Etruscans had no mythology of their own. Homeric battle scenes, anything involving Amazons, fratricidal duels, and other moments of high drama were all popular. Charun and Vanth appear frequently, sometimes on foot, sometimes in a chariot, accompanied by musicians and officials bearing standards. This solemn procession has echoes of the *pompa* at the start of the *munera*.

A version of prisoner sacrifice may have taken place in the sixth century BC, when the people of the Etruscan city of Caere stoned to death the Carthaginian and Greek prisoners of war they had captured after the sea-battle off Alaia, so Herodotus tells us. However, in the earliest purported example of identifiable human sacrifice, Livy writes of the immolation of Roman prisoners of war in 356 BC in the forum of Tarquinian Caere, when the Tarquinians (Tarquinia was an important Etruscan city) were at war with the Romans:

> Nor was the destruction in the line of battle so hard to accept as the fact that the Tarquinians sacrificed 307 Roman captives. (Livy, *Ab Urbe Condita Libri* 7.15)

In an act of carefully taken revenge, and certainly with no hint of ritualised killing or sacrifice, the Romans flogged and beheaded 358 Tarquinian nobles in 355 BC, performing this act of cold-blooded retribution in the Forum. By contrast, the iconographical evidence on the walls of Etruscan tombs and on their pottery shows that the Etruscan interest in the theme of Trojan sacrifice at Patroklos' funeral was strongly represented: it occurs with such frequency that we are entitled to consider it as an indication of their use of ritual killing as a publicly demonstrated custom. Taken with the literary evidence of Nicolaus of Damascus, the Augustan historian who referred to gladiatorial combat as a practice the Tyrrhenians (Etruscans) passed to the Romans, these pictorial proofs of the Etruscan association of funerals with human sacrifice do add a little circumstantial weight to the Etruscan theory. Unfortunately, the weight of evidence does not quite tip the scale.

Even less convincing, in the evidence for gladiator contests at any rate, is the 'Phersu' figure as depicted on several other tomb-paintings at Tarquinia (*17*). In the Tomb of the Augurs, this masked, black-bearded character is dressed in a short, patterned tunic and loincloth, with a tall conical hat. He appears to be holding the leash of a large cat-like creature that is sinking its teeth into the upper right thigh of a man with a sack or hood over his head. The hooded man holds a long club, and blood seems to be dripping from other wounds on his left leg. There is an interesting attachment on the leash nearest the 'cat's' collar. The whole thing is more reminiscent of some kind of *venatio*. It has been interpreted as a sadistic game peculiar, at least so far, to Etruria, in which a helmeted man (if the tall conical hat can be seen as an early helmet), perhaps masked like an actor, as masks were known with beards, performs an enigmatic role. Labelled *Phersu*, he permits a big cat or savage dog (it does more closely resemble a feline) to attack an armed, blinded opponent (if the sack over his head is intended as

17 Enigmatic figure of *Phersu* from the Tomb of the Augurs, *c.*520 BC. This Etruscan tomb painting shows some kind of game, contest or ritual involving wild beasts. *Illustration after the original*

a handicap); it has been thought that the hooded man might be a criminal, and that the game is similar therefore to the Roman penalty of *damnatus ad bestias*. The Latin word *persona*, as in a character in a play, possibly derives from this Etruscan word *Phersu*; it is known that the Romans imported their first actors, *histriones*, from Etruria. The word *histriones* is also Etruscan in origin. It is possible that the Romans also owed a debt to Etruscan theatrical spectacles, in which both bloodshed and buffoonery were featured.

This kind of violent entertainment is suggestive of gladiator shows, although there is no indication of combat. It is puzzling, yet it provides evidence that the Etruscans did at least use bloodshed for show, performances which they saw fit to depict on important tombs. This in itself is not enough to make the case for Etruscan gladiators, although perhaps it may argue for an identification of *venatores*, hunters in the arena, or better still, *bestiarii*, the wild beast fighters.

Lastly, there is a further group of tomb paintings, dating to the fifth and sixth centuries BC, depicting armed men who do not seem to be soldiers. These have been called pyrrhic dancers, performers in the *Pyrrhica*, which was a kind of parade-ground display of battlefield manoeuvres, all done to music. The Romans adopted the *Pyrrhica*, and under the emperors, they were performed in the arena as part of the programme, alongside the slaughter. One of this group of paintings, in the Tomb of the Bigae (named after the two-horse chariot depicted on it), shows nude performers and athletes, but also featured are men in formal clothing, carrying staffs or sticks. Two of the so-called pyrrhic dancers are men with helmets, one of which is plumed; both have spears and one of them has a shield. The effect is of funeral games; the men in robes look like they are officiating at an event, hence the staff or *lituus*.

The Tomb of the Bigae also shows boxing and wrestling, and spectators seated on what looks like bleachers. Other tombs show running, chariot racing, javelin and discus throwing – a veritable Olympic funeral games. The armed men are best understood as participating in these funeral games as combatants (if at all) in an almost balletic, choreographed sense. Whether they fought at all, or if they merely went through the motions without any physical contact, is impossible to fathom. In the picture, the pyrrhic dancers may be waiting to perform some formulaic armed drill, or they may be getting ready to fight. Nothing is certain in this depiction, least of all whether they would be fighting to kill, or just to win. Given the bloodthirsty nature of the Etruscans, the latter seems unlikely. As to the origin of the gladiators, we are left with the feeling that, in terms of hard evidence at least, there is something missing in the case for Etruscan gladiators. Despite the excavation of tombs throughout Etruria, not a single picture of armed combat between two men has ever been found; not a single gladiatorial artefact has been unearthed, apart from some Etruscan seventh-century BC bronze statuettes that have been tentatively identified as pertaining to gladiatorial combat. They are figures of nude males holding a sword in either hand, recalling the gladiatorial fighting style known as *dimachaerius* (fighter with two swords). Unfortunately, the centuries-long gap between the production of these statuettes and the appearance of the *munera* is very difficult to bridge. As with all the fragments of information connecting Etruria with gladiators, the statuettes prove nothing. Because the case rests on so many disparate and flimsy proofs, scholarship has tended to move away from an exclusively Etruscan explanation for gladiatorial combats.

This is not to deny the Etruscans a significant role in the Roman development of spectacles, particularly chariot-racing. It is clear that the Etruscan predilection for spectating rather than performing in games was inherited by their *protégés*, the Romans, as was their preference for using foreigners, captives and slaves to entertain them. This is probably as far as the limited evidence takes us. The Etruscan gladiator trail goes cold.

CAMPANIAN COMBATS

It seems obvious to look for the birth of gladiatorial combat wherever the earliest signs on the ground are. That would indisputably be Campania. Quite aside from the fourth-century BC Osco-Samnite tomb paintings, notably the depictions of armed duels from Paestum, which may well represent the first *munera*, the most significant argument in favour of a Campanian origin is simply that the earliest amphitheatres are all to be found in that region. The oldest is at Capua, dated to the end of the second century BC, as are Cumae and Liternum. Pompeii, the only amphitheatre with an established date, 70 BC, for its foundation, is next. At the time Pompeii's stone amphitheatre was built, the city of Rome still had none. Several others, notably Puteoli and Paestum, appear in the middle of the first century BC. It is therefore reasonable to accept that the earliest examples of stone amphitheatres do appear in Campania before anywhere else. To go further, the probable centre for the origins of the amphitheatre in Italy was around the fringes of the Bay of Naples, in Campania.

Campania had a good supply of stone and an abundance of the raw building materials needed for construction, particularly *pozzolana*, a lightweight, porous volcanic ash used in cement-making, deposited over the centuries from Vesuvius, which would certainly have encouraged building work, but the need for the amphitheatres as locations for combats would have had to precede any construction.

The Paestum duel scenes on the tomb frescoes show something like gladiator fights (particularly one example with what looks like officials refereeing the combats), and the earliest arenas are in neighbouring Campania. More so than the Etruscan theory, this has the look of credible circumstantial evidence. In particular, the quality of the Paestum pictures is convincing; they show helmeted warriors, with spears and shields, in the act of fighting each other; they have wounds dripping blood, and other scars (*18*). They are equipped similarly, so any

18 Paestum: fourth-century BC tomb mural (tomb 10) showing individual combats. *Illustration after the original*

question of this being a portrayal of a military encounter between two opposing sides can be confidently ruled out. What we are left with looks like two men fighting in a controlled bout.

In addition, the well-documented rivalries between Campanian Capua and Puteoli, and indeed other cities in Campania, show determination by the local governments in the region to commit extravagant expenditure on civic monuments, particularly amphitheatres. Some cities even acquired two amphitheatres, such was the popularity and prestige attached to the *munera*. Everything points towards a strong and thriving tradition of gladiatorial combat owing nothing to Rome's influence.

From an early date, amphitheatres were a very important part of the civic set-up in each thriving metropolis of Campania. There is also the fact of Capua's pre-eminent private *ludi*, gladiatorial training barracks, founded long before the imperially-established *Ludus Magnus* at Rome, and the numerous other private training establishments in Campania.

Added to the very substantial argument of form (*amphitheatrum*) following function (*munera*), and the Paestum paintings, there are references from Livy, Strabo and to a lesser degree Silius Italicus, citing the Campanian banquets at which gladiators fought.

Taken as a whole, the case for Campania is very persuasive. Undoubtedly, however, there was a transmission of Etruscan elements at a very early date into the fabric of the gladiatorial combats, but the weight of the evidence suggests Campania is where they first arose.

EARLY SIGNS: GLADIATORS IN ROME

We have Livy to thank for telling us that, in 264 BC, 'Decimus Junius Brutus was the first to put on a gladiatorial combat in honour of his deceased father'; however, we should not assume that the *munus mortis* sprang into being, fully formed, for that specific occasion. Although he was a writer with marked republican and aristocratic sympathies, Livy was also very much a celebrant of Rome's glorious past, which therefore gained him the approval and support of Augustus. His history of Rome in 142 books, of which only 35 survive, is based on religious annals and magistrates' records, and tells Rome's story from its foundation to 9 BC. In his preface, he wrote off the present as a time when ' the might of a long powerful people is beginning to destroy itself'. He claimed to be 'preserving the record of the greatest nation in the world' and he was fiercely patriotic but at the same time pessimistic in the face of what he saw as the moral decline of 'the present day when we can endure neither our vices nor the remedies needed to cure them'. It is quite revealing about Roman attitudes to gladiators that he makes a point of mentioning the combat at the funeral of 264 BC in a generally approving way. He could so easily have omitted all references to gladiatorial contests. However, it is clear that Livy certainly did not think that six gladiators fighting to the death was in any way indicative of a decline in moral standards; quite the reverse, in fact. It was a positive example of *romanitas*, an example he was obviously happy to select rather than reject from the public annals he was using.

There is some faint evidence that combats were held in Rome prior to 264 BC, possibly supplied by Suetonius. A fragment of text that is sometimes attributed to his work, *de Regibus*, credits the Etruscan Tarquinius Priscus, (traditionally 616-579 BC), who was one of the later, less legendary seven kings of Rome, with the establishment of state-sponsored *munera* for a period of 26 years, by the introduction of pairs of gladiators: '*Tarquinius Priscus prior Romanis duo paria gladiatorum edidit quae comparavit per annos XXVI*'. The fragment could equally have come from his commentary on the Roman festivals and games, a book now sadly lost to us. Suetonius was a meticulous and objective historian; at one point in his career, he was the director of the imperial libraries, so he had access to all the archives. However, the text cannot be definitely attributed to him; nevertheless, it is useful when added to the other information.

There is also what might be termed circumstantial evidence of earlier *munera* from the second-century AD writer, Festus, who reports that the *maeniana*, the divisions of seating within an amphitheatre, were named after C. Maenius, censor in 338 BC, because he was the first to enlarge the seating capacity of the Forum for the viewing of spectacles. Linking this Maenius with seating specifically for the better viewing of spectacles, *quo ampliarentur superiora spectacula*, tends to suggest that such combats took place during the later fourth century BC; although *spectacula* could have its meaning of entertainment in general, rather than *munera*, so we need to be careful of jumping to conclusions. Again, it prompts speculation rather than conclusions.

One last piece of evidence to be weighed up is the introduction of the 'Samnite' type of gladiator. It is reasonable to presume that 'foreign captive' classifications came from the introduction of prisoners of war as gladiators; thus, the most obvious and logical period in which the Romans could obtain such prisoners would of course be during the three Samnite Wars, which were pursued between 343 and 290 BC, again, earlier than the first known *munera* presented at Rome.

Adding substance to Livy's account is Valerius Maximus, the first-century historian whose collection of historical anecdotes, *Facta et Dicta Memorabilia*, (Memorable Deeds and Words) provides the further information that Decimus and his brother Marcus were the *editores* putting on the combat, and that it was held in the *Forum Boarium*, the old cattle market down by the Tiber (*2*).

More details surface in the writings of Ausonius of Gaul and Servius, but both men were looking back at the event from their fourth-century AD vantage point, through muddied historical waters. Ausonius claims rather anachronistically, and with poetic licence, that there were three pairs of Thracian-style gladiators. But since the earliest date for this type of gladiator is 171 to 168 BC, when Thracians were probably taken as prisoners of war during the Third Macedonian War, this clearly puts that style of combat much later than 264 BC. He also puts the location of the combats at the tomb itself, presumably outside the *pomerium*, the sacred boundary of the city inside which by law no graves, burials or tombs of any kind could be sited. Servius, the fourth-century AD writer and grammarian, ruminates upon the entire gladiatorial concept, including the derivation of the word *bustuarius*, and the practice of sacrificing prisoners of war to propitiate the shade of the departed:

> *mos erat in sepulcris virorum fortium captives necari; quod postquam crudele visum est, placuit gladiatores ante sepulcra dimicare* – 'The custom was to kill captives at the tombs of great men. Because this, after a time, seemed cruel, it was decided that gladiators should fight before the tombs.'

With these sparse references, we have the first reports of gladiators fighting at Rome itself, although, with the exception of the questionable Suetonius fragment, they throw no light on how the *munera* actually began, other than that they were funeral games, and neither do they give any indication whatsoever of the origin of such combats. None of the commentators ventures any opinion as to whether they came from Etruria, Campania or Rome itself.

POLITICAL GAMES

It would be strange indeed if gladiatorial combat suddenly started up in 264 BC unprompted by the events or influences of the time. However, as this is the first recorded instance we have, it may not be coincidental that it is mentioned as occurring in the same year that Rome entered the First Punic War against Carthage. Even though the combats were ostensibly part of a private occasion to mark Junius Pera's death, his sons used the gladiators not only to pay tribute to their father's standing in the community, but also to enhance it. It made them look good, too; as the *editores* who put on the combats, they, as well as their honoured father, gained prestige. We might think of this as inappropriately exploitative, but again we must remember that our values are not those of the Romans. Mark Antony's oration over the body of Julius Caesar is a perfect illustration of the importance of funerals as opportunities for the heirs and surviving interested parties to serve their own ends by drawing the attention of the public to the importance of the deceased man and his family.

The very fact that this occasion, and many other subsequent ones, is preserved in the public record indicates the ambiguous position in Roman life that gladiatorial displays held, even at this early point in their development. Caught between the public and private spheres, the combats, as we have seen, developed into a spectacular way of highlighting the status of the dead man and his family in the eyes of the Roman public, becoming so popular that each display, in the prevailing political spirit of republican competitiveness, had to top the ones that had gone before it.

This 'first' *munus* in 264 BC was soon followed by others, and the frequency of their occurrence in the historical record increases noticeably. And as they increase, so too does the scale of each spectacle. We are reliant on Livy again for an account of the next one to appear. It was 216 BC when, we are told, 'the three sons, Lucius, Marcus and Quintus, gave funeral games for three days and twenty-two pairs of gladiators in the forum for M.Aemilius Lepidus, who had been consul twice and augur.'

These *munera* were clearly still part of the funeral rites, although the scale of the spectacle has been upgraded from three to 22 pairs of fighters, and naturally therefore taking three days to perform. It is unlikely that the three pairs offered in 264 BC took up more than the afternoon, and whilst the comparatively small space of the Forum Boarium was sufficient to accommodate them and the spectators, the venue for Lepidus' *munera* was the central meeting-place of all Rome, the *Forum Romanum*. This is unsurprising given the high status of the patrician Aemilii Lepidi, a branch of the *gens Aemilia*, which had become a powerful political family with consuls in almost every generation from the third century. We know that one of Lepidus' sons, Marcus, was *praetor* in Sicily in 218 BC, and possibly held office in Rome itself in 217. Livy tells us that Marcus, whose father and grandfather had both been elected consul, ran for the consulship in 216, but was unsuccessful. This is so valuable because it is the first time a link can be made between the electioneering of a political candidate (the very word 'candidate' comes from the Latin for a whitened toga as worn by a political aspirant) and the giving of *munera*; it heralds a gradual progression of political opportunism in the staging of the combats towards the end of the Republic.

The notice of the Aemilian *munera* is to be found next to an account of a dedication of the Temple of Venus Erycina and a report of the celebration of the Roman and Plebeian games, both big state events of that year. Again, Livy is the most important source for these early combats, and he used the public records as the basis for his history, which probably replicated them to a great degree. The fact that the gladiatorial combats appear in this kind of official record strongly suggests that even at that early date the *munera* were regarded as public celebrations.

CANNAE: CATACLYSM AND CATALYST

The significance of the dates of the Junian and Aemilian *munera* must also be appreciated, because one took place at the beginning of the First Punic War in 264 BC, and the other, in 216 BC, was in the year of the battle of Cannae, arguably the worst Roman defeat in history (*3*). Again, it cannot be coincidental that they both appear in the public record at dangerous times for Rome. It is stretching credibility to accept that these two combats, nearly 50 years apart, were the only ones to be put on in all that time. Other *munera* may well have been staged in the ensuing 50 years, but may not have been reported, if no crisis or public event arose to make them newsworthy.

The significance of Cannae cannot be overstated. Rome was left with a legacy of insecurity that acted as a powerful engine for change in military, political and social matters. It would not be an exaggeration to liken Cannae to a Roman 9/11, as the sense of shock and the need for reassurance about national security drove the Romans to extreme measures. Juvenal's remark about the news of the people's favourite chariot team, the Greens, being beaten and plunging the city into shock 'as if Cannae had happened' is as revealing about Rome's persistent memory of the impact of that defeat as it is about the importance of the races. There was a feeling of mass panic and despair, and public anxiety about the campaign weakening Rome by draining resources, with no compensating prospect of replenishment from spoils of war. So many men had been lost at Cannae – at least 50,000 out of 86,000 troops – a levy of young men over the age of 17 was raised, and even slaves were recruited into the army:

> They gave orders that armour, weapons and other equipment should be made ready, and took down from the temples and porticoes the ancient spoils of enemies. The levy wore a strange appearance, for, owing to the scarcity of free men and the need of the hour, they bought, with money from the treasury, 8,000 young and stalwart slaves and then armed them, first asking each if he were willing to serve. They preferred these slaves for soldiers, though they might have redeemed the prisoners of war at less expense.
> (Livy, *Ab Urbe Condita Libri* 22.57.9-12)

The important phrase in Livy's account is 'they might have redeemed the prisoners of war at less expense', because it reveals Rome's contemptuous disdain for soldiers who had failed to keep faith with it, soldiers who should have won or died trying. The prisoners of war in question were 7000 armed soldiers who had failed to take a golden opportunity to fight their way back through the Carthaginian ranks; instead, they surrendered, and that made them worse than slaves who at least served their masters well, and certainly worse than gladiators who fought bravely.

There was a debate in Rome over whether to ransom these captives of Hannibal. The captives' envoy asked that they should be spared because they had shown courage, and that they did value their honour above life; they asserted that no comparison could be made between their value and that of slaves. This was too much of a provocation to the famous general Torquatus. He came from a distinguished Roman military family, with a strong tradition of meeting the enemy in single combat, in the ancient fashion, and by his response, it is clear he felt the envoy was almost making a virtue out of the troops' surrender. Disgusted, he replied:

> You lack even the spirit to be saved!... you have forfeited your status, lost your civic rights, been made slaves of the Carthaginians. Do you think to return, for ransom, to that condition which you forfeited by cowardice and turpitude?

The Senate decided against a ransom; although the envoy had believed that slaves were of less value to Rome, Rome decided it would rather do without the services of men who had disgraced themselves. They were regarded as men who had reduced themselves to the status of the worst kind of slave. Instead, Rome chose the slaves who had proved, by their willingness to give their lives for Rome, that they were more honourable than the soldiers now held prisoner by Carthage. This episode illustrates Rome's unbending attitude towards gladiators. They were expected, as soldiers were, to win or die, with no exceptions or mitigating circumstances.

After 216 BC, Rome wanted to see gladiators re-enacting the stark military imperatives exposed by Cannae: facing death without flinching, volunteering their blood just as the slaves had done, and thus emulating the heroes of Roman legend. For rebels and deserters, an equally graphic demonstration of Rome's reward was laid on for the public good. Prior to the elephant trampling of deserters in 167 BC, there were earlier instances of harsh measures against military criminals. In 214 BC, 370 deserters were publicly scourged and then thrown from the Tarpeian Rock in Rome, and in that same year, the Roman commander of Sicily had 2000 deserting troops beheaded.

As if to compensate for any defeat and loss of face it had suffered, Rome's brutality towards any enemies who did fall into its hands was magnified. There was a need to show the world (and itself) that hostile forces would be utterly destroyed, deserters and cowards, losers and rebels would pay a terrible price for their failures, and that soldiers demonstrating *virtus* would receive the gratitude of Rome, with immortality assured as part of the city's eternal memory.

The defeat at Cannae crystallised Roman attitudes to gladiators in particular; hitherto, the *munera* had primarily been the means by which the provider advertised the importance of his family, but now it was obvious that Rome expected gladiators to demonstrate the virtues of military excellence to its citizens. Everything that Rome demanded of its soldiers, it now required of the gladiators in the arena: *fortitudo* (courage/strength), *disciplina* (training), *constantia* (steadiness/perseverance), *patientia* (endurance), *contemptus mortis* (contempt of death), *amor laudis* (love of glory), and *cupido victoriae* (desire to win), all of which could be expressed in the one word that encapsulated Rome's highest and most desirable moral quality – *virtus*.

The effect of Cannae was to propel *munera* from private functions into the public domain, and to produce a rapid escalation of the number and scale of gladiatorial spectacles held in Rome. So much war had sharpened the Roman appetite for contests to the death; it had not escaped the attention of the politicians and the military (in effect, the same thing) that the gladiator fights were also an effective and popular way of keeping the Roman people 'on message'.

The popularity of these displays spread quickly beyond Rome; many rulers had the opportunity to see how useful a political tool they could become, and so the *munera* became one of Rome's own cultural exports: in one of the earliest, in 206 BC, Scipio put on games at Carthago Nova, in honour of the departed spirits, *di manes*, of his father and uncle, both of whom had died five years earlier, and in 166 BC, the Syrian king Antiochus Epiphanes established *munera* at Antioch, having seen the political advantages of the combats at first hand while he was a hostage in Rome. Decades before Julius Caesar, gladiator games were already taking root in the popular culture.

2

CAESAR'S GAMES

In 105 BC, at Arausio in Gaul, about five years before Julius Caesar was born, Rome suffered its worst military defeat since Cannae. Two northern tribes, from the region of what is now Jutland, inflicted heavy losses on the Roman army. There was public alarm in Rome, and the consuls, Rutilius Rufus and C. Manlius, were forced to call upon the services of *lanistae*, gladiator trainers, in a bid to train as many hastily levied raw recruits as they could find. Marius, the battle-seasoned general, who introduced reforms into the army and made it effectively a professional militia, was reported by Frontinus to prefer the troops trained by the *lanistae* to his own. The use of gladiator trainers at this time of crisis was later misinterpreted as the first occasion of official, publicly sponsored *munera*.

The first century BC saw civil unrest, overmighty generals and warleaders, from Marius and Sulla to Antony and Octavian, and of course Caesar himself, taking advantage of Roman insecurities about invasion by foreigners to build up for themselves political and autocratic powerbases. These rival commanders with their privately raised armies did not stay within the Roman law – they adjusted it to suit their purposes as they saw fit. The republic was slowly decomposing, providing a breeding ground for power struggles, in which gladiators, with their crowd-pleasing abilities, were an important resource.

It was into this state of flux that Gaius Julius Caesar was born, in around 100 BC (*19*). His was an old, aristocratic Roman family, though not wealthy, and one that liked to believe it was descended from the goddess Venus. During the civil wars, the young Caesar, whose family had picked the losing side, was forced to flee Rome to escape from the dictator Sulla and his rule of fear. He served in the army abroad, deliberately staying out of the tyrant's reach, finally returning home only sometime after Sulla's death in 78 BC. It was then that his ambitions started to clear a path for his rise to military and political success.

By 68 BC he was *quaestor*, in an atmosphere of fevered competition, where the republic was a pale shadow of itself, as Rome became a crucible for conflicting political ambitions. The spectacles, whether *ludi* or *munera*, became indistinguishable from each other, because the rival generals just needed to get the people on their side, no matter what outlandish show they had to provide to do it.

19 Bust of Gaius Julius Caesar.
Photograph: Pharos Pictures

The convention that a *munus* was held in honour of the death of a relative had been so eroded that it was observed only in theory. The requirement that the games were to be offered as an obligation to the deceased could be circumvented by staging the *munus* at a much later date, when it was most useful to the giver, usually in terms of political advantage. This meant, in effect, that some *munera* were held years after the deaths of those they purported to honour and commemorate.

Julius Caesar did this very thing in 65 BC, when he held games on the pretext of a *munus* for his long-dead father, whose shade had presumably been patient enough to wait twenty years for the filial duty to be carried out. The historian Plutarch describes this extravaganza, the first of many in Caesar's career:

> And, when he was *aedile*, he provided a show of 320 pairs of gladiators fighting in single combat, and what with this and all his other lavish expenditure on theatrical performances, processions, and public banquets he threw into the shade all attempts at winning distinction in this way that had been made by previous holders of the office. The result was to make the people so favourably disposed towards him that every man among them was trying to find new offices and new honours to bestow upon him in return for what he had done. (Plutarch, *Vitae* 5)

Judging by the popularity it brought him, Caesar's massive investment of funds into this spectacle paid off handsomely. So conspicuous was the extravagance of the show he put on, that the gladiators fought with silver weapons, against each other and against wild beasts. It was the prospect of this event that caused the Senate to take fright. Hearing about Caesar's plans for a gladiatorial extravaganza, and seeing clearly that he could have had, in effect, what amounted to a small private army at his disposal in the city, unnerving the executive, the Senate passed a law in the year of 65 BC limiting the number of gladiators a person could keep at Rome.

Julius Caesar was not the only ambitious young politician seeking public recognition on his way up the greasy pole; so prevalent was electoral bribery of this kind that the Senate passed another law in 63 BC, the *lex calpurnia de ambitu*, making it *ambitus* (electoral corruption) to give shows, feasts or cash gifts within two years of candidacy. Cicero tells of one Vatinius, seeking high office, who'knew what the people wanted' and 'foresaw their applause', and he was certainly not an isolated case.

However, Caesar outclassed his rivals with his instinctive showmanship and willingness to take financial risks. During his rise to power, he was often labouring under vast amounts of debt; the spectacles did not come cheap, and he had to borrow against the future benefits he could bring his creditors. This need to spend huge sums of money prompted him to establish his own gladiator school in the heart of Campania, at Capua (*6*). He rightly saw that it would be cheaper to supply his own fighters than to hire them at a premium.

With political success came physical threats, and like other prominent public figures, notably his future rival Pompey, he started to use gangs of gladiators as personal bodyguards. They didn't confine their duties to guarding Caesar, however, and political intimidation of Caesar's opponents seems to have been part of their job description.

By 50 BC, Caesar had consolidated his political future with military success in Gaul, secured the consulship, and earned the enmity of his main rival, Pompey. It was said that Caesar had 5000 gladiators at the barracks in Capua, a venture that had proved to be a considerable source of profit for him. As well as providing him with gladiators on tap, as it were, it meant he could charge *munerarii*, anyone wanting to give games, for their hire, including a capital sum for any who were killed. To give some idea of the level of expenditure, in a surviving textbook of Roman law from the second century AD, known as Gaius' *Institutes* after the famous jurist, the sums payable for gladiators at that time are given: 80 *sestertii* for every gladiator who survived, and 4000 for every man killed or wounded. Though this was obviously a century later, allowing for some inflation, it is still a fair indication of the sort of sums involved.

Seeing the inherent threat in a private army of 5000 armed and trained gladiators at Caesar's command on Rome's doorstep, Pompey seized them, and had them disarmed and dispersed in pairs to be lodged with his supporters. The bad blood between Pompey and Caesar engulfed the city, dividing the aristocracy and perpetuating the civil disorder.

The civil wars rumbled on until 45 BC, although Pompey was murdered in Alexandria in 48 BC, before Caesar could catch up with him. Caesar continued his conquests, returning to Rome for his fourfold triumph, to celebrate his victories in Gaul with games that outdid even those of his old rival. In 55 BC, Pompey had dedicated his theatre with a *venatio* in which 20 elephants and several hundred lions along with 400 other wild beasts had died. In 46 BC, in a spectacular piece of political one-upmanship, Caesar put on gladiator combats and much more besides (*20*). Suetonius gives a detailed account of the extravaganza:

> He added a popular banquet and a distribution of meat; also a dinner to celebrate his Spanish victory, but decided that this had not been splendid enough and, five days later, served a second, more succulent one.
>
> His public shows were of great variety. They included a gladiatorial contest, stage-plays for every Roman ward performed in several languages, chariot-races in the Circus, athletic competitions, and a mock naval battle. At the gladiatorial contest in the Forum, a man named Furius Leptinus, of an important praetorian family, fought Quintus Calpenus, a barrister and former senator, to the death. The sons of leaders of Asia and Bithynia danced the Pyrrhic sword dance....A broad ditch had been dug around the race-course, now extended at either end of the Circus, and the contestants were young noblemen who drove four-horse and two-horse chariots or rode pairs of horse, jumping from back to back...

20 Gladiators contemporary with Julius Caesar. What appears to be a late republican *Thracian* is depicted in combat with another category of gladiator, possibly a *hoplomachus*. Mid to late first century BC. *Based on an original relief in Museo Nazionale Romano alla Terme Diocleziano, Rome*

> Wild beast hunts took place five days running, and the entertainment ended with a battle between two armies, each consisting of five hundred infantry, twenty elephants and thirty cavalry. To let the camps be pitched facing each other, Caesar removed the central barrier of the Circus, around which the chariots ran. Athletic contests were held in a temporary stadium on the Campus Martius, and lasted for three days.
>
> The naval battle was fought on an artificial lake dug in the Lesser Codeta, between Tyrian and Egyptian ships, with two, three, or four banks of oars, and heavily manned. Such huge numbers of visitors flocked to these shows from all directions that many of them had to sleep in tents pitched along the streets or roads, or on roof-tops; and often the pressure of the crowd crushed people to death. The victims included two senators. (Suetonius, *Caesar* 38-39)

It is hardly surprising that Caesar was popular with his soldiers and the Roman citizens; the sums of money and the presents of food he was distributing amongst the populace exceeded anything ever seen before, and must have cost him well in excess of 60 million *sestertii*. On top of that, the land and rent gifts he paid for would have doubled that sum. And that is before the cost of the games is factored in, including the new wooden seating in the Forum, and the underground passages to facilitate theatrical special effects and the transfer of men and beasts into the arena there. When the cost of excavating the swampy ground in the Campus Martius next to the Tiber in order to create the artificial lake for the *naumachia*, the naval battle, is taken into account, the sums involved must have been astronomical, and of course that does not even begin to reflect the cost of the gladiators themselves, the *noxii* involved in the large-scale battles, and the animals.

NAUMACHIAE

Caesar's wealth by this time must have been fabulous for him to be able to consider that kind of outlay. Naturally, his many foreign campaigns would have amassed vast sums from booty, *praeda*, and its realised cash equivalent, *manubiae*, all of which would have personally enriched him. Even so, it is an extraordinarily breathtaking concept, for one man to put on at great cost a public spectacle of such magnitude that it literally would never be forgotten, and one for which there would seem to be no modern parallel. In so many ways, it was a masterpiece of showmanship and innovation; for instance, the mock sea battle, the *naumachia*, was the first recorded in Rome.

The word *naumachia* meant both the site created for the spectacle and the spectacle itself. It was in this type of mock naval battle that several thousand prisoners of war, doubtless reserved from Caesar's many campaigns, supplemented by criminals and unwanted slaves, were slaughtered *en masse* in a bloody tableau, re-enacting an actual historical sea battle between the Egyptians and the

Phoenicians. Caesar had a lake created in the Campus Martius for this specific purpose, big enough for the biremes, triremes and even quadriremes representing the navies of the opposing sides. The oarsmen manning these replicated warships had little chance of survival, each one a puppet in a lavish aquatic spectacle. The point was not to reconstruct history, but to re-enact memorable sea-battles of antiquity for their entertainment value. Typically, Augustus' answer to Caesar's offering was to have a bigger, better lake excavated beside the Tiber, in which 6000 captives re-enacted the Battle of Salamis. This site became the traditional home to *naumachiae* put on by emperors thereafter, with many different naval battles being staged there, although Claudius arranged a spectacular celebratory display on the Fucine Lake, outside Rome, with many thousands of *naumachiarii* drawn from the ranks of criminals and captives. Companies of the Praetorian Guard, backed up by heavy artillery, were stationed on rafts around the lake to prevent any escapes, and vessels carrying marines patrolled the lake as an extra precaution. It was at this amazing aquatic re-enactment that the doomed fighters saluted the emperor with the words now so familiar to 'sword and sandal' aficionados the world over: '*Ave imperator, morituri te salutant*' – 'hail Caesar, those about to die salute you'. These words, which have wormed their way into the public consciousness and crop up as if they were compulsory in each and every gladiator 'B' movie as well as true epics such as *Spartacus* and *Gladiator*, are recorded nowhere else in the classical sources, and it is reasonable to suppose that they were a one-off appeal for mercy to an emperor known for his obvious enjoyment of executions, rather than a customary form of words universally voiced in the arena. In any case, the fighters on the Fucine Lake were not gladiators as such, but *noxii* sentenced to die. Caught off guard, Claudius, in an attempt at wit that backfired, replied: '*Aut non*' – 'Or not'.

Mistakenly thinking that they had been pardoned, the men refused to fight, and only after some coercion, they reluctantly started the combat, though at first with little enthusiasm for bloodshed. Thus far, the episode has a comical Python-esque flavour, but as it unfolds, it illustrates the sheer unpredictability of the spectacles. Forced to fight, the men began killing each other in earnest, although perversely, the survivors were 'exempted from destruction', according to Tacitus, for fighting 'with the spirit and courage of freemen'. They started out as doomed criminals, but by their show of bravery they transformed themselves into gladiators for the day, with the gladiator's reward of life regained, at least for that day.

There is a persistent and controversial belief that *naumachiae* were held in the Colosseum, but it has no foundation in fact; the theory has both adherents and detractors. Granted, the site of the amphitheatre was Nero's Golden House, with its own lake; water supply would not have been a problem if Vespasian had wanted to turn the lake into a *naumachia*, and there is reason to believe he did, conceiving of the amphitheatre project as a way of encompassing all types of spectacle. Yet the archaeological evidence does not support the existence of any mechanical means of flooding the arena, despite the presence of a large pit beneath it which some have interpreted as evidence for water storage. Though there is no doubt the arena was boarded over, there is just nothing to indicate how a water supply could be channelled up into it, and how it would be drained. Vespasian may well have intended to provide naval as well as land-based shows at his great new amphitheatre, but the logistics defeated his planners. His son Titus did indeed put on *naumachiae* to celebrate the inauguration of his father's project in AD 80, as recorded by Suetonius, Martial and Cassius Dio, but there is no hard evidence they took place in the Colosseum. Sea-battles in the Colosseum remain mythological in every sense; wishful thinking naturally places them in the greatest of all amphitheatres.

SIGNS AND PORTENTS

The assassination of Julius Caesar triggered even bloodier civil war, and was the key event that finally propelled the gladiator contests into the public domain. The city of Rome succumbed to a form of collective panic, an unease and disquiet brought on by the tumultuous political events of the last few years, culminating in the death of a man they had both loved and feared. It seemed as if the gods were communicating divine displeasure at the state of things; the relationship that Rome had enjoyed with its deities seemed fractured and dysfunctional, broken on the funeral pyre of Julius Caesar.

The second-century historian, Cassius Dio, gave a detailed account of the omens, prodigies and upheavals that disturbed the Roman state in the year 42 BC, when the republic seemed balanced on a knife-edge. The significance of these terrible events, the awful signs in the heavens as the sun shone at night as well as by day, expanding and then contracting to a pinpoint of light, meteorites and thunderbolts assaulting the city, and the strange events in Rome, was not lost on the Roman people; the eerie sounds of phantom weapons clashing, the shouts of soldiers and trumpets calls that emanated from the gardens of Caesar and Antony, the dog burying the body of another it had killed, in canine imitation of the political murder so recently committed – all of these signs were messages of divine wrath, ready to fall like an axe on Rome's waiting neck.

Most dreadful of all portents for the unity of Rome, the statue of Jupiter Latiaris gushed blood from its right arm for all to see during the festival on the Alban Mount. The people tried to avert disaster by a ritual expiation and purification, to assure the gods of their devotion. It was at this moment of impending national disaster that the plebeian *aediles*, acting in place of the consuls, decided that the circus races normally held in honour of Ceres were not sufficient to pay tribute to the goddess; instead, they decided to hold gladiatorial combats. Blood should be spilt for blood shed impiously.

For the first time ever, gladiatorial *munera* would be held as part of the official spectacle of the Roman state. It is indicative of the official desperation that the establishment decided to harness the undeniable power of the ritual bloodshed of gladiatorial contests and place it in the service of the state in its time of crisis.

From this point on, gladiator combats took their place in the official public calendar; the link between funerals for public figures and the gladiators was broken, and would never be reinstated. Although *munera* continued to be demanded by the people in the event of the death of a public figure, they were not exclusively associated with the funeral rites. As time went on, they came to celebrate only the generosity of the *editor* of the games, which in imperial Rome was more often than not the emperor himself.

AUGUSTUS: *PRINCEPS ET AMPHITHEATRUM*

Caesar's successor, Octavian, by now nicknamed Augustus in a nod towards the veneration in which he was held, had witnessed the immense public value of the *spectacula*, and he announced the provision of eight *munera* in which 10,000 men fought, thus eclipsing forever the memory of Julius Caesar's grand games. His financial resources were far greater than those of any single ruler before him, and, what is more, he had the authority to impose his will on all such *spectacula*. By 22 BC, he had transferred control of the *ludi Romani* to himself at the hub of power; this is the point at which the *munera* came under the *aegis* of imperial control. He set up an empire-wide administrative system for *munera*, the *procuratores familiae gladiatoriae*.

Every measure he passed tied the gladiatorial games more closely to imperial rule, a relationship that persisted through the Julio-Claudian and Flavian dynasties and beyond. The other side of that coin was that the popularity of the emperors became inextricably linked with the provision of lavish and comprehensive games, and although the caricature of the emperor being forced to keep the mob sweet with games is far from the full picture, nevertheless it contains some truth.

Augustus shrewdly limited the *praetores* to two shows and a maximum of 120 gladiators for their term of office, thereby ensuring that all other gladiatorial games would be produced by the emperor and the imperial family; the people would then clearly see to whom their gratitude was owed.

At a stroke, this got rid of the vast sums of wasted money in political competition; the *princeps* alone would henceforth use the games to demonstrate the Roman *imperium*, in the carefully choreographed and manipulated rituals of the arena. The people exchanged the voice they had had in the traditional forum of the republic for the unpredictable clamour of the amphitheatre under the principate of Augustus. The amphitheatre became the place where the people could get closest to their ruler, and hope that he heard their voice.

As Suetonius tells us, Augustus 'surpassed all his predecessors in the frequency, variety and magnificence of his public shows'.

CARNEM ET VENATIONES

By 216 BC, the tipping point for the progression of the *munera* had been reached, and they started to escalate rapidly in scale and number. The deceased Lepidus had been honoured with 22 pairs of gladiators; in 200 BC, there were 25 pairs at the funeral of Marcus Valerius Laevinius; in 183 BC 60 pairs for Publius Licinius, with a public distribution of meat, *visceratio data*, presumably from an accompanying *venatio*, or beast spectacle. In 174 BC, out of several shows presented, the one that stood out was presented by Titus Flamininus, who, so Livy tells us, put on 74 pairs over four days, with theatrical performances and a public banquet of meats, *cum visceratione epuloque et ludis scaenicis*.

The tradition of distributing a dole of meat, known as the *visceratio*, is recorded as early as 328 BC; again, Livy tells of M. Flavius, who thus rewarded those who walked in his mother's funeral procession. This dole of meat apparently made a big impression, unsurprising in a poor and hungry underclass, and won him the tribuneship at the next election.

From the early days of the republic, its ruling elite had provided funeral banquets; famous generals like Caesar and Sulla gave doles of meat at their triumphs. These feasts and banquets were both a political instrument and almost a social responsibility for the rich. By the late first century BC, the city of Rome contained about a million mouths to feed, with at least 200,000 of them on the grain-dole lists. Because the diet of the *plebs*, the Roman underclass, was protein-poor, the prospect of public celebrations, festivals and banquets where meat would be doled out, was keenly anticipated. Cicero himself underlined the tradition of associating gladiatorial spectacles with games and banquets, and was of the opinion that the people should not be denied these things, as long as candidates gave them out of generosity, *liberalitas*, rather than as bribery, *largitio*. This *visceratio* should not be confused with Juvenal's famous 'bread and circuses' remark, which referred to the Roman lower class dependence on the monthly grain handout, *panem*, and the popular public entertainment of chariot-races, *circenses*.

At this point, where the line between the giving of the gladiatorial display out of duty to the dead, and as a crowd-pleasing opportunity for personal advancement starts to blur, it is interesting to note that there is more than just bloodlust at work in the mob. A hunger for that rare commodity, meat, is accompanied by an appetite for amusement, a diversion from the serious business of keeping body and soul together, in a world where the average lifespan was 27 years. The poor were underfed and malnourished for most of the time; at the *epulum* or *cena*, the public banquet, usually devoted to a god such as Jupiter, as at the gladiator fights, they may have been encouraged to feel they were being treated as honoured guests of the state, and later, of the emperor. The dishes were served up to them just as the events were presented to them in the arena. In the protein-poor daily grind, any sort of show to relieve the monotony was as welcome as fresh meat was to a grain-based diet.

As for the public mood, the legacy of Cannae was a persistent national insecurity that could only be allayed by a carefully constructed embodiment of the traditional military virtues. Since most of the people would never see actual warfare, they needed to see it in the most public of spaces, the arena, where the gladiator had the ritual task of demonstrating to the spectators the military qualities that would ensure Rome was never again defeated. This expectation was never spelt out, though most commentators hinted at it, but it hung in the air all the same. Courage was rewarded, cowardice despised. Skilful gladiators, like good soldiers, demonstrated what Rome demanded of its warriors. In fact, soldiers were encouraged to watch gladiators fighting before they themselves went into battle, because it was thought the sight of blood and mutilation in the arena would desensitise them for the fighting to come.

At the end of the first century BC, food shortages could and did lead to riots, something the politicians were anxious to avoid. Unlike in Greece, where public distribution of religiously sacrificed meats was done on a large scale, in Rome the *triumphi* and *munera* were linked with *viscerationes* because they were the major occasions for the beast spectacles. Poor Romans, in common with most ancient people unburdened by the Judaeo-Christian traditions, would have been quite happy to eat anything that came out of the arena on a hook, even when the beast in question might have been eating humans a short time before, as Tertullian points out:

> (What of) those who dine on the flesh of wild animals from the arena, keen on the meat of boar or stag? That boar in his battle has wiped the blood off him whose blood he drew; that stag has wallowed in the blood of a gladiator. The bellies of the very bears are sought, full of raw and undigested human flesh.
> (Tertullian, *Apologeticum* 9.11)

This would make for occasional exotic eating; that great physician of gladiators, Galen, related an account of the dissection of an elephant at which the imperial cooks removed the heart for a special dish.

Since a world of creatures like ostriches, rhinos, bears, elks, wild horses, hippos and giraffes were all to be found in the *venationes*, sooner or later they would end up butchered and distributed and the Roman poor would be very grateful for this boost to their protein intake. In the world of the gladiator, nothing ever went to waste. With their bellies temporarily full, and their minds occupied with stirring gladiatorial examples of military virtue, the masses could be safely ignored.

CONCLUSION

In order to address the thorny problem of the origin of gladiatorial combat, we may have to accept that it is not just another historical question with a straightforward answer in terms of place of origin (Etruria or Campania), context of origin (ritual, human sacrifice, martial by-product, trial by combat, or athletic competition), or method of introduction (influenced by superior culture, or simply by neighbourly proximity of observed tradition). The phenomenon of the gladiator did not appear on the scene out of nowhere. We know it can't have done. The truth is more complicated, and therefore ultimately more satisfying. Accepting that we may never pin down the gladiator's point of origin, we can nevertheless go on to dismantle the world of that origin, examine each element of it, and see if it fits in with the others to make a plausible and compelling reality. The gladiator was not invented; he evolved, just as Rome itself did.

3

FROM *LUDUS* TO *ARENA*: THE MAKING OF A GLADIATOR

... the art they glorify, the artist they disgrace ...

Anyone who ended up as a gladiator was at the very bottom of the social scale, a man without dignity or value, the despised dregs of humanity, in fact almost without humanity (*21a* and *21b*). Tertullian's description of where the gladiators stood in relation to polite society highlights the ambivalence of the Roman attitude to them:

21a Above left Reconstruction of early imperial *thraex*. *Photograph: author*

21b Above right Oil lamp showing a *thraex* at rest or in defeat. *Taken from the Guttman Collection, with kind permission of Christies Images Ltd*

> Look at their attitude to the charioteers, players (*scaenicos*), gladiators (*arenarios*), most loving of men, to whom men surrender their souls and women their bodies as well, for whose sake they commit the sins they blame; on one and the same account they glorify them and they degrade and diminish them; yes, further, they openly condemn them to disgrace and civil degradation; they keep them religiously excluded from council chamber, rostrum, senate, knighthood, and every other kind of office and a good many distinctions. The perversity of it! They love whom they lower; they despise whom they approve; the art they glorify, the artist they disgrace. (Tertullian, *de Spectaculis* 22)

Although Tertullian was writing from the outside looking in, as a Christian apologist with what we would now call an agenda, his thumbnail sketch of the paradoxical nature of the gladiator's status is illuminating. The interesting point about his scathing comments is that they are all directed at the Roman viewing public; the gladiator is merely the cause of all of those conflicting emotions. Tertullian compares the gladiator to the actor, but he must have been aware that they were not equals in the degradation stakes; the gladiator at all times had the edge over the actor as the most despised, the most loathsome of all creatures. As both Seneca and Juvenal agreed, for a man of good breeding to go on the stage was social death, but for him to go into the arena was scraping the very bottom of the barrel, a fate even worse than death. Even by the second century AD, opinions had not changed, as Calpurnius Flaccus made clear: 'There is no meaner condition among the people than that of the gladiator.'

The satirists and moralists of Roman literature frequently expressed their horror and contempt when a free man, or worse, a free man of noble birth, made the deliberate choice to become a gladiator. From the large number of references to these men, knights and sometimes even senators, who went into the arena of their own free will, a totally misleading impression of the proportion of free men fighting in the *munera* could easily be obtained.

However, as with all public scandals and unusual practices, they take up more column inches in the papers than the ordinary, everyday occurrences. The Roman writers who took such a high moral tone of disapproval, amongst them Juvenal, Seneca, Suetonius and Tacitus, were inclined to be pessimistic about falling standards in Roman society generally; the type of cases they report with such outrage were exceptional, and form only a very small part of the overall picture. In any case, they were not speaking for the average man in the street; it is clear that the lower classes wholeheartedly enjoyed the entertainments provided for them. As intellectuals, the authors tended to belong to the higher orders of Roman society, and their revulsion at the coarse pleasures of the vulgar mob could almost be seen as an instinctive reaction – if the masses liked gladiators, then there had to be something dubious about them.

WHO WERE THE GLADIATORS?

The vast majority of gladiators were taken from three huge reservoirs of humanity that Rome always had at its disposal: prisoners of war, slaves and criminals (*22*). All three categories had one thing in common – their lives were not their own. They were outsiders, non-citizens, to whom Rome's protective laws and customs, *lex et mores maiorum*, were unavailable.

To the Roman way of thinking, prisoners of war were enemies of Rome who had refused to submit to its rule. They were drawn from lands where Rome had imposed its domination by force of arms; each a *provincia*, literally territory won by conquest, each a part of what would become the Roman Empire – the lands of North Africa, Egypt, Judaea, Palestine, Turkey, Syria, Arabia, Gaul, Greece, Portugal, Spain, Germany, Britain; the constant flow of thousands of captives into Rome from its ever expanding conquests was like a terrible life-blood nourishing the arena. In common with condemned criminals, *noxii*, with whom they were, for all practical purposes, interchangeable, war captives were a convenient by-product of victory, just as criminals were a by-product of the judicial process. They were a resource for Rome's entertainment industry, Rome's mines, Rome's public works; nothing was ever wasted – even their non-Roman weapons and armour mutated over the centuries into the standardised equipment of the gladiator (*23*).

22 Roman prisoners of war; relief carving from the base of the Arch of Severus. *Photograph: Pharos Pictures*

23 Reconstruction of provincial *murmillo* gladiator.
Photograph: Pharos Pictures

The dark side of Rome's centuries-long climb to absolute power was its unswerving belief in its right to conquer everything in its path; it would tolerate no resistance, and furthermore, in the eyes of the Romans, anyone who did so had no legitimate basis for opposition. Therefore, anyone who opposed Rome was a rebel, for whom death was the appropriate fate. Yet though their life was forfeit, Rome might choose to save them, *servare*, whereupon they would become saved, or a slave, *servus*. This explanation for the origin of the Latin word for slave as being one who has been saved from a deserved death was asserted by Roman writers, and another example of its application occurs when Augustus talks of choosing to save the nations which could safely be pardoned, rather than eradicating them.

A captured prisoner of war could suffer several fates; many never made it back to Rome and were simply executed *in situ*, usually by crucifixion or being thrown to wild beasts, standard penalties for rebellion against Rome's authority; some were sold off as slaves locally; still others were shipped to Rome and used in the triumphal parades of victorious generals, at the end of which they were slaughtered as part of the triumphal games.

Josephus' account of the fall of Jerusalem is a good description of the way in which Rome sorted its captives by age, ability, and usefulness:

> As the soldiers were now growing weary of bloodshed and survivors were still appearing in large numbers, Caesar gave orders that only men who offered armed resistance were to be killed, and everyone else taken alive. But as well as those covered by the orders the aged and infirm were slaughtered: men in their prime who might be useful were herded into the Temple and shut up in the Court of the Women. To guard them Caesar appointed one of his freedmen, and his friend Fronto to decide each man's fate according to his deserts. Those who had taken part in sedition and terrorism informed against each other, and Fronto executed the lot. Of the youngsters he picked out the tallest and handsomest to be kept for the triumphal procession; of the rest, those over seventeen were put in irons and sent to hard labour in Egypt, while great numbers were presented by Titus to the provinces to perish in the theatres by the sword or by wild beasts; those under seventeen were sold. During the days in which Fronto was sorting them out, starvation killed 11,000 of the prisoners, some because the guards hated them too bitterly to allow them any food, others because they would not accept it when offered; in any case there was not even enough corn to fill so many mouths. (Josephus, *Bellum Judaicum* VI, 423)

Josephus gives a perfect illustration of the sifting process. Of course, Caesar would only want perfect specimens in his triumph; broken-down, weak and ugly captives would certainly not look good in his procession, nor would they enhance his victory. There is an interesting account of how some Germanic prisoners of war were made to grow their hair and dye it red for the *triumphus*; obviously, the parade was not a spur of the moment thing, but an event which was planned as carefully as any election campaign. Even the captives had to look impressive, handsome, beautiful, strong, thereby reflecting those qualities back onto the victor.

Unfortunately, in the case of the ones who weren't picked to go to Rome, Josephus cannot tell us how Fronto decided which men should be sent to hard labour, and which to the arenas. The most interesting part of the account is the massive logistical effort involved in handling such large numbers of prisoners, including the fact that it took so long to sort them out that several thousand starved to death while waiting to learn their fates. There is a useful rule-of-thumb guide; it states that a man can last three minutes without air, three days without water, and three weeks without food. That picture of thousands of captives, held in what amounts to a prison camp outside Jerusalem for weeks while Caesar's representative assesses his living spoils of war for their usefulness to Rome, encapsulates the Roman attitude towards its enemies. In further reports, Josephus talks of Titus arranging for the captives to be held in custody as the summer was over and the voyage to Italy (by sea) impossible for a while, and then:

> Titus marched to Caesarea Philippi, where he stayed a long time exhibiting shows of every kind. Many of the prisoners perished here, some thrown to wild beasts, others forced to meet each other in full-scale battles … Titus Caesar spent some time in Berytus … from

> there he passed through a number of Syrian towns, exhibiting in them all lavish spectacles in which Jewish prisoners were forced to make a show of their own destruction. (Josephus, *Bellum Judaicum* VII, 20,93)

Of the 97,000 prisoners taken by Titus during the Jewish campaign, not many were obviously military combatants; he had given orders that only those who resisted should be killed. Although thousands of Jews perished in the touring spectacles that Titus took round the Middle East, and thousands more were slaughtered back in Rome, their deaths were those of condemned men, not gladiators in the sense we would understand it. However, some who showed promise would have received training in a gladiatorial school, a *ludus*, before being sent into the arena.

There is a crucial distinction to be made between the doomed slave, criminal or captive who is sentenced to die without any real contest in the arena, and the true gladiator, who, although he may have entered his career involuntarily as any of the above, has at least a fighting chance of redeeming himself, if he is good enough. Unlike Livy, therefore, who thought there were just two categories of gladiator, 'slaves, and free men who sell their blood', the only distinction that really matters is between those who had no hope of survival, and those who did. To understand how Rome obtained its slaves and convicts for the arena, and how the sentence of a particular penalty could make all the difference to their survival, we need to examine the operation of Roman criminal law and capital punishment, which ultimately categorised the victims by the penalty to which they were condemned.

CRIME AND PUNISHMENT

From Rome's earliest days, law and religion did not act separately, but complementarily, to sanction and execute highly visible acts of severe public punishment. The extent to which government, judicial authority and religious ritual were entwined and inter-dependent is perfectly illustrated by the fact that the office of *pontifex maximus*, the greatest pontiff, chief priest and head of the Roman state religion, was held by a prominent political figure, such as consul, the most famous examples being Julius Caesar and Augustus. In fact, patricians filled most of the major religious posts. There was no separation between Church and State as we might think of it, and no priestly profession. With the exception of the *flamen dialis* and *rex sacrorum*, archaic priesthoods left over from monarchical Rome, religious offices were carried out by men of state.

Brutal public executions were designed to protect the established order and maintain the security of its citizens, particularly the ruling class; by staging horrendous scenes of violent, judicially approved death, the authorities' intention was to demonstrate that opposition to Rome and its society, in whatever form it took, would not be tolerated. The aim was not to rehabilitate or seek restitution; it was to compel submission and exact the appropriate revenge for whatever wrongs had been done to society. By witnessing the capital punishments, the people were at once reassured that order was being restored, and forcefully reminded of the consequences of rebellion or criminality. And although we would be horrified to see an execution in which there was a strong element of public entertainment, as well as unusual cruelties, these are modern humanitarian concerns. Again, as Bauman's examination of Rome's penal system observed: 'the bottom line is that there were few bleeding hearts in ancient Rome.'

NOXII

The primary source of arena victims was the condemned criminals, of which Rome, due to the severity of its penal system, always had a good supply (*15*). Seneca gives an account of the proceedings at a mid-day show, *meridianum spectaculum*, in which the participants were obviously not gladiators, but *noxii*, condemned to execution in the arena:

> By chance I attended a mid-day exhibition, expecting some fun, wit and relaxation – an exhibition at which men's eyes have respite from the slaughter of their fellow men. But it was quite the reverse. The previous combats were the essence of compassion; but now all the trifling is put aside and it is pure murder. The men have no defensive armour. They are exposed to blows at all points, and no one ever strikes in vain.... In the morning they throw men to the lions and the bears; at noon, they throw them to the spectators. The spectators demand that the slayer shall face the man who is to slay him in his turn; and they always reserve the latest conqueror for another butchering. The outcome of every fight is death, and the means are fire and sword. This sort of thing goes on while the arena is empty. You may retort: 'But he was a highway robber; he killed a man!' And what of it? Granted that, as a murderer, he deserved this punishment.... In the morning they cried 'Kill him! Lash him! Burn him! Why does he meet the sword in so cowardly a way? Why does he strike so feebly? Why doesn't he die game? Whip him to meet his wounds! Let them receive blow for blow, with chests bare and exposed to the stroke!' And when the games stop for the intermission, they announce: 'A little throat-cutting in the mean-time, so that there may still be something going on!'
> (Seneca, *Epistulae* 7.3-5)

The Roman concept of justice ran counter to ours; not for them the principle of equality for all before the law, the 'level playing field' which we hold so dear. We feel that the law should ignore the different degrees of status in those who are before it; the Romans felt that respect was due to people in direct relation to their status, deserved or not. As for our 'level playing field', they would have thought it unjust and the very opposite of equal. To the Romans, justice consisted of treating each person according to his status and worth in society, a concept expressed in the Latin phrase *ius suum tribuere*, meaning 'giving to each his right'; each man was given the rights he was entitled to, even though for the unfortunate lower classes, this meant no rights at all.

From the beginning, Roman society had always been run on extremely hierarchical lines. The familial hierarchy was the state in microcosm; underpinning it was the ancient law of the *paterfamilias* and the *patria potestas*, denoting the absolute power that the head of the household, the father, wielded over his household, the *familia*, and the lives of his descendants, including the power of life and death over his children, even after they reached adulthood, indeed for their entire lives, until death broke the bonds of obligation. This harsh outlook was symptomatic of the Roman attitude to human life generally.

The law of the Twelve Tables, Rome's first written code of law, stood from about 450 BC, and from that we can see that Rome's earliest criminal punishments were designed to be carried out publicly and brutally. They were not casually or accidentally cruel; cruelty was integral to the Roman perception of retribution.

Set alongside the permitted brutalities of everyday Roman life, it is understandable that the popularity of gladiators at funeral games, where foreign captives, convicts and slaves were first made to fight in honour of the dead, naturally projected them into the spectacles, in which law, religion and political advantage all had an interest.

The spectacles and the public punishments had a common aim: to dispose of all threatening outsiders, be they heinous criminals, prisoners of war, disobedient and murderous slaves, arsonists, sacrilegious temple robbers, traitors, deserters – everywhere they looked, the Romans saw threats to the security and dignity of the state.

As the transition from republic to principate started to gather momentum, politicians found they needed to buy the public's support with ever more spectacles and games, and with civil strife increasing on several fronts, the demand for executions and punitive measures also rose. The imposition of *pax romana* was beginning to affect one of Rome's traditional reservoirs of victims: with the vast numbers of captives from foreign campaigns dwindling, the legal system responded to the needs of the arena, compensating for the shortfall by producing more condemned men (and women), *damnati*, to provide arena fodder.

In practical terms, the privileges, protection and penalties of the law were administered to the people in direct correlation to their place in that society: to put it bluntly, the lower class Romans, citizen or not, received swifter and more severe penalties than those higher up the social scale. Aristocrats who transgressed were usually able to depend upon the swift mercy of the sword, usually by beheading, rather than the aggravated executions of crucifixion and the flames, beasts and inventive slaughter of the arena.

Contrary to popular belief, crucifixions rarely took place in the arena, since they were long drawn-out, static deaths with insufficient drama to hold the interest. On the other hand, they were salutary reminders of the consequences of rebellion when located by roadsides and other public places, as Crassus demonstrated when he crucified 6000 slaves after defeating Spartacus and his followers: he had them crucified and placed at intervals all the way along the *Via Appia* between Rome and Capua, where the uprising had started.

As Crassus put it, it was a means of improving 'the morale of the Roman citizens', and doubtless he meant that as a result of the defeat of Spartacus, people could sleep easier in their beds, free from fear of attack and robbery. However, the message of 6000 slaves dying slow and agonising deaths on crosses along the entire length of Rome's major transport artery must have been a powerful one for anyone harbouring the slightest tendency towards rebellion.

As already touched on, the Romans had an idea of justice far removed from our own. Pliny summed up the Roman attitude to justice: *nihil est ipsa aequalitate inaequalius* – 'nothing is more unequal than equality itself'. He would have been horrified at our concept of equality, where a person's status in society is deliberately kept out of the judicial consideration; to him, and to his fellow Romans, that would have seemed like the worst inequality possible, to have one's rank in society ignored, to be treated exactly like everyone else.

Therefore, in its dealings with criminals and convicted slaves, Roman law was constructed to ensure the punishment fitted the crime, sometimes spectacularly so. The *noxii*, the convicted criminals, were *damnati*, condemned just as the professional gladiators were, but to a more predictable fate; unlike the gladiators, their appearance in the arena would not be repeated. The important question is what form their condemnation took.

The *noxii*, as outsiders and non-citizens, could not benefit from the penalties prescribed for those within the reach of custom and law; not for them the simple punishments of exile, enforced suicide, beheading (*ad gladium*); instead, they faced the ultimate punishments, *summa supplicia*. Crucifixion, *crucis supplicium*, exposure to wild beasts, *damnatio ad bestias* and fire, *damnatio ad flammas*, *crematio*, *vivus uri*; all were forms of *summa supplicia*. These were the very worst capital punishments, excruciatingly painful and protracted, reserved not just for those who were sentenced because of crimes committed, but also for those whose mistake was to resist Rome's rule, like runaway or insubordinate slaves, rebels, prisoners of war and traitors.

These aggravated executions did not involve just a simple putting to death; that would not have satisfied the Roman sense of justice, in which the punishment had to match the crime. To us, these executions seem cruel, and we judge the Romans to be callous and unfeeling for imposing them, let alone watching them. However, to the Roman mind, restorative and punitive justice was being visibly enacted upon the wrongdoer, to the benefit of society as a whole. We miss the point if we characterise their very public cruelty as sadism (*24*).

It is at this point that we come to one of the most distasteful (in modern eyes, anyway) aspects of Roman executions. The modern westernised belief is that

24 Line illustration of an execution using wild beasts (*damnatio ad bestias*) from the Zliten mosaic. *Archaeological Museum, Tripoli, Libya*

executions should be conducted soberly, efficiently, almost clinically and with the minimum of distress for the condemned, and certainly away from the public gaze. The Romans however, took the view that by forcing the criminal to act out some myth or legend in which the character comes to a bad end because of their misdeeds, a moral and indeed educational purpose was thereby served, as the spectators watched both the mythical and the actual wrongdoer receive their just deserts, at one and the same time.

This kind of real-life morality tableau was common; Suetonius mentions one that was performed for Caligula just before his assassination in AD 41; in retrospect, the message looked like it was meant for Caligula himself, an omen of his wrongdoings catching up with him. Juvenal also refers in passing to this playlet, when he pours scorn on a member of the aristocratic Cornelia family, 'nifty Lentulus' who 'took the part of Laureolus and did it rather well: in my opinion he deserved a real cross'. In the case of Lentulus, he was a free man acting out a role in the arena, which was shameful enough, and merited true execution, according to Juvenal. However, Martial describes the acting out of this fatal charade, in the phrase coined by Coleman, using a condemned criminal in the role of Laureolus, and the authenticity of the outcome was not in doubt:

> As Prometheus, bound on Scythian crag, fed the tireless bird with his too abundant breast, so did Laureolus, hanging on no sham cross, give his naked flesh to a Caledonian bear. His lacerated limbs lived on, dripping gore, and in all his body, body there was none. Finally he met with the punishment he deserved; the guilty wretch had plunged a sword into his father's throat or his master's, or in his madness had robbed a temple of its secret gold, or laid a cruel torch to Rome. The criminal had outdone the deeds of ancient story; in him, what had been a play became an execution. (Martial, *Liber de Spectaculis* 9)

The unfortunate criminal played the part of the robber Laureolus for real; hung on a real cross, *non falsa pendens in cruce*, he was ripped apart by a real bear shipped from far-off Caledonia. The method of execution was *damnati ad bestias*, rather than *ad crucem*; he was on the cross purely to facilitate the bear's part in the proceedings. Martial very helpfully lists all the possible capital offences that could result in so severe a penalty: murder of a relative or a master, if a slave, temple-robbing and arson. This arresting scene would have been a memorable one for the spectators and therefore all the more likely to be improving in the eyes of Rome's moral watchdogs, like Seneca. In the performance of the 'farce called Laureolus' that Caligula watched, so Suetonius says, the leading character, a highwayman or street robber, 'had to die while escaping and vomit blood' and 'the understudies were so anxious to display their proficiency at dying that they flooded the stage with blood'. No special effects needed.

These fatal charades and myth-clad executions were to become increasingly popular and, by the reign of Nero, they were a regular feature of the spectacles, in contrast to his uncle, the previous emperor, Claudius, who expressed a distinct preference for unadorned, straightforward executions, without any trappings. Claudius also arranged to have gladiators' throats cut on the slightest pretext:

> At gladiatorial shows, whether or not they were staged by himself, he ruled that all combatants who fell accidentally should have their throats cut – above all net-fighters, so that he could gaze on their death agony. (Suetonius, *de vita Caesarum*, *Claudius* 34)

By particularly selecting unhelmeted *retiarii* for execution, Claudius' unhealthy preference for looking into the faces of the gladiators as they died was satisfied. From Nero's reign comes the first recorded instance of an execution performed within the structure of a myth, when, according to Lucilius, a thief called Meniscus was burnt alive, *vivus uri, crematio*, for having stolen three apples, purportedly of real gold, perhaps taken from the *Domus Aurea* gardens, or perhaps, if they were really made of gold, foolishly stolen from Nero's house itself.

He certainly offended Nero, because the penalty was a terrible one: in this type of execution, the condemned wore a garment soaked in pitch, the *tunica molesta*, which was set alight. Comparison was made by Lucilius to the legendary Heracles, whose wife Deianeira murdered him by giving him to wear a cloak smeared with the highly flammable blood of a centaur; it bonded with his skin and he could not tear it off, and thus he was burnt to death.

These *tunicae molestae* were used in the infamous scapegoating of Christians by Nero after the fire that swept through Rome in AD 64. Nero was worried about rumours that he was responsible for starting the fire, as Tacitus reports:

> To suppress this rumour, Nero fabricated scapegoats – and punished with every refinement the notoriously depraved Christians (as they were popularly called). Their originator, Christ, had been executed in Tiberius' reign by the governor of Judaea, Pontius Pilatus....

> First, Nero had self-acknowledged Christians arrested. Then, on their information, large numbers of others were condemned – not so much for incendiarism as for their anti-social tendencies (or, 'because the human race detested them'). Their deaths were made farcical. Dressed in wild animals' skins, they were torn to pieces by dogs, or crucified, or made into torches to be ignited after dark as substitutes for daylight. (Tacitus, *Annales* XV 43)

If the myth was carefully chosen, it could provide a suitably exciting and educational spectacle, although sometimes the story would be altered if the crime didn't quite fit. Equally, the ending might be completely different from that of the myth, as in the case recorded by Martial, where a criminal portraying the lyre-playing Orpheus was chained to a rock in the Colosseum; but instead of being charmed by his music, one of the wild beasts, 'an ungrateful bear', tore him to pieces. A bear was also involved in an unusual re-enactment of the Daedalus myth, again reported by Martial:

> Daedalus, when you are being thus torn by a Lucanian bear, how you wish you now had your wings! (Martial, *Liber de Spectaculis* 10)

A particularly inventive execution was thought up for a Sicilian robber by the name of Selerus, who had been terrorising the countryside round Mount Etna during Augustus' reign:

> I saw him torn to pieces by the beasts in the Forum while a contest of gladiators was being held. He had been put on a high platform as though on Mount Etna, and when the platform suddenly broke up and collapsed, he himself crashed down into wild-beast cages which easily broke open, placed beneath the platform in readiness for this purpose. (Strabo, *Geographica* 6.273)

The punishment of *damnatio ad bestias* was restricted in AD 61 by Nero's *lex Petronia*, which made it against the law to condemn an unruly or disobedient slave to the wild beasts without a permit from the courts. In practice, however, this did not make much difference to the spectacles, since most of the people who ended up in the arena were there by imperial authority anyway. Even as late as AD 372, the emperor Valentinian I kept two favourite man-eating bears in cages outside his bedroom. One he rather ironically named Innocentia, and 'after seeing many people buried whom Innocentia had torn to pieces', he gave the creature its freedom, returning it to the wilderness.

We tend to think nowadays that the function of the execution of a criminal is to expunge that person from the face of the earth, whilst depriving them of the right to live on it any longer; our age-old desire for retribution plays an ever-shrinking role in that process. For the Romans, however, the fact that the executions also entertained and sometimes even titillated them, was no reason to doubt their underlying purpose, of showing society's disapproval of certain acts, and the satisfying triumphant reinstatement of good over evil.

When we hear of truly despicable murderers who have met violent ends, we too may experience that momentary human satisfaction that a price has been paid; however, we baulk from admitting it. The Romans did not hold their noses as they watched the imaginative and cruel slaughter of people who had threatened the peaceful conduct of their society – they felt a sense of restoration and reassurance that the order of things had been maintained.

The gladiator, if he displayed skill and courage, could hope to save himself to fight another day; the *noxii* had no hope. *Damnati* who had been found guilty of crimes would first be evaluated; only those with some degree of spirit or skill at arms might be sent to one of the better *ludi*, maybe even the imperial *ludi*. As Pliny discovered when he was sent by Trajan to Bithynia as governor, some convicted criminals had ended up as public slaves, with annual stipends out of the public purse, a 'cushy number' that the Roman penal system had not intended; Trajan ordered Pliny to put a stop to the practice, and return them to proper punishment, or if ten years had elapsed since their conviction, to allocate them to jobs at the baths, or as street cleaners and sewage workers.

It is likely the poorer specimens were condemned to work in the mines, *damnati ad metallum*, or in public building works, *ad opus*, or sold off to *lanistae* as arena fodder, to be used up, maybe in one of the big set-piece spectacles, the battles or *naumachiae*, within a set time as agreed by the *munerarius* purchasing them.

To be condemned to train as a gladiator, *damnati ad ludum gladiatorium* or *damnati ad ludos*, was a common penalty available in Roman law, for slaves who had displeased their owners in some way. It should be stressed that to be condemned to be handed over to a *lanista* for training at a gladiator school was not an automatic death sentence, unlike those condemned to *summa supplicia*. Compared to death by crucifixion, or being burnt alive or torn apart by wild animals, *damnatio ad ludos* was a penalty which at least held out the hope that if the condemned man survived long enough, he could earn his freedom. After three years, if he lived that long, he would be released from his solemn vow to fight as a gladiator, the *sacramentum gladiatorium*, and would gain the wooden sword, the *rudis*, which signified his discharge from the binding contract, the *auctoramentum gladiatorium*, and after five years he could be set free. The earliest reference to the *rudis* comes from Cicero, showing that, even as early as the republic, gladiators could be valued for their skill. On the other hand, criminals, the *noxii*, could be handed over to the *ludi*, under a sentence of *damnati ad gladium*, and they might survive one fight, or a few, but the *munerarius* had to make sure that they died by the sword when a set period, usually no more than a year, was up.

A variation of this system was that anyone wishing to put on gladiatorial games could apply to the authorities for criminals who had been found guilty of capital crimes, broadly speaking, murder, arson, treason, sacrilege and theft, and incorporate these *noxii* into his show. A set price was paid for each condemned man thus obtained, and as before, the *munerarius* had to undertake on oath to ensure that the *noxii* would be disposed of within a set amount of time, usually a year. Either way, they were put in the arena with nothing but swords, to kill and be killed until no one was left, or to be finished off by properly trained gladiators. This is the insult to expectation that triggered Seneca's rant; he went to the *meridianum spectaculum* hoping for some light entertainment, mock battles with knockabout comedy routines by *paegniarii* with dummy swords and whips perhaps, and instead he got sheer bloody murder with no finesse, no thrills, no suspense and no doubt about the outcome. It was quite the opposite of what the Roman citizen had a right to expect from a professional gladiator.

SERVI

Slaves who were in some way displeasing to their owners might also end up sold to a *ludus*. Under Hadrian, this sale of slaves to a gladiator school was forbidden, unless he had committed an offence meriting it. Some desperate runaway slaves actually sold themselves to a *lanista*, but if discovered, they had to be returned to their master. The idea that a slave's existence might be so bad that they actually tried to escape it by going voluntarily into the risky life of the gladiatorial world is hard to understand, but of course, the risks for a fully trained gladiator were not at all bad. In a world where most people didn't get past their thirtieth year, it might not have seemed too bad a deal – food, shelter, clothing, financial rewards, in return for the risk of death or wounding two or three times a year.

As we have seen, some prisoners of war were sifted, sorted and sent to the *ludi* in the same way as the slaves. Another source of unwilling participants were the captives and hostages of pirates and brigands, and they would similarly have been sold off immediately to a *ludus*.

AUCTORATI

One further type of gladiator was the free Roman citizen who entered the *ludus* and signed up of his own free will. Sometimes this was not so much free will as an economic compulsion brought about by bankruptcy, gambling debts or simple lack of funds to make ends meet. True compulsion was rare; Caligula took one man at his word:

> Someone had sworn to fight in the arena if Gaius (Caligula) recovered from his illness; Gaius forced him to fulfil his oath, and watched his swordplay closely, not letting him go until he had won the match and begged abjectly to be released. (Suetonius, *Gaius* (*Caligula*) 27)

When a free man joined up, he was paid a sum of money, an amount that Marcus Aurelius reduced to 2000 *sestertii* to try to discourage the practice. In addition, he might win prize money if he was good enough. His bed and board were paid for, and all he had to do was survive long enough to win his discharge, usually after five years, if he lived that long. Some men, probably seasoned fighters who genuinely enjoyed the dangers and could live with the risks involved, it must be said, actually signed on again, and for higher fees. Yet no matter how low his place in society as a gladiator was, regarded as *infamis* by the respectable Romans, he never lost his status as a free Roman citizen. However, that citizenship meant nothing while he was bound by the gladiator's formidable oath, the *sacramentum gladiatorium*.

Some people volunteered because they genuinely enjoyed the danger and risks; we call them adrenaline junkies now. These are the people for whom everyday life is too safe to merit the term 'life'. For them, the only way to truly appreciate their existence is to risk it in some dangerous pursuit. These tended to be men from the higher classes, the aristocratic ruling elite, young noblemen with nothing to do once Rome had no more conquests to achieve. The young men from senatorial and equestrian families who fought in the arena did so with the explicit encouragement of emperors like Commodus and Nero. Understandably, the stigma that attached to free men who joined up for money, contracting themselves to a *lanista*, did not so much apply to those who stepped into the arena purely for glory and fame, by the demonstration of the military virtues. Commodus himself exemplified this craze by fighting over a thousand combats with wooden, as opposed to sharp metal, swords (*25*). The emphasis was

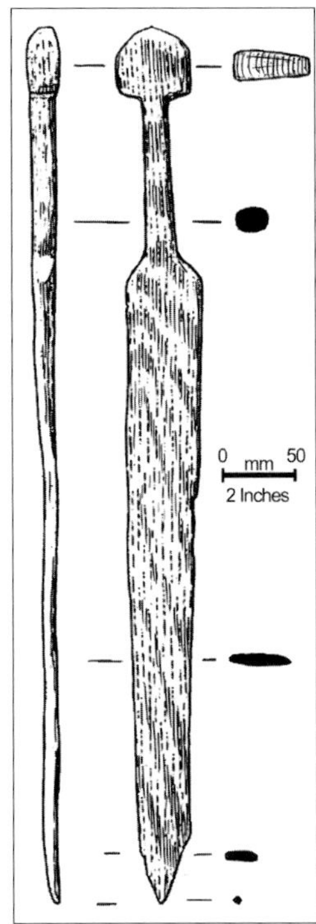

25 Wooden sword, made from oak, AD 72-3. Possibly a surviving example of a training sword. *Illustration based on a line original by S. Winterbottom*

on swordsmanship, which harked back to the military virtues that Rome had always been able to call upon from its young men. Not all emperors thought that it was a good idea for the young men of high rank to disgrace themselves in this way; Augustus prohibited it, as did the later emperor, Vitellius, as Tacitus tells us:

> A severe warning was issued against Roman knights degrading themselves by gladiatorial fighting. Earlier emperors had bribed and, more often, forcibly compelled knights to fight, and numbers of country towns in Italy competed by the offer of high sums to entice really degraded young men to do the same. (Tacitus, *Historiae* 2.62)

Just because it was forbidden, however, did not mean the practice died out. The flower of Roman youth, in its obsession with all things gladiatorial, found ways to disregard the official line.

When a free man wanted to sign on as an *auctoratus* (paid contractee), he had first to inform the tribune of the *plebs*, as the later *Aes Italica* of AD 177 laid down. This may have been an opportunity for the tribune to assess the physical condition of the applicant. On joining, he got a sum of two thousand *sestertii*. If he rejoined after discharge, he could get as much as twelve thousand *sestertii* as a starting fee. Juvenal states this more colourfully:

> Rutilius is the talk of every dinner party, every bathhouse, every piazza, every theatre. The reason? They say that, while his limbs are hot-blooded and strong and young enough for the soldier's helmet, he's about to sign up to the rules and royal decrees of the gladiator-trainer – and with no compulsion from the tribune, but no prohibition either. You can see many like him, of course. Their only reason for living lies in gourmandise. Their creditors, to whom they've often given the slip, always lie in wait for them at the entrance to the meat market. (Juvenal, *Satirae* XI 2-11)

This neatly illustrates the type of young man who signed up: spendthrift, debt-ridden, hounded by creditors and forced therefore to only use the assets at his disposal – youth and strength. In earlier times, it may well have been thought glorious to become a gladiator for the glory and fame of it, however debased that fame might be. But the majority of free men were probably just making the best use of their only remaining saleable asset – their bodies. Another type of young man might dabble in the gladiatorial world without taking that irrevocable final step of signing up as an *auctoratus*, as Apuleius reports:

> From the moment when Rufinus put on the adult toga, he abused adult freedom by attending gladiatorial exercises. He knew all the gladiators by name and knew all the details of their previous contests and their wounds. He even went through a training course under the supervision of a professional gladiator, although he came from a good family.... (Apuleius, *Metamorphoses*)

This gladiator madness was quite common among the upper classes. Presumably, those lower in status and wealth would risk their necks by volunteering only in the event of financial crisis. For them, the noble art of swordsmanship was emphatically not their reason for signing up.

SACRAMENTUM

In all cases of potential gladiators, it is obvious that only the fit and strong would be acceptable to the training school. Anything else would be a waste of time and money. The gladiator recruits, willing or unwilling, were known as *tirones*, or *novi auctorati*. The lower age limit for acceptance was at least 17, and possibly younger in the case of particularly promising individuals. On entering the gladiatorial training school the gladiatorial recruit, the *tiro*, had to swear a binding and solemn oath, the *sacramentum gladiatorum*, to endure being burned by fire, bound in chains, beaten, and killed by the sword: *uri, vinciri, verberari, ferroque necari patior*.

Petronius refers to this oath in the *Satyricon*, although the slaves taking it are not gladiators by any stretch of the imagination. Nevertheless, it is an indication of how strong this oath was thought to be that it could be used to bind the slaves together in their joint deception:

> And so to safeguard the imposture in which we were all involved, we swore an oath dictated by Eumolpus, that we would be burned, flogged, beaten, killed with cold steel or whatever else Eumolpus ordered. Like real gladiators, we very solemnly handed ourselves over, body and soul, to our master. (Petronius, *Satyricon* 117)

In the entire Roman world, there was no more binding oath that could be sworn than that of the gladiator. This oath was by its very nature a consecration of the gladiator. By swearing to suffer the worst forms of death that the arena could offer and finally to agree to give up life itself, he converted his awful predicament into a matter of honour. By voluntarily accepting the fate that was before him, he transformed the compulsion into a formidable and solemn obligation. It was a way of turning the dishonour of being a gladiator on its head. From the moment he swore the oath, he was bound by its terrible consequences. There was a great similarity between the oath of the gladiator and that of the soldier. This latter oath, the *devotio*, was brought in about the time of Cannae, when things were looking bleak in the face of Carthaginian advances. By the *devotio*, the general, and later the soldiers too, consecrated himself to violent death at the enemy's hands. In return, he asked for victory. The gladiator asked for nothing at all. His sacrifice was total and undemanding of anything in return.

FAMILIA GLADIATORIA

The most famous example of a *ludus*, a gladiator training school or camp, is the one set up by Julius Caesar in Capua. At its height it contained 5000 men, most of whom were described as *secutores*. However, this was at a time when the categories of gladiators were not as detailed as they would become under Augustus and the emperors who followed him. As the spectacles grew in scale and popularity, and particularly after the construction of the Colosseum, it became clear to the *procuratores* who managed the *ludi* that Capua and the interconnecting organisational system set up around it in Campania, mostly in the Bay of Naples region, could not cope with the increased demands of Rome.

At this point, Vespasian's younger son, Domitian, took the decision to establish a brand new supply and training school network. He based it in Rome just to the east of the Colosseum, and the centrepiece of the construction was the *Ludus Magnus*, which was specifically designed to replace the imperial *ludus* at Capua that Caesar had originally established, and which Augustus had inherited (*26* and *colour plate 2*). Julius Caesar had wanted to cut out the middleman by running his own gladiator school, and Domitian carried this through to the logical conclusion. Now, not only the gladiators were under imperial control, but also the framework for the supply and maintenance of the wild beasts, and other special services required to put on the spectacle. The emperor had no need

26 The *Colosseum* in relation to the *Ludus Magnus* in Rome (both buildings are shown enhanced by darkening to aid comparison). *Photograph and enhancement: D. Shadrake. From the model of Rome in the time of Constantine by architect Italo Gismondi at the Museo della Civilta, EUR Rome*

to hire or buy in any part of the show – it was all in-house, from the gladiators to the beasts, the huntsmen and animal-keepers.

The imperial slaves were part of the emperor's household, and probably a vast army of *servi* kept everyone and every creature fed and watered, from menageries for the exotic creatures, *vivaria*, to barracks for the gladiators. The imperial *ludi* even called on the army to take on some more specialised tasks of the capture of animals for the arena, including their shipment back to Rome and subsequent storage.

Some guilds, *sodalitates venatorum*, specialised in the capture, sale and transport of particular exotic beasts; one such was the *Telegenii*, professional beast hunters based in North Africa. This travelling troupe of hunters is typical of many such guilds, and they are depicted on the brightly coloured mosaics found in Tunisia, at El Djem. Other specialists supplying the arena were the *ursarii*, special military units of bear hunters from Germany and the Danube region. One such *ursarius*, a centurion from *legio I Minervia*, is recorded on an inscription as having caught 50 bears in six months.

It is impossible to estimate the proportion of slaves, *servi*, and free men, *auctorati*, not to mention criminals, *damnati ad ludos*, in any given establishment. This may have varied in any case according to the prohibitions on *auctorati* at certain times. For instance, the elite classes were forbidden from enrolling or fighting as gladiators in decrees given in 46, 38, 22 BC, and in AD 19.

This did very little to stop the enthusiastic and the desperate from joining. The thrill-seekers still found a way to run the risks of the arena, and the financially strapped still got round the rules. Any attempt to analyse the ratio of slave to free men in a *ludus* by epigraphic analysis of tombstones immediately runs up against the difficulty that not all gladiators had the wherewithal for a grave of any kind, let alone a stone to mark it. So, since it is likely that only rich gladiators had any kind of memorial erected to them after death, usually by family, or failing that friends, it is not a representative way of judging the make-up of the inhabitants of any *ludus*, be it small-town school or imperial establishment.

Most gladiators, taken from the ranks of criminals, captives and slaves, would have lived within the confines of the barracks; however, the free men, and the successful professionals who had signed on for a second or further term were probably not billeted at the *ludus* and could come and go as they pleased. We know from many inscriptions that gladiators had wives and children, extended families that would not have fitted into the training barracks regime; we assume therefore that they lived outside, and, having voluntarily chosen their profession, would not be regarded as at risk of absconding from it.

The compelled and involuntary gladiators were another matter. Although the *Ludus Magnus* is the largest school, it nevertheless is an accurate reflection of the logistical and administrative requirements common to all *ludi*. Gladiatorial troupes were named after their owners, according to Varro; as an example, he mentions the gladiators of the Faustini *familia gladiatoria*, named after a certain Faustus.

TRAINING THE GLADIATOR

When the recruit entered the *ludus*, whether of his own volition or not, he became part of the *familia gladiatoria*. Once he had taken the oath, he became a *tiro*, and would stay in that lowly state until his training period, which usually lasted for around six months, had been served to the satisfaction of the *lanista*. Some time after his first successful fight, the *tiro* became known as a *veteranus*. There is a suggestion from some classical sources that new recruits were ritually beaten in the arena before beginning their gladiatorial career.

The *ludus* was the place where all the training of the gladiators was done. The fighters practiced in a smaller version of the arena. As we have seen from the case of Rufinus, who took lessons from a *lanista*, it may well have been possible to pay for gladiator training without actually signing up. It was probably a lucrative and easy sideline for a *lanista*. Certainly, there were times when the gladiator trainers were used to train soldiers, as when the hard-nosed republican general Marius famously said that the soldiers trained by the *lanistae* were better quality than his own. So it is obvious that the quality of the training could and did surpass that of the average soldier, at least at the bigger *ludi*, anyway.

The accommodation itself could also vary, depending on the size and location of the ludus. The most important example of a gladiatorial training school is that of the *Ludus Magnus* in Rome. Together with the *Ludus Dacicus*, the *Ludus Gallicus*, and the *Ludus Matutinus*, the *Ludus Magnus* made up the complex of the four great imperial training schools. Built in the reign of Domitian, to complement the activities in the Flavian amphitheatre, otherwise known as the Colosseum, they were located immediately to the east of the great amphitheatre, and almost certainly linked to it by underground tunnels (*26*).

Because of the size and scale of these imperial schools, they could afford to specialise in particular types of combat: the *Ludus Dacicus* and *Gallicus* trained gladiators in the styles of fighting and armature associated with those nations, whilst the Matutinus trained the *venatores*, the beast-fighters. The *bestiarii* were at first not wild-beast fighters but animal handlers; over the centuries, this distinction was lost and the terms became interchangeable. The *Matutinus* was so-called because it was the school in which men were trained to fight in the morning games. Traditionally, this meant the animal hunts and beast spectacles, the *venationes*.

The positions of the various activities in the day's programme were never as set in stone as our modern minds, with their tendency to look for patterns, would like to believe. However, it is invariably the case that, when beast spectacles are mentioned in classical sources, from the republic right through to late imperial times, they are recorded as having taken place in the morning, *i.e.* before lunchtime, or midday, *meridianum*, when the interludes, comic or otherwise, took over to keep the audience amused until the afternoon combats started. Given the logistical considerations of keeping so many animals in a state of readiness, and then the subsequent carnage to be cleared, it made sense if they were scheduled for the morning, before the gladiators.

The largest and most important of these four schools was the *Ludus Magnus*. Its overall dimensions were about 75m by 54m, with an arena size of 63m by 42m. In effect, it was like an amphitheatre, at least in terms of the elliptical arena, in which the fighters trained, but with far less seating capacity (*27*). There were several tiers of seats, and it seems likely that smaller private shows, perhaps rehearsals, may have been put on here for invited spectators only – a few thousand people could comfortably be accommodated. Behind and above the seating area were three levels of accommodation and storage, possibly colonnaded (*28*). Much of this area would probably have been given over to barracks; if so, the accommodations were by no means poor. It was common, though not universally seen, for each cell to house two men. Smaller barracks outside Rome might have had up to six men per cell.

In a decent to large-scale *ludus*, there would have been room for a refectory and cookhouse, a heavily guarded armoury (after Spartacus, Romans retained their fear of slave revolts), sophisticated medical facilities rather like the small hospitals of the Roman army, and offices for administrators, staff and slaves of the school, who would have looked after the day to day running of the infrastructure. Under successive emperors, in the imperial *ludi*, this infrastructure came to require the services of a small army of imperial slaves, civil servants who ran every aspect of the administration of the spectacles – epigraphic evidence tells us of the special departments for gladiatorial clothing (*a veste gladiatoria*, *ILS 5160*), for beast fighters' clothing (*a veste venatoria*, *ILS 1762*), even for the adornment and decoration of the spectacles (*adiutores procuratoris rationis ornamentorum*, *ILS 1771*). An inscription from the reign of Commodus (*CIL* VI 631, *ILS* 5084) lists

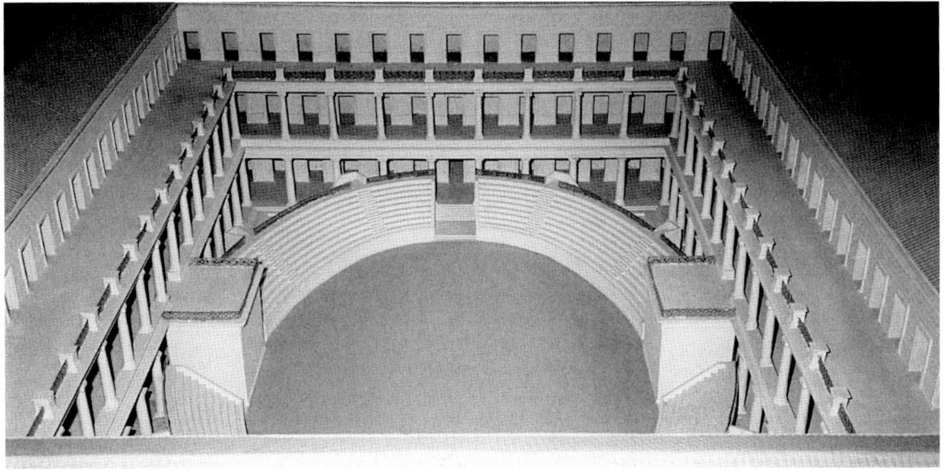

27 Seating and outer colonnaded galleries in the *Ludus Magnus* training school. *Museo della Civilta, EUR Rome. Photograph: author*

28 Surviving cells/storage rooms below what would have been the seating area in the *Ludus Magnus*, Rome. *Photograph: author*

all of the members of the four *decuriae* of a college of gladiators, among them the *manicarius* Demosthenes, of the second grade, *decuria II*; it was obviously desirable to have in-house specialist makers and repairers of the armguards, the *manicae* worn by many gladiators. The impressive remains of the *Ludus Magnus* can still be seen today, in the shadow of the Colosseum (*28* and *colour plate 2*).

What went on in the *ludus* probably varied little except in scale and quality of equipment, wherever it was based. Little is known about the actual training exercises of the gladiators, except for what is gleaned from a handful of references. The late fourth-/early fifth-century AD military historian, Vegetius, is one source for methods of training. Although he was writing centuries after the height of the gladiatorial phenomenon, he was still aware of gladiators, and indeed mentioned them, not in the past tense, but as a contemporary presence. In addition, he used the works of Cato, Frontinus and Varro to inform his commentaries on military practice, and it is therefore possible to extrapolate from his findings a picture of much earlier times. Since the training of the soldier and that of the gladiator both have similar aims, *i.e.* to coach the recruit in use of arms, defensive and offensive, and to ensure his killing potential is maximised, Vegetius' comments are invaluable in a gladiatorial context. In particular, his report on how the ancients trained recruits with wooden swords, wicker shields and with posts is both detailed and relevant (*25*). Similar advice would doubtless have been circulating amongst the gladiator trainers, the *doctores* and *magistri*, at the *Ludus Magnus*:

> The ancients, as one finds in books, trained recruits in this manner. They wove shields from withies, of hurdle-like construction, and circular, such that the hurdle had twice the weight that a government shield normally has. They also gave recruits wooden foils likewise of double weight instead of swords. So equipped, they were trained not only in the morning but even after noon against posts. Indeed, the use of posts is of very great benefit to gladiators as well as soldiers. Neither the arena nor the battlefield ever proved a man invincible in armed combat, unless he was judged to have been thoroughly trained at the post. Each recruit would plant a single post in the ground so that it could not move and protruded six feet. Against the post as if against an adversary the recruit trained himself using the foil and hurdle like a sword and shield,so that now he aimed at as it were the head and face, now threatened the flanks, then tried to cut the hamstrings and legs, backed off, came on, sprang, and aimed at the post with every method of attack and art of combat, as though it were an actual opponent. In this training care was taken that the recruit drew himself up to inflict wounds without exposing any part of himself to a blow. (Vegetius, *Epitoma Rei Militaris* I.11)

As if this weren't detailed enough, Vegetius goes on to emphasise how a recruit should be taught to strike not with the edge but with the point (*29*). This implies the continued use of the *gladius*, the stabbing, thrusting sword, as opposed to a longer, slashing blade like the *spatha*, and as such it would have had as much relevance in the first century AD as in the fourth:

> Further, they learned to strike not with the edge, but with the point. For the Romans not only easily beat those fighting with the edge, but even made mock of them, as a cut, whatever its force, seldom kills, because the vitals are protected by both armour and bones. But a stab driven two inches in is fatal; for necessarily whatever goes in penetrates the

29 Tip of the Pompeii *gladius*; note the raised diamond-section point, thought to have added greater strength and penetrative ability to what was primarily a stabbing weapon. *Taken from the Guttmann Collection: photograph ©David S. Michaels, Legion Six Historical Foundation, Los Angeles, CA*

> vitals. Secondly while a cut is being delivered the right arm and flank are exposed; whereas a stab is inflicted with the body remaining covered, and the enemy is wounded before he realises it. That is why it is agreed, the Romans used chiefly this method for fighting. The hurdle and foil of double weight they gave out so that when the recruit took up real, and lighter arms, he fought with more confidence and agility, as being liberated from the heavier weight. (Vegetius, *Epitoma Rei Militaris* I.12)

Everything that Vegetius says seems to have equal relevance to the training of gladiators, and it is hard to see how his advice could have been improved upon. There are many references by other writers to the *doctores* and the *magistri*, the gladiator trainers, who were likely to have been ex-gladiators themselves. These *doctores* tended to specialise in different disciplines, for instance there were *doctores secutorum*, *doctores thraecicum* and so on through the categories, including the *essedarii* and *sagittarii*, and in each case they taught the use of the particular weapons and defences of their specialism.

References to *primus palus* (and *secundus palus*) seem to have been the gladiatorial equivalent of the *primus pilus*, the senior centurion of a legion, indicating a hierarchy of skill and experience within the *ludus*. The *palus* itself, the wooden post in the practice arena, at which gladiators were expected to train day in and day out, was the primary training tool, and the term *primus palus* seems to have signified an instructor or a highly skilled first-grade gladiator. There may have been up to four grades, with the lowest ranked the most expendable.

Ancient writers do not often go into specific details about the physical requirements of the gladiator, but there are many references to the mental attributes needed. In his Natural History, Pliny the Elder in a discussion of the properties of the eyes, mentions that there were 20,000 gladiators in Caligula's *ludus*, of whom only two did not blink when faced with the danger of cold steel; these two were invincible. This quality of unblinking steadiness under pressure is a well-known indicator of victory in battle; as Tacitus remarked in his *Germania*, 'Defeat in battle always begins with the eyes'. Conversations with the champion boxers Nigel Benn and Chris Eubank during the filming of 'Celebrity Gladiators' at Ostia in 2003 supported this point. Both fighters independently asserted the psychological importance of staring an opponent down. As Nigel Benn confirmed, a fight is often won before entering the ring if an opponent looks away. Exactly the same psychology must have been at work in the arena, the only difference being that, once helmeted, further opportunities for meeting and beating an opponent's gaze were lost.

THE PRICE OF A GLADIATOR

Once a gladiator had proved his worth in the arena, his status would be re-evaluated; it is likely each category of gladiator had its own hierarchy, with the *primus palus* of each discipline representing the best exponent of that particular type of combat, and the *secundus palus* graded one lower. Obviously, a gladiator's individual successes would affect his rank and value within the *familia*, and therefore detailed records of his fights were kept – how many combats, how many wins, defeats and draws, how many times he had gained the ultimate award, the *corona* or laurel wreath crown. This is the kind of information given on the *libellus munerarius*, the programme of the *munera* that was issued a few days in advance of the games, so that people could study the form of the declared fighters. Any betting on individual gladiators may well have relied on this source of information for calculating odds. This detailed account of fight results also appears frequently on gladiators' epitaphs, and in graffiti where individual fighters are named, showing that the public had a good working knowledge of their heroes' careers, which they must have followed avidly. Although the fans did not organise themselves into supporters' clubs, as the chariot racing factions did (the Reds, Greens, Whites and Blues all had their followers, one fan throwing himself on a famous charioteer's pyre to follow his hero into the underworld), they had their favourites; that much is clear from the numerous examples of graffiti.

The market value of a gladiator was especially relevant if he died in the arena, or of his wounds thereafter, because his price was fixed according to rank, status and degree of success. His death then became a chargeable item, for which the owner, usually the *lanista*, would require appropriate payment.

Successive emperors, notably Marcus Aurelius, did their best to establish a legal framework for gladiator prices, grading the types of *munera* and the associated costs. With imperial encouragement, the senate passed a law between AD 177 and 180 to take control of prices paid by *editores* for gladiators, the *senatus consultum de pretiis gladiatorum minuendis*. The evidence for this law is found in the fragments of two inscriptions of its text, one from Spain (the Italica) and the other from Turkey (the Sardis).

So by the end of the second century AD there were four official grades of *munera*, with the very smallest, privately funded shows, the *munera assiforana*, not even meriting classification. They remained outside the imperial control, being too modest to require regulation, and generally they cost less than 30,000 *sestertii* (about £200,000) to put on. The calculation of the equivalent in today's prices is necessarily rough and ready, using four *sestertii* as an average day's pay, representing about £25-30.

The lowest official class of *munera*, class IV, cost between 30,000 and 60,000 *sestertii* (roughly £200,000 to £400,000), and the highest, class I, cost between 150,000 and 200,000 *sestertii* (around £1,000,000 and £1,250,000), though at that level the sky was sometimes the limit. In the lowest class, a first grade gladiator would have a maximum price of 5,000 *sestertii* (about £32,000), and a second grade fighter, 4,000 *sestertii* (about £26,000), with the third and lowest grade being priced at 3,000 (about £19,500); in the class I *munera*, the top grade gladiator would have a price of 15,000 *sestertii* (about £97,500), and the second grade gladiator, 12,000 *sestertii* (around £78,000), again with the lowest fifth grade gladiator priced at 6,000 *sestertii* (about £39,000). There were five grades of gladiator within the top two classes, and three grades in the two lower classes.

In the most lavish display, anything from four to 12 pairs of each of the five grades of gladiator would be presented in matched pairs. There was another, cheaper type of gladiator known as a *gregarius*, who fought only in a group, *gregarii* or *gregatim*. Their starting price was considerably less, at 1000 *sestertii*, or £6,500, because they were not so skilled. At any *munus*, a rule was imposed that at least half the number of gladiators had to be *gregarii*.

So a typical class IV show might have one pair of each grade of gladiator, there being three grades, with a mêlée of anything up to 12 *gregarii*, or alternatively, two pairs of each grade, with correspondingly fewer *gregarii*. By contrast, the very best non-imperial (*i.e.* provincial) show might boast between four and 12 pairs of each grade of fighter, there being five grades, and many more *gregarii*, in multiples of ten, from 20 to 60, if the Augustan decree limiting gladiators to 120 in a single *munus* still held.

To put the prices in perspective, it is helpful to consider the buying power of the currency at the time the law was trying to curb gladiatorial inflation; four *sestertii* (which equalled one *denarius*) would probably feed a family, including breadwinner, for one day. A loaf of bread, depending on size, would cost between one and two *asses*, about the same as a provincial prostitute, or a cup of wine. The *as* was a small bronze coin; four *asses* equalled one silver *sestertius*. Even criminals had their price, and *noxii* who were *damnati ad bestias* or *ad gladium* could therefore be purchased for private shows at a cost of 600 *sestertii* each.

Although Marcus Aurelius and successive emperors strove to keep the price of gladiators down, it was symptomatic of the economic downturn to which the empire eventually succumbed that inflationary pressures took hold of the markets – and that included the market in gladiators. It was this relentless rise in prices that contributed, in part at least, to the gradual phasing out of gladiatorial combat in later centuries in favour of the (relatively) cheaper animal spectacles.

MEDICUS

No self-respecting gladiatorial school would have been able to function without doctors. Quite apart from the deliberate wounds sustained during actual combat, there would also be the accidental injuries from training. Depending on the size of the training school, one doctor, *medicus*, might be employed, or several.

The pioneer of surgical procedures as well as other, less invasive treatments, was Galen of Pergamum, who rose to prominence at the time of Marcus Aurelius. The emperor was impressed by his work, and appointed him court physician to his son and heir, Commodus.

Author of the *Ars Medica*, his medical research and subsequent findings remained the unchallenged foundation of medical knowledge until as late as the seventeenth century. Whether or not it was approved by Galen, Pliny the Elder records a remedy for stomach pains and bruises, 'a draught of lye made from ashes of a fire' which he said would 'set you right, and one can see how gladiators benefit from drinking this at the end of a contest'. Ashes were often used in medicine; as Varro said, 'let your hearth be your medicine-box'.

Earlier in his career, Galen had completed his studies and had been appointed physician to the gladiators in his hometown of Pergamum, now in modern Turkey. This afforded him excellent opportunities to observe a variety of anatomical conditions, wounds and other injuries of all kinds, and to record his findings. After this post, he took up an assignment as surgeon to the legions fighting in the Germanic wars, and it was here that his extraordinary skill brought him to the attention of Marcus Aurelius. His long experience as a physician to gladiators and soldiers was recorded in his work *de methodo medendi*, which remained the standard reference work for the treatment of wounds for generations. Galen put heavy emphasis on the importance of diet, exercise and hygiene in the maintenance of good health, and his work with gladiators was doubtless emulated and transmitted by other *medici* who studied under him or followed his work.

Thousands of examples of Roman surgical instruments have survived; they are mostly made of copper-alloy (bronze) or a combination of copper-alloy and iron, in the sense that the scalpels, for example, have copper-alloy handles and iron blades (*colour plates 3* and *4*). Surgical scissors, vein hooks, cauterising instruments, probes, tweezers and specialist bone levers are just some of the wide variety of instruments found (*colour plates 5* and *6*). Some are specifically mentioned by Galen; as is the case with the bone levers, *mochliskos*. From Galen's remarks on these instruments, it seems they were used for levering fractured bones into position, doubtless a quite common occurrence in a large school where training with heavy shields and swords was common.

It is clear that the gladiator at a reasonably large school would have sophisticated medical treatments available to him; ironically, this is far more than the average Roman citizen could expect. Galen developed techniques that repaired muscle injuries by suture, and staunched deep wounds (*colour plate 7*). Such techniques would have been appreciated at the average *ludus*, where an expensive gladiator could not just be invalided out.

The recent discovery of the gladiator graveyard in Ephesus and subsequent analysis of the bones by Professor Karl Grossschmidt revealed a particularly interesting fracture on a radius, the thicker and shorter bone of the forearm, of a gladiator who was buried there. The fracture had healed so perfectly with the help of physiotherapy that it is almost invisible to the naked eye. This is surely a testament to the skills developed and taught by Galen.

Physiotherapy and massage were both advocated by Galen, and from many inscriptions of the time we know that gladiators had their own in-house masseurs, *unctores* and *tractatores* (or masseuses!) as well as doctors.

The diet of the gladiator seems to have varied very little from *ludus* to *ludus*. The analysis of the gladiator bones at Ephesus, not far from where Galen practised, also included a technique called elementary microanalysis; this allowed the scientists to identify what an individual gladiator had eaten during his lifetime. The results reflected the accepted Roman belief that gladiators ate mostly barley. In his *Natural History*, Pliny the Elder tortuously argued that this grain was the oldest food known to man as proved by the fact that it was given to gladiators, 'who used to be called *hordearii*', or barleymen. There are many references to their special food, *sagina*, or barley stew. Barley contains less gluten than wheat, which may have a bearing on the ability of the gladiators to eat large portions of it without becoming obese, although it was recommended that gladiators put on a layer of subcutaneous fat before a contest, in order to protect their vital organs.

The 2004 excavations and analysis of the gladiator bones appear to indicate that the gladiators ate very little meat and that their diets in fact consisted mostly of barley, beans and dried fruit, established by the proportions of zinc and strontium present in the bones; a balanced diet of meat and vegetables leaves equal amounts of strontium in the cells, while a mainly vegetarian diet would leave high levels of strontium and little zinc, according to Professor Grossschmidt.

Barley is an ancient food crop dating from around 6000 BC in the Middle East, and although it has good levels of nutrients, it produces dark, dense bread or stews, and a high level of flatulence. It was thought of as a foodstuff more fit for animals, which effectively is what the gladiators had become when they entered the *ludus*.

MORTALITY RATES

The chances of dying in the arena were by no means as high as our preconceptions would have us believe. However, chances of survival varied at different times in the history of gladiators. When they first fought in the early days of the republic as *bustuarii*, it was still a religious obligation, and their death was part of the offering to the deceased, as sustenance for the departing soul, so at least one, if not both combatants, could expect to die as a matter of course.

As the political value of the *munera* increased in the later republic, the issue was one of conspicuous consumption, in order to impress the voters, and so the gladiators had to die as part of the display of extravagance. Once Augustus ushered in the imperial period, he reformed the *munera*, and prohibited combats *sine missione*, that is to say, to the death. This prohibition was partly in recognition of the investment value of the skilled fighter. Unfortunately, it did not last, and whilst the first century AD was therefore a time when fewer fights ended in death, this altered with the later emperors, who reinstated the combats fought to the death. Once again, the gladiator's chances of survival deteriorated. From a gladiator's point of view, therefore, early in the first century AD under Augustus was the most desirable era in which to enter the arena, in terms of risk of death.

Statistics on survival of gladiators can never be trustworthy; there are too many unknowns. For example, whilst tombstones and epitaphs generally can be useful, they do not tell the full story – not everyone could afford a proper funeral, so the tombstones and inscriptions only testify to a certain proportion of the gladiatorial profession.

The inscriptions in particular indicate that quite a considerable number of fighters died only after several years as a gladiator, and it is by no means clear that they all died in the arena. If we accept as a general rule that a professional fighter probably fought two or three times a year at most, then that is not the mortality rate that Hollywood would have us believe. This is, after all, a world of lowered life expectancy where many people died in childhood, and where only two out of five would live into their twenties. Placed against that backdrop, the gladiator's life does not seem quite so severe. He was, after all, subject to the same vagaries of health and accident as the rest of the population.

Assuming that the gladiator was a skilled practitioner of his profession, then if he were lucky, he might survive his two fights a year for several years. Equally, the inscriptions record a number of gladiators who seem to have had many fights in a short period, such as a man aged 22 who had survived 13 bouts, whilst another commemorates a gladiator who had died aged 35 after 20 wins. In Trajan's games, there was a gladiator who is recorded as having fought nine times on nine consecutive days. Inscriptions show many deaths between 18 and 27 years, whilst one records that another lived to the comparatively ripe age of 45. One particularly busy fighter, in a Sicilian inscription, died at 30 after 34 fights, of which 21 were victories. All that these kind of details tell us is that some survived, some didn't, and the very fact that they were successful enough to have tombstones put up in their memory means that they were probably at the better end of the life-survival curve.

By analysing the results of contests, the scholar Georges Ville calculated that a gladiator had a 9:1 chance of surviving, though if he lost, that went down to 4:1, again depending on whether he won an appeal for *missio*. This was the situation in the first century AD at any rate, but in the second and third centuries, the death rate rose, with the loser almost certain to be killed, rather than be sent out.

On the other hand, there are references to gladiators who felt that they had gone to seed through lack of combats. The more successful a gladiator became, the more likely it was that he would survive; his reputation would give him the edge in any contest with an intimidated unknown, and his supporters would ensure that, in the event of his defeat, he was allowed to leave the arena (*missio*). So, if a gladiator managed to keep himself alive for the first four years, then he had a pretty good chance of staying that way for a lot longer. Every fight that he won was a boost to his status and rank, and assisted his reputation further, so that when he stepped out into the arena, win or lose, he was well-known and hopefully well-loved enough to get the spectators on his side. Equally, for a rank outsider to be paired with a veteran, who was a survivor of many contests, the intimidation may have been so crushing as to take away the will to win. The fate of Urbiscus, a *secutor* from Milan, as recorded on his tombstone, is salutary: *Te moneo ut quisquem vicerit occidat* – 'I warn you that you had better kill the man you have defeated'. Obviously, his beaten opponent had turned the tables on him in a later fight.

Despite the statistics, and the rare exceptions, it seems reasonable to assume that most gladiators must have died in the arena, or of their wounds thereafter, before they were about 25 years old, and furthermore, a great many of them probably died, unrecorded, in their first fight. The fortunate few managed to avoid the attentions of Nemesis, but they were definitely in the minority. Anyone reaching the age of 27 years old, or thereabouts, was no worse off than the average Roman citizen.

Perhaps the last word should go to the gladiator Glauco, whose tombstone tells a familiar story:

> To the revered spirits of the dead. Glauco, born at Mutino, fought seven times, died in the eighth. He lived 23 years 5 days. Aurelia set this up to her well-deserving husband, together with those who loved him. My advice to you is to find your own star. Don't trust Nemesis; that is how I was deceived. Hail and farewell.
> (*CIL*, 5.3466)

1 Above Achilles slaughtering prisoners of war. *Reproduced with kind permission of Misha Nedeljkovich, Associate Professor, College of Journalism and Mass Communication, University of Oklahoma*

2 Right The *Ludus Magnus* in Rome, looking west towards the Colosseum. *Photograph: author*

3 Left Iron-bladed, bronze-handled scalpels. *Courtesy of Historical Collections & Services, Claude Moore Health Sciences Library, University of Virginia*

4 Below Bronze probes. *Courtesy of Historical Collections & Services, Claude Moore Health Sciences Library, University of Virginia*

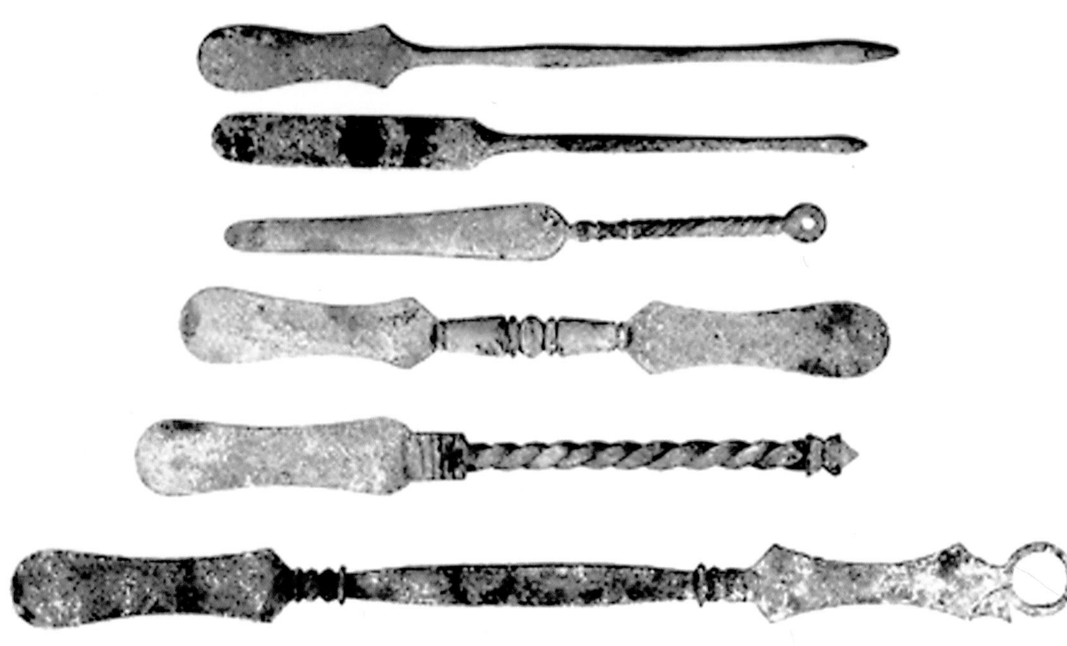

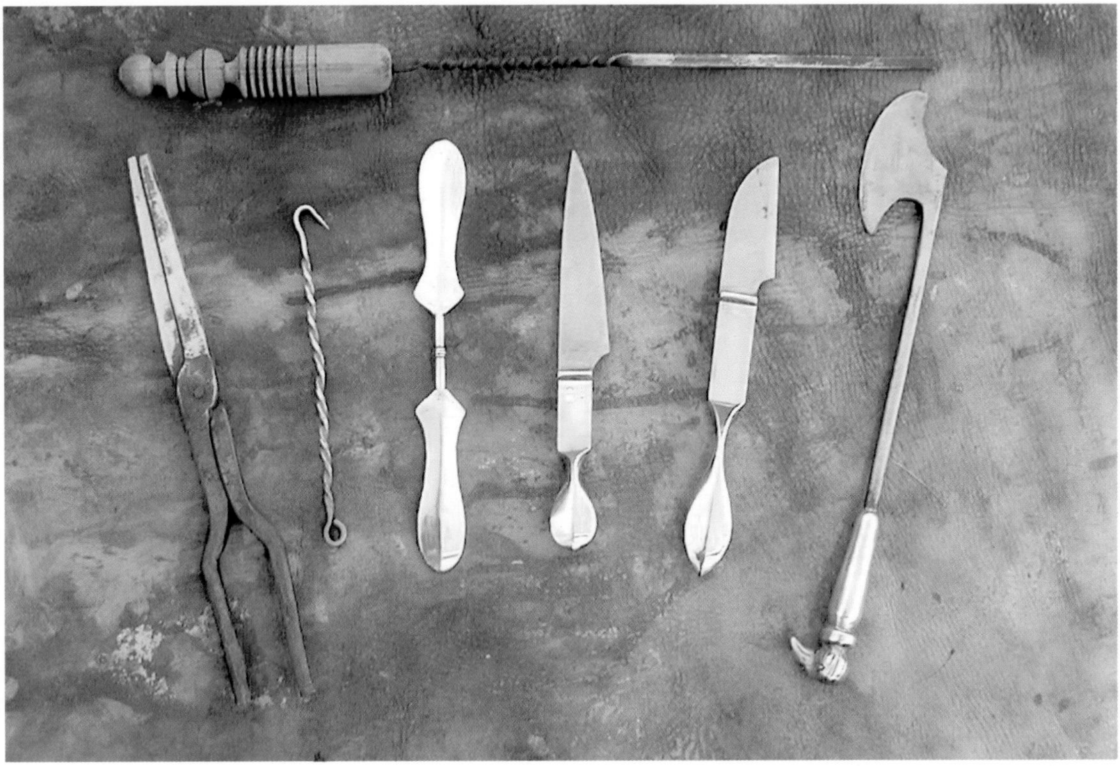

5 Probes and scalpels reconstructed for modern demonstrations of ancient surgery. *Photograph*: *Matt Bunker, ERA*

6 Reconstructed scalpels. *Photograph: Matt Bunker, ERA*

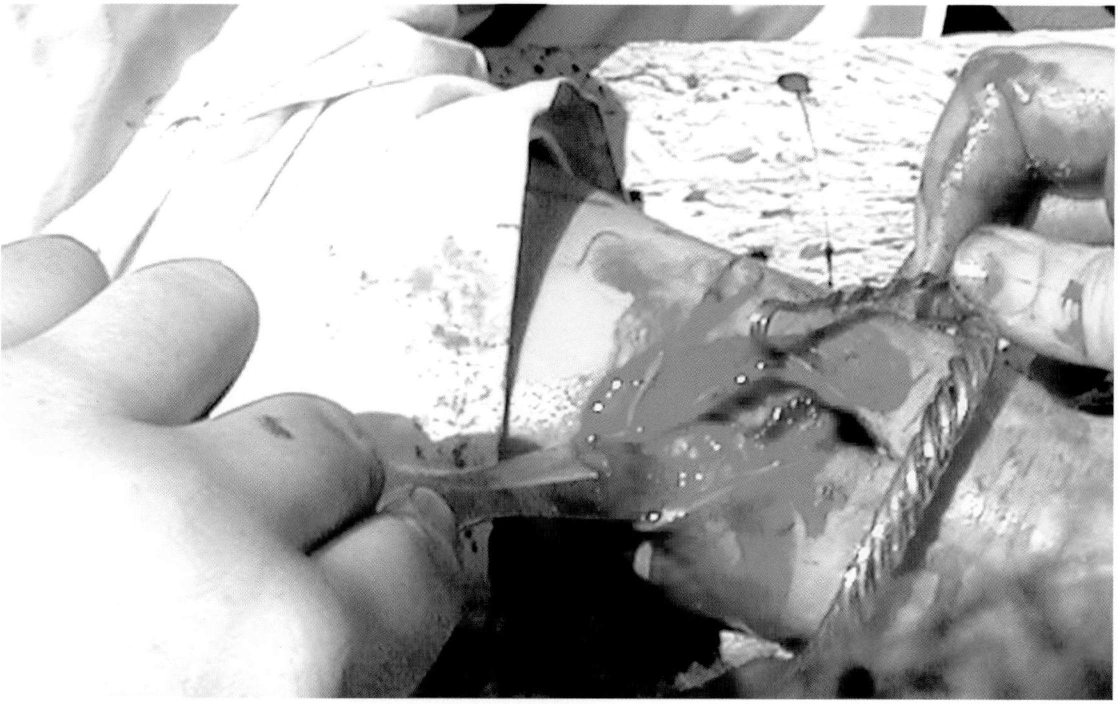

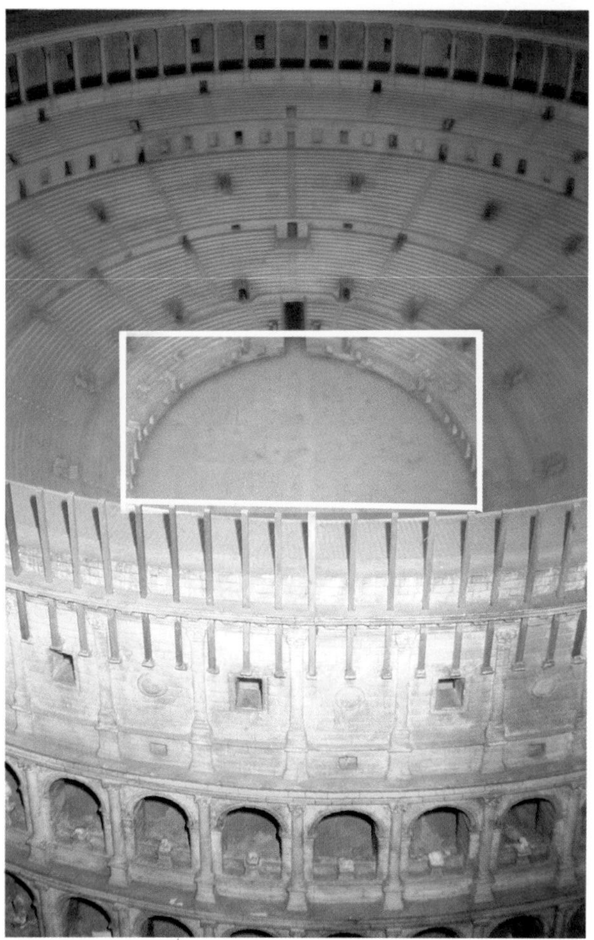

7 Above Prosthetics are often used to dramatic effect at re-enactments. These are not for the squeamish to view but serve to illustrate not only the physical consequences of combat in the arena, but also the skills of the ancient surgeon. *Photograph: Matt Bunker, ERA*

8 Left Reconstruction of the *Colosseum* in the form of a model at Rome's *EUR Museum. Photograph: Pharos Pictures*

9 *Above* The same area seen highlighted in colour plate 8 photographed in the Colosseum in 2005. *Photograph: Pharos Pictures*

10 *Right* *Eques* gladiator. *Thanks to: Marcus Junkelmann, Steve Rogers, in association with Rheinisches Landesmuseum Trier, Treves, Deutschland, Archäologoischer Park Carnuntum, Petronell, Niederösterreich*

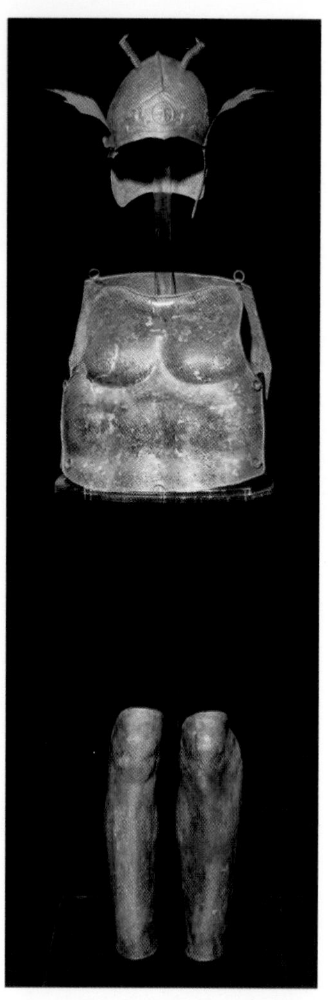

11 Left Samnite armour of fourth to third century BC. *Taken from the Guttman Collection, with kind permission of Christies Images Ltd*

12 Below Wide Samnite belts in bronze (copper alloy). *Taken from the Guttman Collection, with kind permission of Christies Images Ltd*

13 Early helmets worn by Samnites, Campanians and indeed Romans were undoubtedly of Hellenistic influence like this fourth- to third-century BC Phrygian-crested Attic helmet in bronze. *Taken from the Guttman Collection, with kind permission of Christies Images Ltd*

14 The Colchester Thracian. *Courtesy of Colchester Archaeological Trust*

15 *Above* The Hawkedon Helmet. *With kind permission of the Board and Trustees of the British Museum*

16 *Left* Exploded view of a *murmillo* helmet

17 *Above Retiarius* trains against a *secutor* gladiator. *Reproduced with kind permission of Marcus Junkelmann, in association with Rheinisches Landesmuseum, Trier*

18 *Right* Relief of a *secutor* defeating a *retiarius*. *Photograph: Professor Chris Grocock*

19 Left The Piddington Knife; with an iron blade and bronze handle fashioned like a *secutor* gladiator the circular plate over the left hand side of the chest may have been a stabilising plate for the arm guard. *Photograph: Roy Friendship-Taylor. Courtesy of Upper Nene Archaeological Society*

20 Below left Piddington Knife replica. *Courtesy of Nodge Nolan*

21 Below right Interpretation of the Piddington *secutor* at Chester amphitheatre with circular stabilising plate illustrated. *Reconstruction: Britannia and Tony Wilmott (English Heritage)*

22 Marker illustration of the stabilising plate on the chest of a later gladiator. *Copied from a detail of the Villa Borghese mosaic*

23 *Above* Carved stone plaque from Chester, now in Saffron Walden Museum, showing a *retiarius*; the depiction of the armguard has led to differing interpretations of how, and indeed whether, the elbow joint may have articulated. *Reproduced with kind permission of Saffron Walden Museum, Essex*

24 *Left* Detail of the armguard from colour plate 23

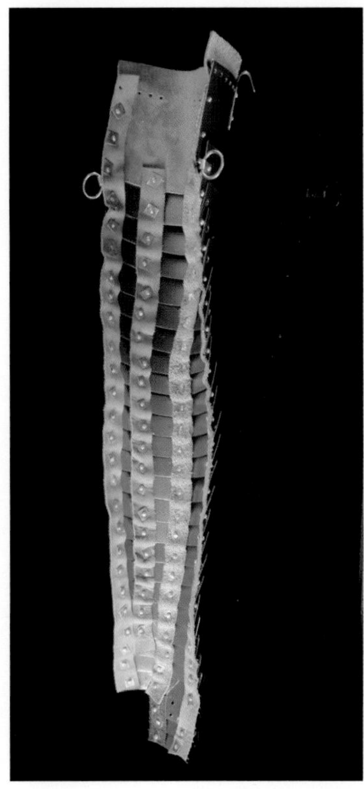

25a Above left Replica *manica* based on the Carlisle finds. *Reproduced with kind permission of Michael Hardy*

25b Above right *Manica* inner surface showing riveted and belted construction. *Reproduced with kind permission of Michael Hardy*

26 *Secutor* gladiator on a glass fragment from Vindolanda showing what the author believes to be a combination of padded fabric and metal armour on the arm. *Courtesy of Vindolanda Trust, Chesterholm Museum*

27 Replica of a *murmillo* helmet. *Taken from the Guttman Collection, with kind permission of Christies Images Ltd*

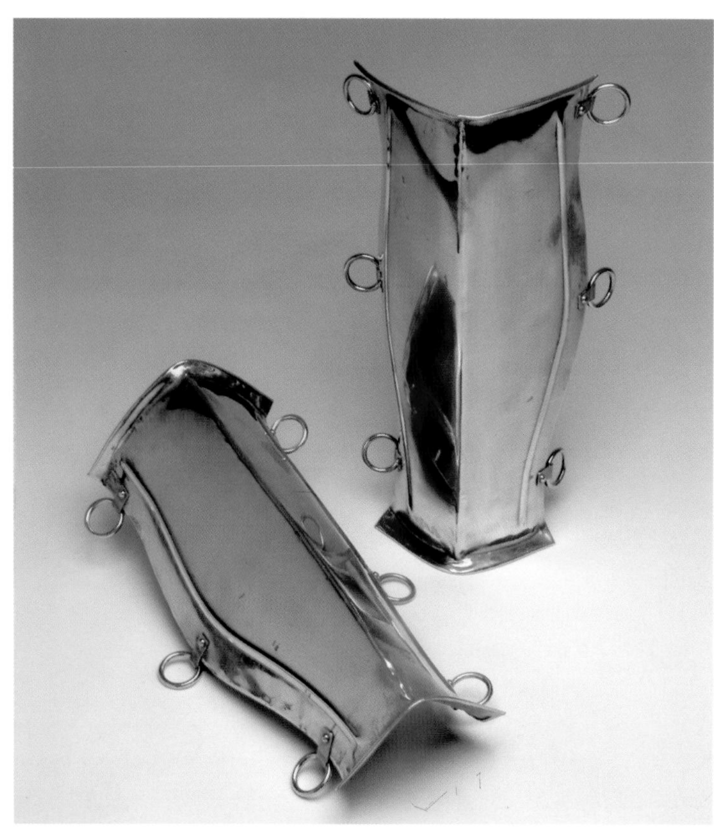

28 Replica leg greaves in bronze. Despite the angle down each shin, they are surprisingly comfortable and a universal fit. *Photograph: Michael Hardy*

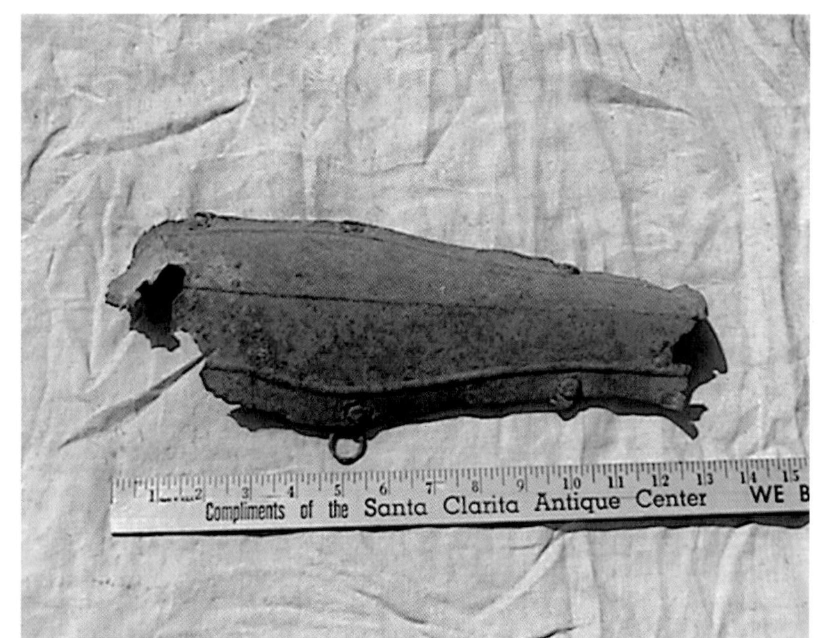

29 Original leg greave in bronze, (copper alloy). *Taken from the Guttmann Collection, with kind permission of Christies Images Ltd. Photo (copyright): David S. Michaels, Legion Six Historical Foundation, Los Angeles, CA www.legionsix.org*

30 Above left Murmillo gladiator. *Reconstruction: Britannia. Photograph: Pharos Pictures*

31 Above right The index finger was raised (*ad digitum*) as a plea for mercy. *Reconstruction: Britannia. Photograph: Fraser Gray*

32 An assortment of gladiator helmets with a battered, 'provincial' look. *Photograph: Fraser Gray*

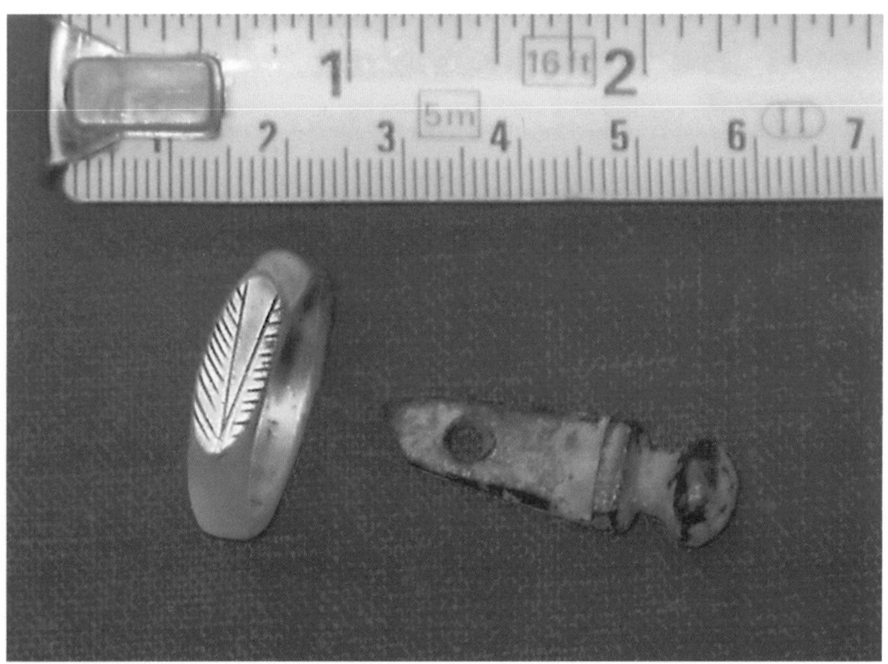

33 Souvenirs of the games. Left, a silver adult's ring bearing the unusual emblem of a split victory palm. Second and third century AD. Right, a votive miniature *gladius*, pierced with a hole for wearing around the neck. *Photograph: author*

4

BEHIND THE GAME OF DEATH: ORGANISING THE SPECTACLE

The enduring words of the Venerable Bede, even though they were written in the eighth century, hundreds of years after the high summer of the Roman Empire, are always recalled in connection with the colossal amphitheatre that we now know as the Colosseum: *quamdiu stabit coliseus, stabit et Roma; quando cadet coliseus, cadet et Roma; quando cadet Roma, cadet et mundus* – 'while stands the Coliseum [*sic*], Rome stands; when falls the Coliseum, Rome falls; when Rome falls, so falls the world'. These are stirring words, eternally binding together the fates of the Colosseum, Rome and the world. Unfortunately, Bede was not referring to the monumental remains of the amphitheatre commissioned by Vespasian in AD 70, but to the huge bronze statue of Nero, the work of Zenodorus, standing 119ft (35m) high in the grounds of the *Domus Aurea*, his outrageously extravagant palace. This overblown, and now non-existent, statue of Nero as Helios, god of the sun, the largest bronze statue of its day, was inspired by the well-known Colossus of Rhodes. It was this statue that became known as the *coliseus* or *colosseum*; it was not until the turn of the millennium that the great amphitheatre, built on the site of the hated Nero's infamous Golden House, the *Domus Aurea*, at the order of the new emperor Vespasian, acquired the name by association, after the statue had collapsed and left no trace. Thereafter, the amphitheatre of the Flavian dynasty of emperors became known as the Colosseum, the name it has retained to the present day.

Rome without the Colosseum is inconceivable. It is the one monument that says 'Rome' without a shadow of ambiguity, and, if asked to name an amphitheatre, most people would unhesitatingly answer, 'The Colosseum'. Over two millennia, its rearing monumental outline, the roundness of its construction echoing the city and the globe of the world, has become a visual metaphor for the city of Rome itself (*30* and *31*). In the public mind, it has always been associated with gladiators, and yet, for several centuries before it was built, Romans had already been enjoying spectacles in and around the city. Rome had not been built in a day.

30 Colosseum model. *Museo della Civilta, EUR Rome. Photograph: author*

31 Surviving section of the *Colosseum*'s outer wall, Rome. *Photograph: author*

GLADIATORS WITHOUT AMPHITHEATRES

The earliest combats did not need much space, if the ancient sources are to be believed; they took place after the death of some important man, and might even have been conducted at the site of his pyre, the *bustum*, hence their nickname, *bustuarii*.

This would inevitably have placed the combats outside the city limits, since one of Rome's most ancient laws forbade any kind of burial within the city. The Law of the Twelve Tables laid it down: *HOMINEM MORTUUM IN URBE NE SEPELITO NEVE URITO*. The funeral rites for the dead had to be conducted outside the *pomerium*, the city's ancient boundaries. Burial within the city was an honour granted only very rarely to individuals who had rendered exceptional service to the state.

Because there were only small numbers of fighters involved in the early gladiator contests, the entire event could easily be staged in any convenient field with room for plenty of spectators, although the historical record is silent as to how they were accommodated. It would have been easy enough to pace out a level fighting area, and cordon it off, and as the whole thing took place outside city walls, there would have been no planning or regulatory constraints from the authorities. But as for details on seating or numbers in the audience, we are in the dark. It is only when the *munera* transfer to the city that information starts to build.

However, the *munera* needed a permanent home, not just a temporary berth in the theatre or the circus. Neither theatre nor circus was custom-built for the kind of spectacle that gladiators provided (*12*). It was all about focus. The theatre stage was impractically small; the circus was not intimate enough to allow the audience to concentrate on two gladiators.

FORUM FIGHTS

As we have seen, the increasing popularity of the combats saw them transfer to open spaces within the city, notably the Roman Forum, with its strong identity as a public meeting place. It was an all-purpose centre of civic activity, with farmers' markets, government headquarters, temples and altars; it was the best place to meet, talk, shop, exchange ideas and be entertained. Temporary seating was often erected in order to create an arena for the staging of *munera*, and was removed afterwards. Unfortunately the space available for spectators was limited to that not already taken up by monuments, statuary and Roman municipal street furniture. The wealthy and well-connected probably avoided the scrum by obtaining reserved places, but the vast majority of the spectators had to take their chances, if they wanted to see the spectacle; the area of the arena and surrounding seating was not able to accommodate more than a tiny proportion of those who wanted to get a good view. That was the problem with using *fora*, and it remained unsolved. It was not helped by the local magistrates' practice of renting out the seats they were providing at steep prices unaffordable by the lower classes.

The Forum may well have been used for *munera* as early as the fourth century BC, as the second-century AD writer Festus suggests in a reference to C. Maenius, the censor of 338 BC, in which he says that the specific term for the seating in amphitheatres, *maeniana*, is named after Maenius because he was the first to increase the seating capacity of the Forum to improve public access to the spectacles. If seating really was being increased as far back as 338 BC, then the history of the *munera* as an established social feature is older than the earliest direct references to it would indicate. However, gladiatorial combat in Rome cannot be regarded as separate from the public funeral, *funus publicum*, of some important civic figure until at least the late republic; for this reason, that most public of all spaces, the Forum, was at first the ideal site for such an occasion, guaranteeing maximum publicity, that *sine qua non* of politicians down the ages.

It was in the Forum that that the *munera* were polished and honed; their practical requirements of ample seating with a good view for all, and architectural control of the space to enhance the spectacle were tested and modified, to achieve ever more impact on the spectators. So although the gladiator combats did not have a settled location, a dedicated building specifically designed and built for the purpose of displaying the contests and shows to best advantage, with every oversubscribed spectacle that took place in the Forum, the necessity for a permanent, specially designed structure became ever more acute.

Even before the days of the great amphitheatres, it was still counted as a perk to be granted access to the better vantage points of the Forum for the *spectacula*, and this honour is recorded as having been bestowed upon one Servius Sulpicius, a senior administrator rewarded posthumously for services to the state:

> … since so excellent a man met his death while an ambassador on behalf of the state, it was decided by the Senate that a bronze standing statue be set up at the Rostra at their expense and that around this statue a space of five feet in all directions be reserved for his children and his posterity at *ludi* and at gladiatorial combats, because he had died in the service of the state. (Cicero, *Philippics* 9.7.16.)

The rectangular ground plan of the Forum, situated between the Basilica Sempronia to the south, and the Basilica Porcia and Basilica Aemilia to the north, meant that the arena was laid out, first as a rectangle within it, delineated by two long banks of wooden seats and two short ones, and then, as the short ends curved in to become semi-circles, the classic elliptical shape was achieved. The colonnades on the long sides of the basilicas were ideal for seating spectators, and the tribunals at both ends of the central open space helped to form a natural, stadium-like arena, though small in size; it must have measured roughly 200ft

(60m) long, by 120ft (35m) wide, with the arena covering an area, again, roughly 160ft (48m) by 60ft (18m). Using an estimated seat allowance per spectator, known as the *locus*, of approximately 16in (0.4m), based on the incised seat dividers still found in many amphitheatres, these dimensions would allow for approximately 330 people in the front row. Further, if we assume, conservatively, that at least ten rows would be set up, then the Forum could hold 3300 spectators. As Rome in the first century AD is thought to have had a population of around one million, of which adult male citizens would have constituted about a quarter, and not very much less in the late republic, this implies the Forum was only capable of holding a very small proportion of its potential audience. It is hardly surprising that the transition to amphitheatres, when it came, was a popular one, making the spectacles available to many more people than ever before.

The whole area may have given the general impression of a provincial arena, bounded as it was by great municipal buildings, including the Regia. By about 170 BC, the Forum had developed into a regular venue for spectacle, along the lines described above, a basic form that it would retain through the escalating permutations and consequent logistical demands of the games and combats that would be held there as the political temperature of the late republic steadily climbed.

Though there were a few modifications, the Forum kept to this basic form until a fire in 52 BC gave Julius Caesar the chance to carry out the reconstruction that he had in mind: one that would promote him personally, rather than indirectly. The most intriguing of Caesar's makeover projects was his personal commissioning of four underground passages beneath the Forum, specifically designed to enhance the *spectacula* he was planning, by providing a series of ramps and steps into the arena by means of which wild beasts, batches of doomed captives and criminals taking part in the big set pieces, stage sets, props, and even gladiators, could be quickly transported up into the arena from a subterranean holding area as if through the floor.

Vitruvius, the early imperial writer whose 10-volume treatise on engineering and architecture was dedicated to Augustus, believed that the *fora* of Italian towns had been deliberately laid out in such a way as to accommodate *spectacula*. He pointed out that the elongated shape was ideal for gladiatorial combat, with a length:width ratio of 3:2 giving the best results. Implicit in his assertions is the concept that the *munera* were important enough to merit serious consideration at the town planning stage, even though the main activities of the *forum* would always be commercial and political rather than cultural.

FROM BLEACHERS TO THEATRES

Before the advent of the amphitheatre in Rome, the earliest type of seating layout for the *munera* in the Forum would have consisted of two long banks of seats opposite each other, with two shorter banks of seats at the ends, which later curved into semi-circular sections. These would have been wooden structures, like the bleachers, *ikria* to the Greeks, erected on convenient hillsides for their sporting contests. But the Roman theatre-builders did not want to depend on the lie of the land for suitable locations.

Therefore, from the very first examples, the Roman theatre is a freestanding structure, supporting itself by means of vaulted galleries on which the banks of seats themselves sit. Hillsides were redundant and the shape of the terrain irrelevant; the Romans could put their theatres anywhere they wanted. This was to be a key factor in the development of the Roman amphitheatre, as shown by the actual appearance of the first one a few years later.

The oldest surviving Roman theatre, dated to the last half of the second century BC, is actually in Campania, where the oldest known amphitheatres were first built. Pompey ordered the construction of Rome's first actual stone theatre, in fact a huge theatre complex, as part of the sanctuary of his Temple of Venus Victrix in 55 BC. In this way, he got round the ban on theatre building; that ban may have applied to amphitheatres as well, given the intense political atmosphere surrounding the *munera* in the late republic. By housing the gladiator combats in purely temporary short-lived structures, the *editores* may have reckoned that they could ring the changes more easily and also cater to the public appetite for novelty.

One of the earliest reports of how the Romans organised their seating arrangements comes from Plutarch. He describes an incident in 122 BC, when Gaius Gracchus, scion of the famous Gracchus family and an ambitious politician who understood the people, staged a piece of political drama when he tore down the seating of the aristocrats at a *munus*, because the tall wooden structures were taking up all the room and blocking the view of the common folk in the cheap seats (that is, standing room only), the *plebs* who were trying to get a look-in.

By tearing down the special VIP seats, Gaius Gracchus made himself unpopular with his political opponents, the local magistrates who had had the seats put up at their expense, but made himself very popular with the ordinary Romans; it was a clear demonstration that he saw his true constituency was the people, the *plebs*, and not the wealthy ruling classes. And all of that was conveyed in a row about seating; in time, the *munera* would supply plenty more opportunities for politicians seeking power via the entertainments of the *plebs*.

By 67 BC, the *lex Calpurnia de ambitu* had to be passed, imposing severe restrictions on the provision of gladiatorial games and limiting the candidates' distribution of seats at spectacles, in an attempt to curtail the blatant electoral bribery that had been rife. The *lex Calpurnia* was followed in 65 BC by another law passed by the Senate to limit the number of gladiators any one particular *editor* could keep in the city while *munera* were being held. More legislation in 63 BC, the *lex Tullia de ambitu*, which was sponsored by the lawyer Cicero, proscribed the provision of *munera* within two years of running for public office.

All the signs of the times were pointing towards the fact that the games were no longer seen as just a duty to the dead, if indeed they ever had been; they had become far too influential to be kept outside state control. The laws stayed on the statute books, but were regularly circumvented by *editores* keen to show their generosity to a grateful public. There is, however, the slight possibility that some of this legislation carried an element of concern for public order; *munera* were escalating in size and scale all the time, and to have 320 pairs of armed, trained gladiators in the city, as Julius Caesar planned to do in 65 BC, presented a risk of public injury or civil unrest – there was no police force or urban militia to deal with such a threat. Gangs of intimidating thugs, ostensibly bodyguards and gladiators, could all too easily be diverted into violent disorder to further the aims of politicians.

THE FIRST AMPHITHEATRES

Amphitheatres had already existed outside Rome, in neighbouring Campania, since at least the end of the second century BC, and certainly from around 70 BC, when Pompeii's amphitheatre was constructed (*32*). By the end of the republic, there were already more than 10 amphitheatres in Campania, Lucania and Etruria, with the majority of those in Campania, the main candidate for the origin of the gladiatorial combats, as well as for the amphitheatres themselves.

By virtue of the Vesuvian eruption of 24 August AD 79, the amphitheatre at Pompeii is unique amongst its contemporaries as time stopped abruptly there, and preserved its fabric at an exact and known date (*33*). Inscriptions, still *in situ*, tell us that it was constructed at about 70 BC. It was financed by two political

32 Interior of the Pompeii amphitheatre. Seating and exits are remarkably preserved. *Photograph: Judith Wade, courtesy of Pharos Pictures*

33 One of the main gates into Pompeii's amphitheatre today. Note the brick re-enforcing arch added to strengthen the amphitheatre's structure after earlier earth tremors. *Photograph: Judith Wade, courtesy of Pharos Pictures*

placemen of the dictator Sulla, after he quashed an uprising in Pompeii taking place as part of the Social War (91-88 BC). Rome's former Italian allies in southern and central Italy, the Osco-Samnites, had rebelled against their second-class treatment; they wanted equality and parity with Roman citizens. They failed, and lost much of their land, and control of their lives, to the despised Romans.

Sulla allocated confiscated lands of the Pompeii district to his retired legionary veterans, establishing a loyal, armed veteran colony to secure the area. This was the context of the newly built amphitheatre at Pompeii. Interestingly, on the inscription of dedication, the term used for the amphitheatre is *spectaculum*. This was the usual word for the place where the gladiatorial combats and wild beast hunts were held. The word *amphitheatrum* came into use much later, in the late first or early second century AD.

In respect of an amphitheatre construction programme, Rome was lagging behind, perhaps because of the restrictions put on the exhibiting of *munera* by a jumpy executive, fearful of the influence they exerted. Out in the countryside, such political pressures did not have the same power. Campania had natural advantages when it came to amphitheatre building, but the fact that Rome did not get its first permanent theatre till fairly late on in the republican period does not mean it was in some way deprived or lacking in the technical ability to initiate such a building programme. Rather, it was the special political situation that pertained in Rome, and the part played by the *munera*, which delayed its acquisition of a theatre or amphitheatre. Typically, a great deal of the political unrest at the time the first amphitheatre was seen in Rome was down to Julius Caesar.

During his ascent to political power, Caesar saw the value of acquiring and keeping his own gladiators, rather than paying to hire them whenever he needed to give a display; in this way, he saved great sums of money by cutting out the middle-man who would normally supply the beasts and gladiators for spectacles. He was clever enough to see that it was better to source his own spectacle-fodder, given that he also realised that it was necessary to put on shows of great extravagance and lavishness in order to win popularity and elections. Therefore, he carefully built up a portfolio of gladiator training camps, or schools as they are innocuously called, the most notorious establishment being the *ludus* at Capua, where he kept 5000 gladiators.

It was a magnificently useful legacy, and one which Octavian, Caesar's adopted son, and the future emperor Augustus, inherited after Caesar's assassination in 44 BC. This network of elite fighters, based at Capua, remained the emperor's personal property to be handed down to his successor, and gladiators who trained at the Capua *ludus* were given the title *Iuliani*, which signified they were at the top of their profession.

Caesar's interest in spectacles did not stop at his remodelling of the Forum in 52 BC. To celebrate his fourfold triumph in 46 BC, he had something he called a hunting theatre built, a *kynegetikon theatron*, a temporary building of wood. The historian Cassius Dio called it an amphitheatre because it had seating on all sides and no stage; he clearly felt it differed from Caesar's Forum. Originally, it had been created for the staging of wild beast hunts, but gladiator contests were held in it as well. But it was still only a structure with a short shelf life, unlike the amphitheatres out in Campania. It was sited out on the south side of the Campus Martius, but soon after the first permanent stone amphitheatre was built in 29 BC, it fell into disuse. Movement towards the ultimate amphitheatre, the Colosseum, began with the architectural and technical advances of freestanding Roman stone theatres and implicit in that, the development of *opus caementicum*, a type of concrete exploiting the properties of volcanic *tufa*. *Opus caementicum* was a new, high-quality building material, which permitted the curved shapes of vaulted structures so important in the magnificent municipal buildings being commissioned. It was this miracle material that would alter the face and character of Rome, because best use was made of it in the two new building types embodying the curvilinear style of vaulting – the theatre and amphitheatre.

Punctuating the development of the amphitheatre proper is a strange episode involving a supposed revolving double theatre. This odd novelty, built by C. Scribonius Curio, at about the same time that Julius Caesar was having tunnels excavated under the Forum, was the only one of its type, a failed experiment in the story of the amphitheatre.

In 52 or 53 BC Curio, a friend of Caesar, commissioned the construction of a pair of large wooden theatres, which were placed back to back, on pivots. Theatrical performances, *ludi scaenici*, were scheduled for the first day of the programme in the individual theatres, and then on day two, while the spectators remained in their seats, the theatres were swung round, the two 'halves' creating an *amphitheatrum*, 'a theatre on both sides' in which gladiators fought. Then athletes competed in the created amphitheatre. Finally, planking on the stages was removed and the previous day's victorious gladiators were brought back to fight again. According to Pliny, the audience was in greater danger from the precariousness of their mobile seating than the gladiators were from their combats.

It is said that this revolving procedure was operated several times, whereupon the strain proved too much for the mechanism and it jammed, never again to pivot, revolve or swivel. This at any rate is Pliny's explanation for the origin of the *amphitheatrum*. It is patently not true, because there were already amphitheatres in stone outside Rome more than a hundred years earlier. He was obviously not that impressed with it, as he called it 'a great lunacy'.

There is no doubt this curiosity existed, as Cicero also refers to it in one of his letters, but it was just that – a curiosity, an illustration of the insatiable Roman appetite for novelty and exotica. At most, it might have been the origin of the word *amphitheatrum*. And it does demonstrate that by 52 BC, the amphitheatre was regarded as the appropriate venue for *munera*.

REAL AMPHITHEATRES

It was not until after the republic had given way to the principate that the first stone amphitheatre was built at Rome in 29 BC by a trusted general of Augustus, Titus Statilius Taurus. Like Caesar's wooden hunting theatre, it was sited at the southern end of the Campus Martius. It is doubtful that it was made entirely of stone; there is some suggestion that the seats were wood on a stone framework. This would make it a halfway house between the temporary structures and the first true permanent amphitheatre, the Flavian. However, it seems to have been unsatisfactory in some way, because although it was used occasionally, the *munera* continued to be staged in other venues for the next 80 years or so.

Caligula was said to dislike the Statilian amphitheatre; he ordered specially built lavish temporary structures in which he presented a series of spectacles, and as he discovered, they made him very popular with the people, if only temporarily, rather like his structures. He then initiated the construction of an amphitheatre near the *saepta*, the people's meeting place and voting area on the Campus Martius, but it was never finished, and according to Suetonius, Claudius abandoned the project.

In AD 58 Nero had an immense and opulent wooden amphitheatre built near the Pantheon, a non-event in the eyes of Tacitus, who felt it was an anti-climax, something that ought to be left to the newssheets, the *acta diurna*, rather than be dignified as history. As he put it, in the year it was built nothing much happened, 'except in the eyes of historians who like filling their pages with praise of the foundations and beams of Nero's huge amphitheatre in the Field of Mars'. The less hardboiled writer, Calpurnius Siculus, enthusiastically sang its praises: 'It rose into the sky, and looked down on the Tarpeian Rock.' If that is an accurate observation, it must have been extremely tall for a wooden building. At its inaugural games, there were reports of a remarkable exhibition of gladiators fighting, at which nobody whatsoever was killed. The audience reaction to this display was not recorded.

No doubt the gladiator contests and wild beast fights continued to find expression in the Forum, the Circuses, and temporary enclosures, as they had done for the previous centuries. General Statilius' amphitheatre never quite set the Roman imagination on fire. Finally, it was put out of its misery when it was burnt down in the fire of AD 64, during the reign of Nero.

COLOSSEUM

After the (slightly) assisted suicide of the emperor Nero in AD 68, the first thing that occurred to the survivors of his miserable reign was to obliterate all traces of him, the customary Roman reaction to a hated ruler. He suffered the fate of many hated emperors, that of *damnatio memoriae*. There followed a fairly short and brutal bout of civil war, lasting 18 months, in which three equally unsuitable aristocrats and one capable general (Vespasian) vied with each other for the permanent position of emperor. This became known as the 'year of the four emperors', and in their enthusiasm to grasp the crown, contributed to the wrecking of central Rome, before the three unsuccessful candidates lost their lives in the process.

Titus Flavius Vespasianus came to power as the result of a coalition to support him. He had the reputation of a blunt, straightforward military man, and his celebrated victories spoke for him. He was the extremely able general who had commanded the Roman army in putting down the Jewish uprising in Judaea in AD 66.

With the booty and spoils of war after the sack of Jerusalem, Vespasian decided to build a new stone amphitheatre on the site of the lake at Nero's *Domus Aurea*, the Golden House. This was a canny move; at a stroke he was putting right the wrong that had so outraged the Roman people and turned them against Nero – the public land he had grabbed for his own personal building programme. As a symbol of the return of the land for the people's entertainment, the amphitheatre was a good choice; it was to be a public space, part of the city, and therefore a monument for all to take pride in. At the same time, Vespasian chose a monument that had strong military associations to commemorate his accession.

The building work was started in or around AD 75, and so immense was the task, that each day, it was calculated, 200 cartloads of stone had to be brought in during construction. There is a suggestion that the deep ruts still visible in the stone of the *Via Sacra* were caused by the continuous traffic of heavily laden carts and wagons. It has recently been estimated that 30,000 tonnes of earth had to be removed during the excavation of the foundations, which were about 40ft (12m) deep.

The Flavian amphitheatre, which we know as the Colosseum, was serviced by a series of tunnels to bring animals and scenery discreetly in and out of the arena, although when it first opened to the public, the lifts transporting wild beasts and theatrical props were incorporated into the perimeter wall running around the outside of the arena itself. A complicated maze of walls and arches was later constructed under the wooden floor of the arena as a more sophisticated method of bringing animals and scenery into the arena (*colour plate 9*). The lifts and trapdoors would have been controlled by a complex series of winches, pulleys and windlasses powered by a small army of slaves who would have spent much of their time in the dark, hot, stinking, cacophonous guts of the Colosseum.

Some provincial amphitheatres such as Capua in Campania and Trier in Germany show evidence of this system of trapdoors and underground vaults (*34* and *35*). On a more modest scale, the smaller amphitheatres such as Chester and London, in Great Britain, show no signs of any system in the arena floor more complicated than drains, indicating that in the less sophisticated amphitheatres, such animals and props as there were, would have been brought in from gates in the arena walls. The construction itself was made possible because of the *opus caementicum* that the Romans had developed, using the special properties of the volcanic lightweight rock known as tufa.

The entire structure used three basic building materials, concrete, brick and travertine limestone, and for lower tier seating and surface decoration, polished and dressed marble. Before the building could even begin, the land had to be drained and over 3000yds of water channels and tunnels to serve as inflow and outflow conduits for the internal water supply had to be built. Traces of lead piping are suspected as having been present in the stonework, but this material was robbed from the site soon after its dereliction. The water supply would have been needed for the many fountains of which traces have been found on the lower levels. The reports of sea-battles being held in the temporarily flooded Flavian amphitheatre are a matter for debate; the water system would have needed to deliver and dispose of prodigious quantities in a short space of time; there is no evidence of any such mechanism.

Vespasian died before the completion of the amphitheatre, although the first two storeys were built by then. By the time of its completion and dedication under the emperor Titus in AD 80, the whole structure had three storeys of outer arcades, a podium, and three levels of seating, the *ima cavea*, *media cavea*, and the *summum maenianum in ligneis*. So it seems probable that Titus added the third

34 Trier arena, Germany, today. The floor has been restored and is a modern interpretation. *Photograph: S. Wade, courtesy of Pharos Pictures*

35 Modern restoration/interpretation of the beams that supported this provincial amphitheatre's arena floor in antiquity. *Photograph: S. Wade, courtesy of Pharos Pictures*

storey. His brother, Domitian, who succeeded him as emperor in AD 81, put the finishing touches to the monument by adding yet another storey, often called the attic storey. This took the height of the Colosseum to over 150ft and visitors to modern Rome are still able to detect in its ruins the monumental and awe-inspiring presence that brooded over the rest of the city; even today, it dwarfs the surrounding buildings.

The most important features of the upper storey added by Domitian, decorated as it was with Corinthian pilasters and bronze shields (of which all that now remains, sadly, are the holes in the masonry where they were once fixed) were the 240 holes and carved stone brackets for the masts that supported the huge canvas awnings, the *velaria*.

The awnings were an essential element of the Colosseum, as indeed they would have been for any Mediterranean amphitheatre, where temperatures could soar, causing great discomfort for spectators who might be sitting all day under the sun. To give some idea of exactly how important shade was, Suetonius gives an account of Caligula's cruel sense of humour:

> During gladiatorial shows he would have the canopies removed at the hottest time of day and forbid anyone to leave. (Suetonius, *de vita Caesarum, Gaius* (*Caligula*) 26)

As a sunshield, it was at least partially effective; it was certainly advertised as an added attraction on bills and leaflets advertising a show: *vela erunt* – 'there will be awnings' was a proud boast particularly of smaller amphitheatres like Pompeii. In fact, the only known depiction of awnings *in situ* is on a fresco at Pompeii, in the peristyle garden of the 'House of the Gladiator Actius Anicetus'. It depicts the riot of AD 59, between the locals and their neighbouring rivals, the Nucerians, which took place in the amphitheatre (*36*).

There was already bad blood between the Pompeians and the Nucerians. During a spectacle put on by a former Roman senator, Livineius Regulus, in which a troupe of gladiators performed, verbal abuse was exchanged in the crowd, turning quickly to stone-throwing, and then to real weapons. As the Pompeians had local reinforcements nearby, the Nucerians got the worst of it and many adults and children were killed and wounded. They sent a delegation to Rome to complain to Nero, who ordered an official enquiry, as a result of which the Senate found Pompeii guilty of public order offences. As a penalty, Pompeians were banned from having public gladiator shows for 10 years. The abolition of illegally formed Pompeian clubs, *collegia*, thought to be behind the worst of the organised violence and the banishment of Regulus, who was suspected of orchestrating the whole thing, were other penalties imposed by the Senate.

The fresco itself shows the amphitheatre from an overhead perspective, and the details are not all faithfully rendered, for example the amphitheatre had six arches under the double staircase, whereas eleven are shown. However, in its

36 Pompeii amphitheatre fresco depicting the riot in AD 59 between Nucerian and Pompeiian members of the audience. This is a detail taken from a larger section of fresco in the house of Actius Anicetus (possibly a gladiator himself). This depiction of the arena's awning may be the best surviving representation of *velaria. Photograph: S. Wade, courtesy of Pharos Pictures*

general portrayal of the structure, it is in agreement with the extant remains, so the inclusion of the awnings is probably to be trusted, though again, they are depicted only partially covering the auditorium, but this is likely to be due to artistic licence. There is certainly evidence for masts all round the structure, with sockets and ring consoles for mast support still in place.

Because each awning was in effect nothing more than a giant sail anchored to the Colosseum around its outer rim, it required a lot of manpower to operate, and the ideal crew for this task would have been detachments of sailors seconded from Ravenna and Misenum, where the Roman navy was based. Scholars still cannot agree on the exact method of rigging the awnings, although it must necessarily have involved at least 240 ropes attached to the masts meeting at an oval-shaped loop of rope in the centre. This would form the *oculus*, the eye of the awnings, through which the sun would be able to shine at various times of day. Because total cover could not be achieved, there would always be areas which didn't get any shade at the hottest times of day, and ironically, if the design of the awnings is correct, these uncomfortable seats were more likely to be in the better seating down at the front. The people up in the 'gods' would at least have the benefit of permanent shade even if they couldn't make out what was going on in the arena.

SEATING AND TICKETS: SOCIAL STATUS SET IN STONE

As Fronto remarked, 'Government is proven no less by its shows than by serious matters ... the entire populace is united by spectacles'. The problem with that statement is that the entire populace did not get the chance to be united by spectacles, because they could not all gain admission. Far from being an open-door policy, Roman custom and law worked together to effectively exclude various groups; a high degree of selectivity was in operation at all times, so that in actual fact the result was a carefully chosen cross-section taken mainly from the representatives of the upper reaches of the Roman hierarchy. As ever, Augustus had been the driving force behind these social regulations. His aim had been to restore the traditional values and moral rectitude that he felt had disappeared from Roman public life. He abhorred, for instance, the disorder and bad behaviour in the theatre, *spectandi ac solutissimus mos*, and his subsequent imposition of the *lex Julia theatralis* was just part of a bigger package of reforms that he extended to cover the seating at *munera* as well as *ludi*.
The rules he laid down remained in force, unchanged, for a significant period extending into the reigns of emperors who succeeded him.

It was Augustus who imposed a certain amount of order on the seating arrangements within the amphitheatre; in that area, as well as so many others, he introduced lasting improvements to the existing system. Suetonius describes why and how Augustus did this:

> He issued special regulations to prevent the disorderly and haphazard system by which spectators secured seats for these shows; having been outraged by the insult to a senator who, on entering the crowded theatre at Puteoli, was not offered a seat by a single member of the audience. The consequent senatorial decree provided that, at every performance, wherever held, the front row of seats must be reserved for senators. At Rome, Augustus would not admit the envoys of independent or allied kingdoms to seats in the orchestra, on learning that some were mere freedmen. Other rules of his included the separation of soldiers from civilians; the assignment of special seats to married commoners, to boys not yet come of age, and, close by, to their tutors; and a ban on wearing dark cloaks, except in the back rows. Also, whereas men and women had hitherto always sat together, Augustus confined women to the back rows even at gladiatorial shows: the only ones being exempt

> from this rule being the Vestal Virgins, for whom separate accommodation was provided, facing the praetor's tribunal. No women at all were allowed to witness the athletic contests; indeed, when the audience clamoured at the games for a special boxing match to celebrate his appointment as chief priest, Augustus postponed this until early the next morning, and issued a proclamation to the effect that it was the chief priest's desire that women should not attend the theatre before ten o'clock. (Suetonius, *de vita Caesarum*, *Augustus* 44, 3-4)

This reform of seating arrangements, known as the *lex Julia theatralis*, took place at a time when the only amphitheatre in Rome was that of Statilius Taurus, built in 29 BC.

It was just one small part of his programme of social reform, which he saw as a way of returning to the traditional values of the Roman people. By restricting access to certain groups of people, Augustus was attempting to make the spectators conform to his idea of the ordered Roman state in microcosm; the hierarchical structure accentuated and status emphasised by selective placement within the amphitheatre. His rules were intended for all games, the gladiatorial shows, the *munera*, as well as the religious and festival games, the *ludi*.

What this amounted to was that women, as well as non-citizens and slaves, were indeed confined to the 'gods', the back rows at the very top, except of course for the Vestal Virgins, priestesses of the state religion, who had a reserved area of seating, truly ringside seats, the *tribunal editoris*, opposite the imperial box, the *pulvinar*. In effect, therefore, no respectable Roman matron was going to be inclined to frequent the games, if it meant relegation to a seat with a terrible view of the action in the arena and a sea of *plebs* down below. This would have had the effect of ensuring a practically all male audience; probably the very thing Augustus had in mind. In the provinces, however, it is unlikely that women's seating was so restricted.

Before Augustus, things had been a bit more free and easy at the theatre; the dictator Sulla had supposedly met his future wife at a gladiator show, as Plutarch tells us:

> A few months later there was a show of gladiators and since at this time men and women used to sit all together in the theatre, with no separate seating accommodation for the sexes, there happened to be sitting near Sulla a very beautiful woman of a most distinguished family. Her name was Valeria.... (Plutarch, *Sulla* 35-)

After a lot of flirting, Sulla proposed marriage to Valeria, but Augustus made sure that games of that kind would not be going on in his theatres. Obviously, the traditional values practised by Sulla would not have met with Augustus' approval.

As for the unusual ban on the wearing of dark cloaks, except at the back, the term *pullati* as used here may mean those in mourning, and therefore wearing dark cloaks, it may mean the 'great unwashed', the rabble, as the word also has the meaning of 'clad in rustic or dirty clothes', or it may mean foreigners as in those not wearing togas, but dark un-Roman coloured cloaks instead. All three possibilities would have the virtue of emphasising the sense of order and status which Augustus so desired, so that when he surveyed the audience in their allotted seats, he could literally be sure that they knew their place in Roman society. Part and parcel of the spectacle was the need for the audience to be in place, to see and be seen. Without the spectators to witness their agonies and life and death dramas, the gladiators were meaningless.

Contrary to the popularly held belief that the Colosseum was filled with the screaming mob, it is more realistic to assume that seats in this amphitheatre, as in most others, were allocated according to status, and in line with the client system of patronage which ran through every relationship in Rome, people of high status were given a certain number of tickets, which they would then distribute amongst family and friends. The importance of the person was reflected in the number of tickets allocated to them. They would then give them to friends, relatives and clients, who would in turn hand them out. In this way, status and influence were maintained and emphasised.

Humbler Romans without family or business connections may have got in to the *munera* only by paying through the nose for the privilege. Some magistrates rented seats out, but this system was in use mainly in the republic. The principle was that blocks of seat passes would be handed out to influential members of the community, who would then pass them to others, and so on. Some tickets undoubtedly filtered down to the lower orders, but not in significant numbers.

The actual tickets, if they can be called that, were *tesserae* giving the location of the seating area and precise directions on how to get there, by specifying the number of the arcade entrance offering the most direct route to it; the Flavian amphitheatre was such a complex structure that a high level of crowd control was needed to avoid potentially dangerous and chaotic crushes on the stairways, the circular galleries (*ambulacra*), arched entry passages (*vomitoria*) and gangways (*praecinctiones*). In fact, the design of the amphitheatre was itself a masterpiece of pedestrian traffic circulation, keeping people moving and allowing easy access to every part of the structure. Seventy-six numbered public entrances (I to LXVII) ensured a steady rate of access. The four main entrances, which were not numbered, consisted of two on the short sides and two on the long sides of the ellipse, and were for the performers, the emperor and magistrates. This great amphitheatre was constructed in such a way as to segregate the classes using it, not only in the allotted seating areas, but also in the routes to those seats. A patrician senator had direct access to his seat on the *podium*, the zone at the very edge of the arena with ivory seating (*subsellia*), without ever having to come into contact with the great unwashed. On the basis that the best seats are always given to the most important people, it comes as no surprise to find that the *podium* was where the senators, priests, ambassadors and distinguished foreign guests had their seats. In the 14 rows behind them sat the equestrian ranks, in the area of the amphitheatre known as the *ima cavea*. There was even a special area set aside for socially unacceptable equestrians who were bankrupt, so they could not taint their more respectable peers. Thus, at a glance it was possible to assess a person's social progress or otherwise, just from their position in the amphitheatre. Once discharged from bankruptcy, they were allowed to resume their previous social status and the seat that went with it. Behind the equestrians in the *ima cavea* was the *media cavea*, where the *cives Romani* sat. Sub-divisions in this zone separated married men, boys under seventeen who were seated with their tutors (*paedagogi*), and soldiers; sons over seventeen who could therefore wear the *toga virilis* may have sat with their fathers, just as girls and young women would have accompanied their mothers in the colonnaded purdah of the topmost level, hidden from the gaze of anyone looking up from the cheap seats below.

5

THE VIRTUE OF WORTHLESS BLOOD: TO PLEASE THE CROWD

You are making your way towards the Colosseum, along the *Via Sacra*. You aren't alone, because anyone who's got a *tessera* to get in, or who thinks they can afford one from a ticket tout, is headed in the same direction. A sea of bobbing heads moves excitedly in front of you. Of course, it isn't called the Colosseum yet; it's Vespasian's monument, the amphitheatre of the Flavian dynasty.

As you approach, you can't see the massive structure properly yet, because the basilicas and temples lining the route obscure its shape. All you get are tantalising glimpses of the enormous mass of stone rearing up into the sky. Then the narrow streets of the Forum suddenly open out onto the broad expanse of pavements around the amphitheatre, and you can just about make out the figures of men, like tiny ants at the very top of the stone walls, running round, tying up ropes, getting the awning just right for the afternoon's performance. After all, there's a rumour that Domitian himself is going to be there today.

The slope of the *Via Sacra* leads you down, pace quickening in excitement, towards the great amphitheatre. Now a wave of sound, colour and smells hits you as you come into the open, and take in the scene – thousands of people milling about, ticket touts, sausage sellers, flute players, souvenir hawkers, children playing with little wooden swords, a detachment of soldiers, probably Praetorian guard, splitting the crowd as they move up the *Via Sacra*, as the sounds and smells of the great stone plain are magnified and mixed in a wave of sensation that is almost palpable. The smell of the sausages from the small covered stall where they are being cooked reminds you that you haven't managed to eat since leaving your riverside apartment on the Aventine. There was an advertised banquet on offer, an *epulum*, earlier in the day, as is usual at these anniversary occasions, thoughtfully provided by the emperor, but so many people were jostling for a share in the meats and loaves on the trestle tables in the Forum that you gave up. You have your *tessera*, assuring you of a fairly decent position, in the middle tier of seating, on the long axis, admittedly, but quite near an entrance, if the directions on the tessera are to be believed. The ticket, the *tessera* of baked clay inscribed with the seat and entrance details, is a present from your well-connected landlord for prompt payment of rent. As you slow down in the crush at one of the 80 arched entrances, the cool darkness of the amphitheatre's outer colonnades feels fresh, and has the smell of damp stone. Ignoring the touts, the *locarii*, because you have your seat guaranteed, you are waved through by amphitheatre staff.

You have timed your arrival at the amphitheatre for the afternoon show, the *munera*. Plenty of adverts about this show, *edicta muneris*, have been painted everywhere; all the walls in the shabbier districts of the city seem to have at least one, in very nice writing, too. According to the notices, this show is in honour of the tenth anniversary of the death of our beloved emperor Domitian's dear departed elder brother, and it is he who is therefore the provider, the *editor*, of these games, as the notice makes plain. There will be 100 pairs of gladiators, *paria gladiatorum*; 10 pairs for every sad year since the glorious Titus departed for Elysium so unexpectedly. And it says there will be awnings, *velaria*; but of course, there are always awnings at this great amphitheatre. It is unthinkable to do without them, even at this time of year, when the Ides of March have been and gone but the festival of *Parilia* in late April has yet to come. Luckily, there is a slight breeze; the stone holds the heat of the day, and any respite is welcome. Apparently, there will be *sparsiones*, which is just as well – the smell of rosewater sprayed around the arena might just stop the rank odour coming from the pits underneath the great wooden floor; no matter what the *arenarii* do, they never can quite get rid of the smell of old blood and droppings.

From the sounds now coming to you as you walk around the interior looking for your stairway, the lunchtime interludes are still in progress. You hear the click clack of wooden swords, and shrieks of laughter as the people already in their seats relax as they enjoy the absurd sight of a single *paegniarius*, the buffoon in tight-fitting costume with his wooden sword and whip, trying to fight off a cohort of dwarfs in specially made armour with huge plumed helmets.

Trying to find your seat, amidst row after row of *togati*, men of Roman citizenship like yourself, at the same time as you watch the last moments of this ridiculous spectacle, you manage to avoid treading on toes and tripping on your own toga. With relief, you get out your little cushion as you locate the actual space on the marble seat that, for the next couple of hours or so anyway, belongs to you. You realise you've timed it just right. Just as you settle, *tubae* blare out brassily to signal the entrance of the emperor. Behind and above you, the serried ranks of the *pullati*, the non-toga-wearing urban poor, slaves and strangers cheer and wave and generally make a din out of all proportion to their numbers. You never fail to marvel that though they represent well under a quarter of the total spectators, they make so much more noise.

But to the business of the day – you try to get a look at the *libellus munerarius*, listing the pairs of gladiators in order of appearance, over the shoulder of the old man in front, as he uses it as a makeshift fan. The *compositio* will have been decided days in advance, depending on who's on form, who's injured and withdrawn, who's going to make a good show of it. The editor would normally decide that sort of thing in consultation with the *lanista* and the *doctores*, the specialist weapons trainers, but as the *editor* is Domitian, it's a safe bet he's left it to his *procurator* for the imperial *ludus*.

Talking of safe bets, there's been plenty of betting on the favourites here today, with odds being laid in corners and shadows at quite a few of the 80 entrances. You see your favourite gladiator, Crescens the *retiarius*, is paired with a *secutor* you've never heard of (*37* and *38*). What's more, their contest is in the first 10, so if it gets too hot you can creep out, and pray to Fortuna that Domitian doesn't notice and make you join the gladiators on the sand.

Both are first grade fighters, *primi pali* of their *ludus*; the *procurator* is a clever man, kicking off proceedings with a tried and tested formula. You squint as you adjust your eyes to the harsh glare of the sun like an angry eye in the dead centre of the arena. The whiteness of the specially imported mica-sprinkled sand reflects the light, but at least under the awnings, flapping slightly like the sails of a ship about to sail away, everything is cooler and bearable.

By now, the emperor and his entourage are comfortably settled on couches in their luxury imperial box, the *pulvinar*, not that you can see them very well, from the far end of the arena. And so the games begin. In the old traditional way, the *munera* start with a solemn procession, the *pompa*. The emperor's *lictores*, the officers of the holder of the games, lead out through the *Porta Sanavivaria*, the Gate of Life, as the massive studded wooden doors swing open. Dressed in togas, the *lictores* bear on their left shoulders the signs of their authority, the *fasces*, the bundle of rods surrounding an axe, symbolising the power they wield (*4*). Four trumpeters, *tubicenes*, follow them out, and four men bearing a platform, the *ferculum*, with painted figures of the deities being honoured here today. It looks like Nemesis Fortuna and Hercules again. Then another 10 groups of bearers emerge, staggering under the weight of some fabulous looking armour and weapons, glinting on the purple cloths, all for the gladiators. Then, as they slowly make their way round the vastness of the ellipse, more richly costumed figures emerge from the Gate. They are carrying an assortment of palm branches for the victors and glinting silver trays of cash prizes in little leather purses, again for the favoured winners. Of course, if this was a little country arena, the *editor* would be out of his seat in a flash and round the arena to take the applause and gratitude of the locals – but this is Rome and Domitian has no need of recognition.

More wind instruments, this time the curved *lituus* and then following up the rear, five pairs of mounted *equites*, the gladiators on horseback (*colour plate 10*). And then, just as it looks like the procession is going to meet itself, like a serpent swallowing its tail, out come the other 90 gladiators in all their finery. The mounted gladiators look glamorous, but the cheer that greets the fighters on foot practically shakes the *podium*. They are wearing the purple and gold cloaks that

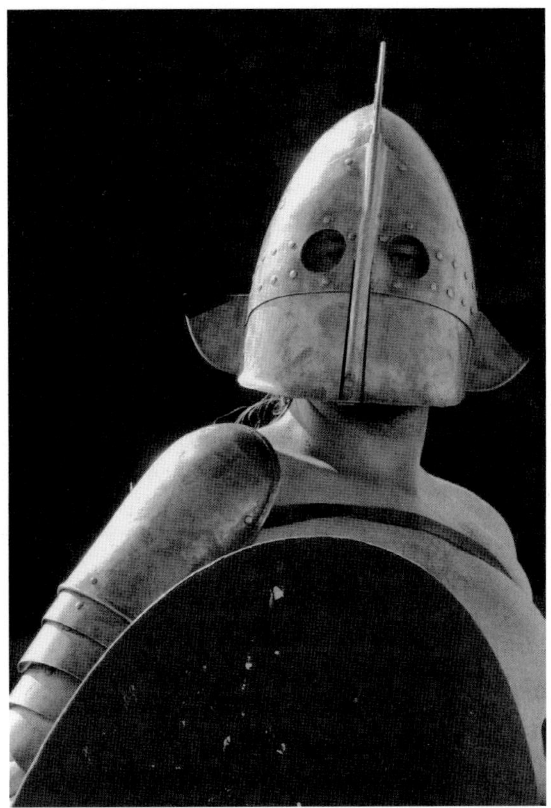

37 Secutor category of gladiator. *Reconstruction: Britannia. Photograph: I. Burridge*

38 Retiarius stands ready with net. *Reconstruction: Britannia. Photograph: Simon Barnes*

Domitian likes to kit them out in, and they strut a lap of the arena as the rest of the *pompa* peels off, back into the gloom. Last night, you could have gone to have a look at them eating in the *cena libera*, the public banquet for gladiators. People gawp at the combatants, to see whether the prospect of imminent death affects their appetites or not. Some fighters eat like there's no tomorrow, which may very well be true for at least half the diners. Some have obviously gone off their food. All are conscious that the men they eat with may be their executioners before the next sunset. It is a strange custom.

Now the only people left out in the open are the arena staff, the *arenarii*, anxiously checking that everything is in order. Meanwhile, the *probatio armorum* is being performed in the very middle of the sand, so everyone can see the weapons are sharp; there's no question of any rigging of matches today, particularly with Domitian watching.

While this is going on, the gladiators have started to warm up with mock weapons, to the accompaniment of a water-organ, the *hydraulis* and the four *tubicenes*, playing very loudly and keeping good time, for a change. The combination of the shrill brass and the piping of the water-organ carries all around the arena, giving the scene below an unreal dimension. There is a cluster of imperial-liveried *tibia* players by the Gate of Life, ready to announce the individual combats with their shrieking double reed-pipes. The acoustics in this amphitheatre have always been superb; every gasp, grunt and clash of metal is as clear as if it was happening at the smallest of provincial arenas.

Without the benefit of the *libellus munerarius*, you can't make out all of the gladiators, but you do notice that it looks like standard pairs, in the traditional manner; *provocatores* against *provocatores*, *thraeces* versus *murmillones*, and right in the centre of the arena, standing in the hot eye of the unshaded sun, is your favourite gladiator, Crescens, casually flicking his net and loosening his limbs. Unlike all the other *retiarii* you have ever seen, Crescens has never caught his own net in the prongs of his trident. He is a pleasure to watch, a craftsman of his profession, with many wins under his jewel-encrusted belt.

The *tubae* blare out stridently, signalling that the gladiators should go back in to get their armour fitted and to be given the sharp weapons they are not otherwise trusted with. As they file off, the *summa rudis*, the arena official who will keep order in this arena and regulate the contests so that the emperor's will is done, comes out to check the sand one last time. With him walks the *secunda rudis*, his second in command. They both wear the distinctive voluminous white tunics with the *clavus*, the red stripes, indicating their office. They are in charge of proceedings, and have a team of *libitinarii*, arena slaves in bright tunics, whose job it is to clear the sand and cart off the dead bodies between bouts (*39*). On either side of the Gate of Death, the *Porta Libitinensis*, lurk the men whose job it is to play the demon Charun and the god Mercury. Both wear masks and Charun has a heavy bronze mallet. At the moment, they have nothing to do, but that will change; as the deaths mount up, they will have solemn duties to perform. *Tubae* sound again: the arena is cleared.

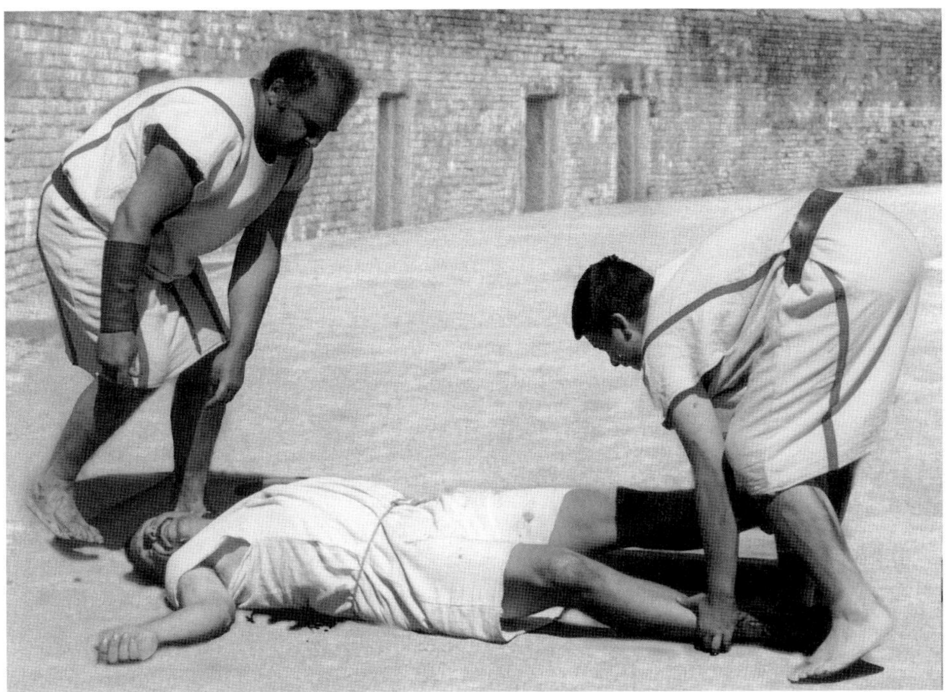

39 Libitinarii clearing a body from the arena. *Reconstruction: Britannia. Photograph: Simon Barnes*

The 50,000-strong crowd packed in to the amphitheatre today quietens and settles down in anticipation, even the scruffy street merchants and lowlifes, the *pullati* in their distinctly drab undyed woollen tunics and cloaks up in the standing room only section at the very back. You thank Fortuna that you were not born so low as to have to take an unreserved place, rubbing shoulders with the *plebs*.

Above them, even further back, behind the topmost colonnade, you get a glimpse of rainbow silks and peacock feathers, signalling the presence of some high-class ladies watching today, from their secluded vantage point, the *summum maenianum in ligneis*, 75ft above ground level. There, the full effect of the awnings combined with the shelter of the colonnades topping the theatre will be protecting their well-bred palest of skins. No suntanned working women will ever get into this exclusive hideaway. From that pinnacle at the very top of the amphitheatre, the respectable wives and daughters of Rome's senators, equestrians and other worthies, won't be able to see or hear very much which, for ladies of good breeding, is probably just as well. The smell, however, is a different matter; after the bloody mayhem of the morning beast show and the midday executions, in which at least 100 criminals met imaginative ends involving big cats and a creative retelling of several of Hercules' labours, the arena reeks of blood, with its peculiar metallic taint pervading the hot afternoon air. To counteract the nausea-inducing odour of scattered blood and flesh on sand, not only has the arena been cleared of the detritus of fatal human and animal conflicts, but also *sparsiones* have been liberally provided, rosewater periodically sprayed by armies of slaves throughout the amphitheatre. It masks, but does not eradicate, the odour of death.

The Gate of Life opens and just two gladiators enter the arena, now made ready for their bout. Both are equipped after the manner of their speciality; one of them is only protected by the gilded bronze *galerus*, *manica* and single greave of the *retiarius*. With a start, you realise that it is Crescens, facing the standard opponent of the net and trident man, the *secutor*, in his menacing fully enclosed helmet.

Tibia wail in unison to signal the start of the bout, and the unnamed *secutor* rushes forward. Crescens appears not to offer any defence, but just as it seems the *secutor* is about to stab him with his *gladius*, the graceful *retiarius* side-steps like a Cretan bullfighter and lightly jabs his opponent on the back of his head, the trident glancing off the *secutor's* smooth, egg-shaped helmet, though with sufficient force to send him sprawling into the dust. A great roar goes up in appreciation of the move, and even the emperor leans forward in interest.

The *secutor* jumps to his feet and is instantly stopped by the *summa rudis*, who has noticed his leg-guard is trailing a strap. He summons a *libitinarius* to come and secure the *ocrea*; the delay is not well received, bringing whistles and shouts from the crowd higher up, but Crescens, ever the showman, fills the moment with a perfectly executed theft of a *tuba* from one of the musicians, dancing round his increasingly angry opponent and blowing comical notes and sending the crowd wild. They adore Crescens; his reputation is detailed on many walls in the city.

The *secunda rudis* mildly remonstrates with Crescens, who swaps the *tuba* for his trident, the lead-weighted net still trailing from his wrist by its loop. The fight is back on. The *secutor* plunges forward in a mad charge, and Crescens, observing the custom that only *retiarii* are allowed to take advantage of, turns and runs. Normally a cowardly act, and scorned by the crowd, it is acceptable when performed with panache by a skilled *retiarius* such as Crescens. A variation on this is when the *retiarius* stands on a bridge-like wooden structure, known as the *pons*, and is forced to defend himself against *secutores* at either end of the bridge. Height is not necessarily enough of an advantage in that situation.

Meanwhile, Crescens retreats to a safe distance and waits for the *secutor* to exhaust himself in pursuit. As the gap is closed, Crescens casts his *rete* low, and it wraps itself round the *secutor's* legs, tripping him so that he goes down like a felled ox at the festival of Jupiter *Latiaris*. The net-man, now netless, seizes the advantage and closes on his enemy, because now the fight has turned from playful to deadly. He stands over his fallen opponent with *fuscina* and *pugio* at the ready. Hogtied by the net, and unable to free himself, the fallen *secutor* casts his shield down and raises his right index finger, *ad digitum*, the customary appeal for mercy to the *editor* (*colour plate 31*).

The crowd have mixed loyalties and they voice them very loudly. The cries of '*mitte!*' (let him go!) accompanied by waving hands and napkins, corners of togas, anything that will flap and catch the attention of the *editor*; all are deployed by the *secutor's* supporters, but they are drowned out by a huge chorus of '*iugula!*' (kill him!) and a forest of thrusting thumbs , imitating thousands of killing blows. You are among this seething mob, and as one, you will the emperor to do away with this shameful amateur of a *secutor*, obviously no real match for the all-conquering Crescens. But then, who could be, but Hercules himself?

It's getting hot down there and Crescens is obviously keen to make lion food of the *secutor*, and go back in for a well deserved rest, and in his eagerness to finish it, he steps in to deliver the death blow. Immediately, the *summa rudis* blocks his way with his staff of office, and the *secunda rudis* restrains his right arm, the *pugio* blade ready to strike. Life is the gift of the *editor*, in this case the emperor, alone. It is not uncommon for gladiators to rush in and finish their opponent in hot blood before receiving the order to do so, but it is not advisable – the crowds can turn against an unsporting victor, with fatal consequences. Crescens sensibly suspends his attack and keeps his eye on the emperor, waiting politely for the signal to kill or let him go.

Usually, these gladiators, coming as they do from one *familia*, one *ludus*, will have trained together, drank together, shared meals and friendship, so it is just as well that, at the moment of truth, the *secutor* keeps his helmet on so that his opponent will not have to meet his gaze. The anonymity of the visored helmet helps to keep the distance that these combatants need in order to be able to fight each other fiercely, without emotion. Neither of them can afford the weakness of pity. All eyes are on Domitian, and so far he has been very sedate, unusually for him. A silence of massive proportions falls on the spectators, as they wait for the emperor's verdict. Not even a cough disturbs the anticipation. With no ceremony and thinly veiled contempt, Domitian turns his thumb outwards, *pollice verso*, as the satirist Juvenal put it, and thrusts the air. You join in the approving roar of the mob. The fate of the *secutor* is sealed. Without removing his helmet, accepting his death as he has been trained to do, he bravely offers his neck to the blade. From a kneeling position he receives the efficiently dealt deathblow to his jugular and slumps sideways onto the sand. A cheerily triumphant shout of '*Habet!*' from thousands of throats fills the hot afternoon air, as it does whenever the crowd appreciates a telling blow, fatal or not. A grimly jubilant Crescens runs round the arena, bloody *pugio* held high, acknowledging the acclaim of his adoring fans. He hasn't worked very hard today; despite that, you fervently hope Domitian won't take it into his head to make him fight fresh opponents, *suppositicii*, until he loses and is killed. He's in luck; Domitian is preoccupied with the distribution of his little gifts to the mob, the *sportulae*, surprise packages that he's arranged for the *arenarii* to lob into the higher seats. Anything from a gold coin, an *aureus,* to a side of ostrich meat, from sets of jewellry to a season ticket for the games is literally up for grabs. Outstretched hands scrabble to catch the parcels as they fly through the air.

All that remains is the task of clearing away the body, which the *libitinarii*, the funeral men, perform with quiet efficiency. The corpse is lifted onto a *sandapila*, a kind of stretcher with legs, then un-helmeted, covered, and carried out. Being dragged out with hooks is reserved for heinous criminals, the *noxii*, and carcasses of beasts, of course.

If only the *secutor* had won his life by fighting more bravely, if only the few of his supporters crying '*mitte!*' and waving frantically to catch Caesar's eye had successfully appealed to the emperor, then he might have left the arena on foot, honourably discharged, *missio*. As the *libitinarii* struggle out with their dead weight, you reflect on some really exciting fights, which have gone on for so long that the two gladiators so equal in skill have literally fought themselves to a standstill. Such combatants deserve to leave the arena on their feet, and usually the *editor* rewards their courage and determination by letting both go, in the *stans missum* result that can be very popular with the spectators.

Even if the *secutor* had been wounded, but had pleased the crowd and the emperor, he might have been stretchered off and hospitalised. Doctors who treat gladiators are at the top of their profession, so the best medical help in the empire is available for those who leave the arena alive, however weakly they cling to life (*40* and *41*). The price of a top-class gladiator is reason enough to try to save his life. No *lanista* in his right mind would let one of his stars die for want of good medical attention.

But the *secutor* failed to get the crowd on his side, a fatal lapse, and goes to his grave a nonentity. Nevertheless, the manner of his dying has provided over 50,000 Romans with an example of a good death, *exemplum virtutis*.

On his last journey out through the Gate of Death, the *Porta Libitinensis*, the bearers pause as customary checks are made to ensure he really is dead and not feigning. Nobody likes to be cheated. If there were any sign that he was pretending death or serious injury to get out of the arena, then it would be a test with the hot iron, the *cauterium*, guaranteed to reveal shirkers. In this case, the demon figure of Charun, with his mask of strange blue skin and ringletted black wig, ceremoniously approaches the stretcher and symbolically strikes a single blow to his head, to claim his soul for Hades (*16*). The arena official acting the part of Mercury Psychopompus, as conductor of souls, stands by. The corpse is stretchered off to the mortuary, the *spoliarium*, a few yards away within the amphitheatre's rooms. There his armour will be stripped, his throat cut just to make sure of death and his body taken to the communal pit outside the city limits, unless some family member or friend claims his body for a decently arranged funeral. Tombstones for gladiators are not unknown; sometimes friends from within the *familia* club together to pay for the funeral.

Crescens has been presented with his victory palm, the *palma*, and his cash prize, the *praemium*, brought in on a silver tray, the amount calculated according to Crescens' ranking within his *familia gladiatoria*. He lives to fight another day. He has fought well, but has won too easily perhaps, and in any case, Domitian prefers Thracians to all other types of gladiator, to the point of obsession, so he is not inclined to award the ultimate accolade, the laurel wreath crown, the *corona*, to a mere *retiarius*.

As Crescens completes his triumphant lap of honour, waving the palm and clutching his bag of money, he runs out of the arena to screams and cheers, his weapons already taken from him by the *arenarii*, who are busy raking the sand

40 Roman surgeon extracts a weapon tip from a combatant's thigh. *Photograph: Matt Bunker, courtesy of ERA*

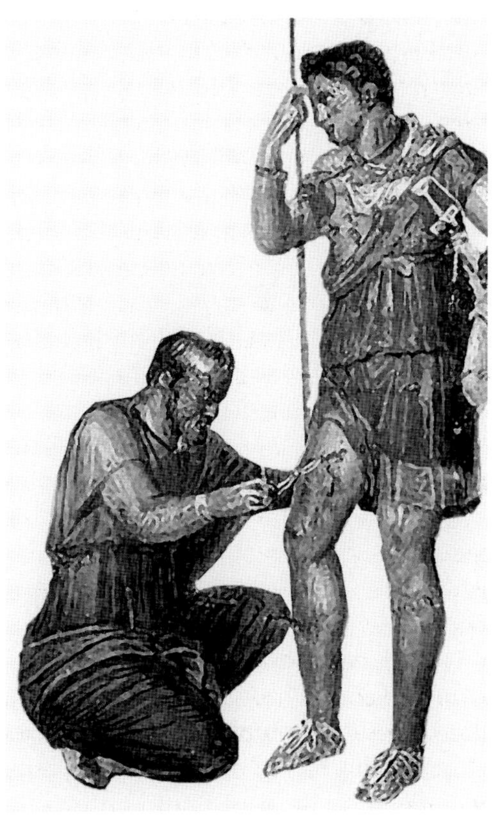

41 Watercolour illustration of the wounded hero Aeneas, based on a fresco in Pompeii

and sprinkling buckets of it over the red stain left by the *secutor*. That bout must have taken 10 minutes from start to finish, five of which was actually fighting, but nobody minds when the standard is high; it's better than some poor *familia* from out in the sticks, with their winded troupe of staggering hack fighters and no decent moves. It's all about finesse, and unpredictability. Who wants to watch evenly matched, careful plodders with an eye on their pensions?

Two hours after midday, and now it's swelteringly hot. Looking up, and squinting into the orb of white-blue sky encircled by canvas, you can see the awnings aren't doing any good at all for those lower down in the amphitheatre. Ironically, the good seats with the best views, the ones with names inscribed on them, down the front and centre of each long side of the ellipse, are the ones least covered by the shade provided by the awnings. The truly wealthy have their own solution; enough seats for their attendants with parasols and fans, to compensate for the shortcomings of the *velaria*, but you haven't even got a straw hat.

The emperor's got the luxury of his *pulvinar*, the imperial box with all its opulent hangings and cushions, slaves with ostrich feather fans, snacks and cooling drinks, and so his comfort is never compromised. The divine Augustus used to enforce the social distinctions by the seating arrangements, but after his death, they became lax and were not so rigidly applied – until now. Domitian has made a point of bringing back the recognition of status in the allocation of seats. The *pulvinar*, situated on the north side of arena, is reserved for him as *editor* and his immediate retinue, the male members of his family and honoured guests.

The box on the south side of the arena, facing the *pulvinar*, is called the *tribunal editoris*, and that's for the empress, her female entourage, the Vestal Virgins and the magistrates officially giving the games. Years ago, in the old amphitheatre, the emperor Gaius (Caligula) used to have the awnings removed at the hottest time of day, and forbade anyone to leave; at least Domitian hasn't thought of that yet. The air is now shimmering with heat, even though it's early in the year. No wonder most games are scheduled for the winter and spring months. Summer in the amphitheatre would be unbearable. Even the marble seats have lost their usual chill. You pick up your cushion and leave. Down the outside staircase, in the cool shadows and then out into the unbearable sunlight. A souvenir hawker tempts you with a tiny terracotta statuette of Crescens, complete with name. You are too tired too haggle and the statuette is yours for one *as*, the price of a loaf and other small physical comforts.

Inside the great amphitheatre a sudden roar goes up – '*Habet! Hoc habet!*' – and you know that somewhere on the hot sand, another gladiator has 'got it' and has just received a killing blow from a sword, *ferrum accipere*, to give the correct term. It's going to be an expensive afternoon for Domitian, with two fighters dead already. As you walk back along the *Via Sacra*, the sounds of the crowd and the combat, the pipes and trumpets merge, and then you realise – this is the voice of the Great Amphitheatre, the voice of Rome itself.

6

NOVELTY AND VARIETY: GLADIATORIAL CATEGORIES

The word 'gladiator' itself derives from the Latin word *gladius,* meaning sword, although not all gladiators fought with that weapon (*42*). However, it is a strong indication that the first gladiators used swords, and that the word became associated with them. One of the best descriptions of an early type of *gladius* comes from Polybius, the historian. Initially a Greek hostage, he became a close friend of Scipio Aemilianus Africanus, the Roman general who destroyed Carthage. As an historian and in a sense, war correspondent, Polybius was well placed to record the workings of the Roman army. Here is his observation of the *gladius*:

> A sword, which is carried on the left thigh and called a Spanish sword. It has a blade which is sharp on both edges, and thus suitable for upward and downward thrusts, and which is strong and stable. (Polybius, *Historiae* 6.22)

Here he is referring to the *gladius hispaniensis*, the forerunner of the military weapon *par excellence*. The first references to gladiators using the actual word *gladiator* rather than a synonym, like *bustuarius,* comes from Cato (234-149 BC).

42 *Gladius* with parallel double-edged blade, (Pompeii type). Flattened diamond in section with a raised point on the blade tip and long tang (passing through a modern Perspex hilt interpretation). The overall length is 25in (63.6cm). The *gladius* is the primary weapon of most categories of gladiator, although this excellent surviving example is almost certainly military in origin, from the first century AD. *Taken from the Guttman Collection, with kind permission of Christies Images Ltd*

Also, Lucilius in the second century BC refers to gladiators in the context of a particular bout, whilst in the same century the playwright Terence, in his *Phormio,* uses the phrase *gladiatorio animo,* with the spirit of the gladiator, as a metaphor for someone who lives with neither hope nor fear, in the fierce desperate strength that the abandonment of both those emotions can bring.

To put the single combats of the gladiators into some sort of context, it should be borne in mind that the Roman method of waging war had evolved at a very early point in its history from the rigid phalanx of the Greeks, into a sophisticated organisation of men in which each individual soldier confronted the enemy face to face in a single combat, even though he was within a well-disciplined formation. This was very much in keeping with the Roman concept of *virtus*, where a man was defined by his prowess at arms. In the case of the Roman soldier, his customary weapon came to be the *gladius*, rather than the spears favoured by other Mediterranean peoples. This inevitably defined the fighting style of the Romans, therefore, and it is not surprising that the single combats of the gladiators should resonate with the Roman spectators; after all, the fights were an echo, however debased, of the heroic hand to hand conflicts which punctuated Rome's past and which every Roman schoolboy knew off by heart. In a sense, the gladiators re-enacted that tradition, reminding the people of the martial qualities on which Rome was built.

We tend to base our concept of the stereotypical gladiator on the images culled from the imperial period of Rome's history, yet gladiators were in existence for at least 300 years before that. However, all of our ideas about what a gladiator should look like derive from the written descriptions and visual representations of the first 300 years or so of the Roman Empire, supported by archaeological finds.

To appreciate fully the significance of the gladiator we must not fall into the trap of thinking that they sprang into existence fully-formed in the imperial era. That is why it is so important to evaluate the proto-gladiators of the republic, as their appearance, equipment and style of combat was the foundation for the gladiator at the height of his popularity.

In parallel with the political convulsions that helped to transform them from a funeral sideshow to a manipulative crowd-pleasing spectacular, the gladiators' popularity increased accordingly, and by the time Augustus took power solely to himself, it was already obvious to him that their usefulness could be enhanced by the restructuring, classification and regulation of the entire gladiatorial system.

His decision to harness the popularity of the *munera* and to restrict its use, so that the prestige it created would not assist any rivals to challenge his authority, is a an indication of how central the *ludi* and the *munera* were to anyone in public life with political ambition. As early as 22 BC he set a limit for the *praetores* of two shows for their period of office, and a maximum of 120 gladiators, while he himself gave eight shows with a total of 10,000 gladiators. He created a virtual state monopoly in gladiatorial contests, as in so many other public and private institutions that he brought under his control. As always, the emperor could pass laws that he himself had no intention of keeping.

It was Augustus who instituted the imperial gladiatorial schools, confusingly called *ludi,* set up legislation to regulate the *munera*, and an effective empire-wide system of procurators, *procuratores familiae gladiatoriae*, to administer them. These changes were vital to the transition from republican to imperial period gladiators, because they imposed a semblance of uniformity on the gladiatorial categories hitherto lacking and certainly not in evidence up till then. Finally, it was Augustus who oversaw the building of Rome's first permanent stone amphitheatre through his trusted commander, T. Statilius Taurus in 29 BC, another step towards turning gladiators from doomed amateurs into professional celebrity killers. As his biographer Suetonius says, he 'surpassed all his predecessors in the frequency, variety and magnificence of his public shows'.

The trap that we must resist falling into is the assumption that everything was standardised and regimented at the behest of Augustus, and that, once established, the gladiatorial categories were rigidly adhered to, and unchanging. How much we can infer from the visual images of gladiators scattered throughout the ancient media of mosaic, sculpture, tombstones, wallpaintings, graffiti, and pottery is open to debate. Even more difficult to judge is the weight we should give to the literary sources, as they tend to reflect the attitudes and bias of their times – they are rarely impartial to the degree we expect of reference works today.

The conclusions that can be drawn as a result of assessing all of the archaeological, literary and iconographic evidence do not represent anything but a core-sample of the gladiatorial world. Distinct types of gladiator are recognisable, but until the day comes when a twenty-volume papyri '*de gladiatoribus*' is discovered, we should be wary of imposing a bogus set of generalisations in our desire to bring order to the confusing and sometimes contradictory evidence, because the order we impose is based on entirely different value judgements.

Following on from Augustus' reorganising of the *munera* came images and descriptions of gladiators whose categories can sometimes be discerned with a degree of confidence. To put it any higher would be a misuse of the facts.

The figure of the gladiator that comes to mind today is almost an icon of imperial Rome, but his origins go back to those early fighters, slogging it out in market-places and by the side of funeral monuments and pyres in the Latin and Campanian countryside.

PROTO- GLADIATORS OF THE REPUBLIC

The fourth-century tomb paintings found at Paestum, in Lucania and in Campania, show duels or combats between warriors armed with spears, richly helmeted in the hellenized Italic style common to the peoples of the Italian peninsula (*18*). When helmets of this type are found, they are always of copper-alloy (bronze) construction, which ties in with their representations on the tomb paintings (*43*). The combatants rarely wear body armour, save for greaves on the legs, though they usually carry the large round shields akin to those of the Greek hoplites; some are clothed in tunics, others have bare torsos and wear loincloths and a few are naked. In this type of depiction, the fighters tend to look almost identical, and have more in common with the images of heroes in Homeric legend than with gladiators.

Yet those tomb paintings are regarded as the main evidence for early gladiatorial bouts, and whilst the appearance of the combatants is ambiguous, there is no doubt that the fights are not showing episodes of war; they are too ritualistic in composition and the opponents have no distinguishing martial insignia to indicate differing loyalties –indeed in most cases the fighters look as if they have been recruited from the same ethnic group, which adds weight to the gladiatorial theory, if they can be identified as prisoners of war, the original source of fighters.

It is therefore open to us to make the leap of faith that what we see on the walls of Lucanian and Campanian tombs is a form of gladiatorial contest, whether for the appeasement of the dead or as part of a liminal rite to assuage misfortune or avert military disaster. After the third century BC the evidence for gladiators is thin on the ground, and this gap causes problems in tracking

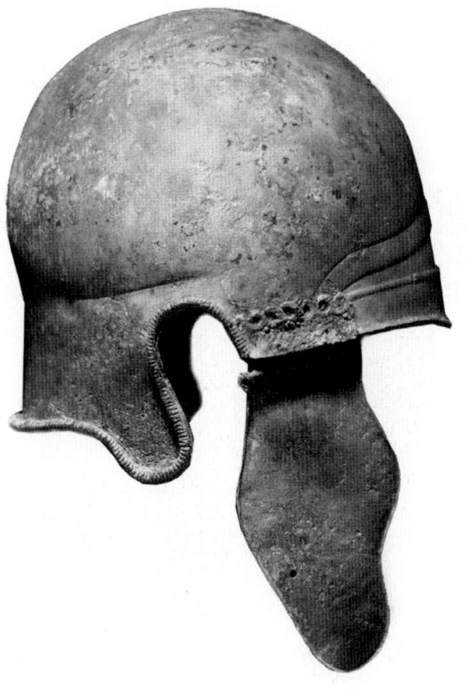

43 Samnite-type helmet dated to fourth century BC; traces of a riveted plume holder survive on this bronze helmet. *Taken from the Guttman Collection, with kind permission of Christies Images Ltd*

their evolution. It is only in the late republican era, with its massive political investment in the *munera,* and the subsequent gladiatorial scenes recorded on the funeral monuments of the rich, famous, and important, that a light starts to shine on the gladiatorial world (*44* and *45*).

44 *Above* Illustration of a section of a relief carving showing a first-century BC gladiatorial contest. *Upper section based on an original relief in the Glyptothek Museum, Munich*

45 *Right* Republican gladiators; one combatant, positioned unusually under a shield seems to be kneeling in defeat. *Illustration based on a relief carving in the Museo Civico Archeologico, Bologna*

Whether or not the tomb paintings depict gladiators, it is certain that the early gladiators were prisoners of war; their complete expendability made them ideal fighters in a fatal combat, and initially these captives would have used their own distinct weapons and armour to emphasise the point that they were humiliated and defeated foes. There are many literary references to gladiators categorising them as Samnites, Gauls and Thracians – all three ethnic groups were originally persistent and notorious enemies of Rome. In time, these categories came to identify the equipment and style of combat rather than ethnic origin; once the Romans absorbed these peoples into its territorial fabric, they were no longer perceived as outsiders or different, and it would have been considered archaic and inappropriate to think of them as alien to Rome. When that happened, within the imperial period which saw Augustus' reorganization of gladiatorial contests, these terms simply became labels for types of gladiator, whatever their country of birth. Even leftover equipment from bygone ages would slowly have corrupted and changed to accommodate the needs of the arena rather than the field of battle.

This re-ordering of the contests was not intended to dispense with what had gone before; it adapted and developed the elements already present, deliberately selecting from the confusing diversity in order to impose definitions of armatures and standardization of procedures. In this way the Samnite, and Rome's other enemy, the Gaul, may both, over time, have contributed to the *secutor* and its relative, the *murmillo*; it is even possible that the *hoplomachus* arose from this miscegenation. Opinion is divided, because we just do not have sufficient information about the cultural context driving the changes, nor can we now fully appreciate the subtle differences of type that may have been so obvious to the Roman spectators. It is easier to see the results of Augustan reform than to trace the traditions they inherited. In fact, the Thracian, or *thraex,* is the only category derived from tribal captives and traditional enemies to make its way into the era of imperial gladiators unchanged in name.

SAMNITES

The Samnites, or Osco-Samnites, were a tough hill-people organised into a loose confederacy of tribes who occupied the hinterland of the central Apennine mountains, overlooking neighbouring Campania. They were an offshoot of the Sabines, though rougher, more rustic and less sophisticated. They coveted the fertile lands of Campania, as did the Romans, and this inevitably brought the two into conflict many times in the fourth and third centuries BC when the Samnite wars were fought. In his account of a battle between Campanians and Samnites in 308 BC, Livy describes the Samnite warriors:

> The Samnites, besides their other warlike preparations, had made their battle line to glitter with new and splendid arms. There were two *corps*: the shields of the one were inlaid with

> gold and the shields of the other with silver. The shape of the shield was this: the upper part, where it protected the breast and shoulders, was rather broad with a level top; below it was somewhat tapering, to make it easier to handle. They wore a *spongia* to protect the breast and the left leg was covered with a greave. Their helmets were crested, to make their stature appear greater.

There are many surviving examples of Samnite weapons and armour but they are unfortunately at odds with the description given by Livy (*colour plate 11*). He was writing about two centuries after the event, and his account of specific details of armour and weapons is not to be trusted as definitively descriptive of actual Samnite warriors of 308 BC; the best that can be said for it is that Livy may well have inadvertently provided some information about the gladiators known as Samnites in his own time.

The odd reference to chest protection which Livy calls *spongia*, or sponge, to translate it literally, may indicate ring-mail, as this has a multi-perforated surface appearance, so the term may stem from the similar appearance of ring-mail to a sponge. Alternatively, it could be some kind of slang terminology for a circular metal breastplate, or simply an error of translation.

In other texts it would seem, to judge from context, that *spongia* is cognate with *pectorale*, and *cardiophylax*; this latter is the heart protector mentioned by Polybius a century earlier in his description of the Roman army from his *History of the World*. In all cases the protective plate, whatever it was made of, would be fastened by leather straps going over the shoulders and crossing at the back with some form of buckle. The conventional view is that any armour of ring-mail at that time would be an anachronism.

To help build up a picture of standard Samnite military equipment, as opposed to the later gladiatorial re-enactment of it, we should bear in mind that most finds of Samnite breastplates are of a solid copper-alloy (bronze) construction. There are several types, of which the following are most common: the classic 'muscle' cuirass giving total upper torso protection, back and front with either shaped and 'muscled' features; shorter versions of this cuirass, with less abdominal protection; trilobate (three disc) breastplates, usually back and front, connected by links and smaller plates (*46*); the alternatives would be small square plates, or circular discs, perhaps suspended by leather strapping, which just protected the area of the heart. This armour was not peculiar to the Samnites; it is found in the archaeological contexts of Campanian, Roman, Greek and Carthaginian military campaigns. In fact, as we have already seen, Polybius, writing in the second century BC, makes it clear in his description of the Roman soldiers that the small square breastplate was commonly worn even then:

> Most of the soldiers also wear a bronze breastplate, one span square, which is placed in front of the heart and therefore called a heart protector. This completes their equipment. (Polybius, *Historiae* 6.26)

46 Triple-disc bronze body armour, probably Samnite *c.*fourth century BC, comprising front-plate, back-plate and surviving shoulder-plates. Main body 11.2in high (28.2cm), shoulder-plates 8in long (20.4cm). *Taken from the Guttman Collection, with kind permission of Christies Images Ltd*

Interestingly enough, he goes on to mention the mail-shirt as being exclusively worn by soldiers with enough personal wealth to qualify, those with a property value of more than 10,000 drachmas. Again, we must remember that Polybius is talking about Romans of nearly two centuries later than those Samnites in the battle Livy was trying to describe.

It is tempting to think that different armies were equipped with distinct, easily identified armour and weapons, to facilitate differentiation on battlefields. A reminder that good defensive ideas were constantly being adopted, modified and improved comes from the writing of Varro; in his *de lingua latina*, he says that he believes that the Romans acquired their knowledge of mail-making from the Gauls, who invented it.

Depictions of the original Samnites, soldier or early gladiator, are thin on the ground. However, from the archaeological finds, it is possible to build up a picture of the standard (if such a thing could be said to exist) Samnite warrior (*47*). From that, we can track the transition to gladiator of that type. As we have seen, there were several types of body armour in use at the time the Samnites were in conflict with Rome. About 15 examples of the triple disc cuirass have been found and one of those is from Alfedena, in the central highlands of Samnium. The other is from nearby Lucania. So many artistic representations of this style of cuirass exist that it is fair to assume that it was a common one of the time. So our Samnite has his breastplate (*48*). The rest of his equipment consists of helmet, belt,

47 Interpretation of a Samnite warrior

48 Detail of a warrior featured on a Campanian red-figure Bell Krater. The warrior is shown wearing the distinct triple-disc body armour with wide belt, from the fourth to third century BC. *Taken from the Guttman Collection, with kind permission of Christies Images Ltd*

shield and weapons. Taking the belt next, it is clear from the enormous numbers of wide copper-alloy (bronze) belts found throughout central and southern Italy that they were an essential item for the warrior, whether Samnite, Campanian, Lucanian or other southern tribe. These impressive belts, varying between 2.5–5in wide, are thought to be typically Samnite (*49* and *colour plate 12*). They are so distinct and robust that they seem to convey a sense of strength of purpose, symbolic of manhood or prowess in battle. As with the gladiator belts, they may have provided protection whilst allowing flexibility of movement.

As the Samnite belts are often seen together with breastplate, helmet and greaves, forming the panoply – meaning a complete set of armour and weapons, from the Greek *pan* for 'all' and *hopla* for 'arms', it is reasonable to assume that the belt and breastplate complement each others function – giving a modicum of defence against injury whilst permitting normal range of movement. The Samnite belts have an appearance strongly reminiscent of the ubiquitous wide gladiator belts of the centuries-later imperial period as depicted in mosaics, glassware, stonecarvings, even figurines and lamps. It is worth mentioning, however, that no actual confirmed gladiator belts or belt fittings as depicted have ever been positively identified, because the main substance of these later belts would doubtless have been organically fragile leather, and also because of the difficulty in distinguishing between military and gladiatorial fittings when found.

49 Trilobate cuirass in relation to wide belt, both copper alloy, fourth to third century BC. *Taken from the Guttman Collection, with kind permission of Christies Images Ltd*

The early armies of the peoples of the Italian peninsula, particularly the Etruscans, Samnites, Romans and Campanians, were undoubtedly influenced by the Greek fashions in military equipment, particularly via the conduit of the Greek colonies of southern Italy. The earliest Samnite helmets owe a debt to the Greek ones they replicate; occasionally, it is impossible to distinguish between them (*43*).

Samnite warriors were certainly depicted in helmets more often than not. The earliest sort of helmets worn by Samnites, Campanians and indeed Romans were undoubtedly of Hellenistic import or at least influence (*colour plate 13*); Attic, Boeotian, Chalcidian, Illyrian, Corinthian and many other 'Greek' helmets, shields, body armour and weapons are readily associated with Etruscan, Latin, Campanian, and indeed Samnite peoples, in fact the helmets themselves were often worked from one sheet of copper alloy (bronze) into a bowl with fixed and later articulated/applied cheek guards.

Many of the more decorative examples of headgear, such as the Attic, Macedonian and Corinthian styles with wider brims, high crests and elaborate plume holders were later superseded by lighter, plainer and more functional head protection such as the later Montefortino helmet on the battlefield, which was in effect no more than a form of bowl with added cheekguards, and thus more economical to produce and repair *en masse*.

It is not hard to see in the surviving distinctive elements of the early period headgear a possible origin for the elaborate and stylised nature of the gladiatorial helmets of the Imperial period, particularly the great crests of horsehair and feathers, and the wide brims which became even more exaggerated (*50*); since it is known that many arena combats were often theatrical re-enactments from the earlier classical periods, such flamboyant elements would have been allowed to persist in the anachronistic, ostentatious and highly theatrical world of the Roman arena.

The Montefortino helmet of the second and first centuries BC took over from the Hellenistic styles worn by the Samnites (*51*). Where this helmet originated is uncertain, but it is strongly present amongst the Gauls, who brought it with them in their incursions into the Italic peninsula from the fifth century onwards. Due to their practicality they became very popular throughout Italy and mutated into the standard issue Roman helmet of the late republic and early Empire. In this way, the Montefortino style found its way into the arena, as an all-purpose gladiatorial helmet, in the days before the differences in gladiators were not, so to speak, set in stone.

Lastly, the primary weapon of the Samnite was the spear, if the rare depictions of what appear to be Samnites are to be relied upon.

In favour of the case for a distinct Samnite identity in at least one example is an account by Livy of the aftermath of the afore-mentioned battle in 308 BC between an alliance of Romans and Campanians against Samnites. The Samnites lost:

50 Brimmed bronze helmet, Hellenistic in influence, second or first century BC. *Taken from the Guttman Collection, with kind permission of Christies Images Ltd*

51 Montefortino helmet, second to first century BC. This may have been a Celtic helmet introduced into Italy and subsequently adapted into the standard issue Roman helmet of the late republic and early empire. *Taken from the Guttman Collection, with kind permission of Christies Images Ltd*

> So the Romans made use of the splendid armour of their enemies to do honour to the gods: while the Campanians, in consequence of their pride and in hatred of the Samnites, equipped after this fashion the gladiators who furnished them entertainment at their feasts, and bestowed on them the name of Samnites.

The Romans at this time had clearly not adopted gladiators – whilst they took the captured arms of their old enemies and decorated the Forum with them, they did nothing with the captives to provide themselves with gladiatorial entertainment. Sometime between 308 BC and 264 BC that attitudes changed. The Campanians, however, expressed their keenly felt hatred of their foes by having gladiators equipped and named as Samnites. This event, if Livy is to be trusted, seems to record the inauguration of the category of gladiator thereafter known as Samnite. And the Romans may well have caught the habit of gladiatorial combats, with the insulting use of enemy captives and their armature, from their allies, the Campanians.

This history of enmity between the Campanians and Samnites provides a possible explanatory background to a fourth-century BC tomb painting from Paestum in Campania that shows a combat between two men, and possibly at least two more, who appear to be gladiators. The two better-preserved figures are both wearing winged or plumed Attic-style helmets; are naked from the waist up, one seems to have a greave on his left, or leading, leg; both carry large round Greek-style shields, and spears which, if accurately represented, may have been extremely lightweight judging from the fact they are being wielded from the base in a one-handed grip with no obvious sign of any counterweight.

Given what we know of the hostilities in the region, it seems plausible that this painting in Campania shows two Samnites, taken captive and made to fight in an early example of gladiatorial combat, possibly in connection with a *munus*, since it appears on a tomb. This would explain why both are equipped in the same manner.

Spears feature strongly in a first century BC relief on the side of a funeral monument, from Amiternum near Aquila, Abruzzo (*52*). This region falls within Samnium, although by the time the monument was set up, it would have long been under Roman control. It shows a combat between two gladiators – because of the funerary context we can be fairly sure this commemorates in graphic form the *munus*, depicting the actual *bustuarii*, gladiators who fought at the funeral games of the man whose tomb they decorate.

The gladiators are often identified as of Samnite type; however, as the tomb is located in Samnium, it would be strange to show locally sourced gladiators. At first glance, they are equipped almost identically, with long spears, a definite Samnite trait, metal-edged rectangular shields with winged strap bosses, greaves on their leading left legs, and body armour. Curiously, they are both bareheaded, although they both have some kind of headdress.

The body armour worn by the gladiators is intriguing, as one, the fighter on the left, has what appears to be a mail-shirt reaching the top of the thighs, with typical

52 Illustration of a funeral monument, from Amiternum near Aquila, Abruzzo, first century BC. A possible representation of early gladiators, Samnites or perhaps Gauls

shoulder doubling, fastened by an oblong-shaped chest clasp (53); the unusual clasp is almost identical to one depicted on Galatian mail on a frieze of the second-century BC temple of Athena in Pergamum (54). This aspect, coupled with the distinct, winged strap boss, which is normally associated with the Gauls of this time, and the very fact that the armour is chain-mail, seem to suggest that this gladiator may not be Samnite at all; if anything, he is reminiscent of an early Gaul. His opponent may be wearing a mail-shirt, but it is shorter than the other, and has the appearance of muscling, though this may be artistic rendition of movement.

They both have distinctive swept-back hair – is this a representation of a barbarian hairstyle commonly associated with Celtic peoples such as Gauls? If the mid-first century BC dating of the tomb relief is reliable, perhaps the scene shows two prisoners of war from one of Rome's victories over the invading Helvetii tribes, which occurred at about that time. So, rather than Samnites, this might show one of the first depictions of original Gallic gladiators.

It is clear that to the Romans, by the end of the second century BC, 'Samnite' was an actual category of gladiator, and if the following quote is any guide, not a popular one:

> In the public show given by the Flacci was a certain Aeserninus, a Samnite, a nasty fellow, worthy of that life and station. He was matched with Pacideianus, who was by far the best of all the gladiators since the creation of man. (Lucilius, *Remains of Old Latin* 4.2.172-5)

This is a very useful reference, as it shows that the category of fighter known as a Samnite was in existence at the time of Lucilius (died 102 BC), and also that the gladiators were fighting under real, rather than stage names. That would come later, with the development of the *munera* under the emperors.

53 Illustration of an oblong-shaped chest clasp fixed to the shoulder doubling of a mailshirt, (highlighted) on the Amiternum funeral monument. This is typical of features associated with representations of Celtic mailshirts in the republican era

54 Illustration of clasp featured on Galatian mail on a frieze of the second century BC

By the time the Samnite was regarded as a gladiator type, rather than an enemy, he had probably lost his original authentic trappings and had evolved into a heavily armed fighter with sword arm protection, a plumed and/or crested wide-brimmed helmet, a single greave, a sword, *gladius*, rather than a spear, *hasta,* large rectangular shield, *scutum*, yet with a bare upper torso; whether the name for this type of gladiator.

GAULS

Like the Samnite, the Gaulish enemy tribes gave their name to another category of early gladiator, the *gallus*. Little is known about what the *galli* actually looked like, since no certain depictions or descriptions have been identified, although the comments above concerning the identity of the fighters on the tomb relief at Amiternum are relevant (52 and 55). The Gauls had been a thorn in Rome's side from the very beginning of the Republic; the bitter memories of the Gallic sack of Rome in 390 BC, the supporting role they played to Hannibal when he invaded Italy, and their own attempted invasion of Italy in 225 BC, go some way to explaining the brutal treatment they received at the hands of the Romans when finally the Gauls were conquered in their heartlands, Gallia Cisalpina, the valley of the Po.

55 Interpretation of a Gaul using the Amiternum funerary monument as reference

Given that they were based on successive waves of Gallic prisoners of war, which were again sent to Rome in their thousands after Julius Caesar conquered Gaul, their initial appearance would have followed the traditional image of the Gallic warrior; in Roman art celebrating famous victories over the Gauls, they would generally be pictured bare-headed, though not always, with a long slashing sword, *spatha*, or spear, large oval, rectangular or lozenge shaped shield, and with body armour of mail, if armour was worn at all, otherwise bare-chested, or even naked, as in the Dying Gaul sculpture.

As with the Samnite, by the time the Gaul transformed from hated barbarian enemy of Rome into the *gallus* category of gladiator, he had lost all semblance of the original warrior. By the Augustan period, the *gallus* became defunct; old enemies were no longer seen as different or dangerous enough, as they had become assimilated into the Roman mainstream. It has often been said that the *murmillo* was descended from the *gallus*.

THRACIANS

The dictator Sulla is credited with introducing the Thracians as gladiators, and Cicero's reference to a barbarian, 'tattooed like a Thracian' is the first literary reference to these savage fighters. To Romans of the late republic, Thracians were at first just another conquered people from a far off northern land.

Thrace occupies the territory now known as Bulgaria. On the western side of the Black Sea, it had a reputation for producing fearless and ferocious fighters. The Thracians were a belligerent people and this often brought them into conflict with Rome, resulting in them being captured and shipped to Rome as slaves, to be trained as gladiators. The archetypal Thracian is Spartacus, who has earned his place in history by leading an ultimately doomed rebellion of gladiators against the might of Rome:

> The rising of the gladiators and their devastation of Italy, which is generally known as the war of Spartacus, began as follows. A man called Lentulus Batiatus had an establishment for gladiators at Capua. Most of them were Gauls and Thracians. They had done nothing wrong, but, simply because of the cruelty of their owner, were kept in close confinement until the time came for them to engage in combat. Two hundred of them planned to escape, but their plan was betrayed and only seventy eight, who realised this, managed to act in time and get away, armed with choppers and spits which they seized from some cookhouse. On the road they came across some wagons which were carrying arms for gladiators to another city, and they took these arms for their own use. They then occupied a strong position and elected three leaders. The first of these was Spartacus. He was a Thracian from the nomadic tribes and not only had a great spirit and great physical strength, but was, much more than one would expect from one in his condition, most intelligent and cultured, being more like a Greek than a Thracian. (Plutarch, *Crassus* 8.1-2)

Plutarch, being Greek himself, brings a strong sense of admiration for the Thracian rebel into his history. By the time he was writing, Spartacus was long dead, yet the story of the slave who became a gladiator was a compelling one. Even at the turn of the next century, the fame of Spartacus was still bright, as the historian Florus indicates:

> ... the man who, from being a Thracian mercenary, had become a soldier, and from a soldier a deserter, then a highwayman, and finally, thanks to his strength, a gladiator. (Florus, 2.8.8)

This high praise encapsulates the tenacity and fighting spirit of the original Thracians. Again, like the Gaul and Samnite, the Thracian lost his connection with ethnic origin as the combats developed and were regulated in the Augustan era; he didn't have to be from Thrace to qualify as a *thraex* – it was a style of fighting with a particular armature. Unlike the *samnis* and *gallus*, both of which changed out of all recognition, however, the *thraex* persisted in name certainly, and in a form not too far removed from the fierce fighters of Spartacus' homeland.

The *thraex* of the pre-imperial period started out in all probability just as the *samnes* and *galli* did; captive Thracian warriors who were forced to fight with their native weapons and armour, using the techniques peculiar to their ethnic origin. He was a far simpler combatant than the later imperial incarnation of the same name, having the *sica*, small rectangular or square shield, two greaves, or shin-guards, reaching above the knee, and helmet. It is unlikely the helmet was the same in appearance as the curving, griffin–decorated, deep-brimmed example of the classic Thracian. In common with most early gladiators, the helmets were generally derived from the Hellenistic types, with identifiable elements of the Attic and Boeotian styles (*56*); the broad, curving brim of the former with the cheek-guards (and occasional crest) of the latter. The special inheritance of the Thracian was, however, the Phrygian style, which is discussed in the analysis of the imperial era headgear.

To attempt any greater description of the *thraex* in the early republican period would open the door to a blurring of the early and Augustan types. Suffice it to say that the *thraex* retained his name, his fighting style, and possibly his identity. Because Thracians were very popular with the crowds, their style of fighting, together with important elements of their combat traditions, persisted, though with modifications. However, it would be wrong to think, in view of the persistence of the *thraex* category when other enemy warrior types were gradually absorbed, that all *thraeces* were at all times exclusively Thracian in nationality; there is an interesting inscription found in a gladiatorial context, dated to approximately the first half of the first century AD, in which this is summed up: *Thelyphus samnes natione Traex* (*CIL*,VI.10187; *ILS* 5085).

Thelyphus, a misspelling of Telephus, was Thracian by nationality, but fought as a *samnis*. Quite apart from the seeming perversity of a Thracian adopting the

56 Illustration of Thracian helmet, from the fourth century BC, found at Kovachevitsa in Bulgaria. Note the distinct Phrygian style of crest and pronounced brim. *After Christopher Webber*

fighting identity of a different category of gladiator, it shows, as a bonus, that the Samnite type had not disappeared or been incorporated into a later category at that stage. Also from the *Inscriptiones Latinae Selectae*, is a similar, though much later, case, where a Roman citizen, though Alexandrian by birth, called Marcus Antonius Exochus fought at Rome as a Thracian in Trajan's triumphal games (*CIL* VI 10194; *ILS* 5088).

This is part of an inscription of a dedication on a tombstone; it has an interesting feature in addition to the above ethnographic information. It contains all the symbols of Exochus' profession – the *sica*, a pair of tall greaves decorated with gorgons heads, *ocreae*, a victor's crown and three victory palms, and a griffin, *gryps* – the Thracian and his griffin, hovering over his head in life, and protecting his tomb in death.

The *sica* was the native weapon of the Thracian, typically a very short, curving, dagger-like sword, designed for close-quarters combat as it was solely used for thrusting (57). Whether it had two cutting edges or one is not known. This weapon can often be confused with the *falx* from Dacia, a country almost adjacent to Thrace, corresponding to modern Romania; the *falx* like the *sica*, was a traditional weapon of the Black Sea tribes but although it had a curved blade, it was much longer, with a scythe-like appearance, and a hooked end.

Variations in the shape and size of examples of the *sica* are known only from depictions in art, including graffiti. Unlike the mass-produced *gladius*, the *sica*

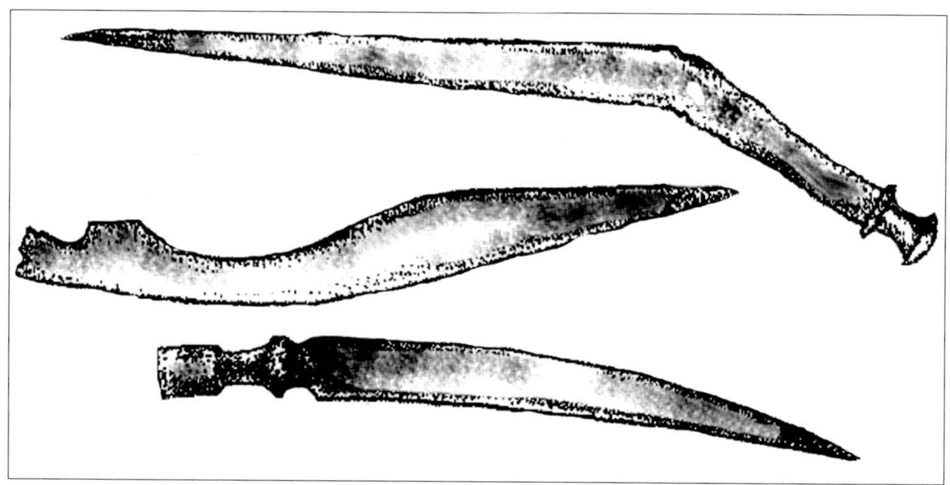

57 Sword blades found in Thrace, third century BC. *Based on the research of Christopher Webber and representations by Daniella Carlsson.*

was a specialist weapon, probably manufactured in traditional fashion in Thrace and imported for gladiatorial use. In the countries of the Black Sea, iron was a scarce commodity, and archaeological finds of *sicae* are hence rare, as recycling of weapons must have occurred as a matter of course.

There is an iron curved-blade weapon in the Romermuseum, Augst, Switzerland, although at approximately 2ft or 60cm long (including the handle), it does not conform to the depictions of *sicae* in art; whether it is of gladiatorial provenance is uncertain. A possible wooden practice *sica*, around 14in or 34cm long, was found in a ditch at the legionary camp, Oberaden, in Germany (*58*). This is a more plausible size for a *sica*, and it matches the look of the artistic representations; it may therefore show the true dimensions of a working iron version (*59*). As a variant on the curved blade, an angled or bent blade is known from the imperial period, although amongst their own tribespeople, the Thracians seem to have had *sicae*, curved swords and knives of all shapes and sizes, including angled blades, for centuries before they were subdued by the Romans. These were also variously called *machairai*, *kopis*, or even *falces*, which they shared with the Dacians. Ironically, it was said to have been a Thracian who killed M. Licinius Crassus at the battle of Carrhae in 53 BC; considering that years earlier, Crassus had pursued and destroyed Spartacus, the most famous Thracian of all, it was perhaps fitting he should meet his end at the hands of another. Crassus' head was allegedly severed by a single blow of the greatly feared Thracian *rhomphaia*, which was a long, straight or slightly curved sword, similar to the Dacian *falx*, used by Thracian cavalry.

58 *Above* Illustration of possible wooden practice *sica*, found in a ditch at the legionary camp, Oberaden, in Germany

59 *Right* Interpretation of an early Thracian gladiator with distinct curved iron *sica*

PROVOCATOR

The *provocator* is a gladiator of late republican type. There is a military style to these gladiators; their equipment mirrors standard issue legionary armature. The *provocator* always fought another *provocator*, never other types of fighter. This unusual trait was shared with the *equites*, mounted gladiators, who, similarly, were never matched with any other kind but their own. The most detailed depiction of *provocatores* is on a marble bas-relief dated to the Augustan period around 30 BC; usefully, it belongs to the pivotal point in time when gladiatorial combat was becoming an imperial monopoly. It was found in the Tiber between Ostia and Rome, and is now in the Museo Nazionale Romano at the Baths of Diocletian

(*60*). It originally formed part of a funeral monument, and in that context it is almost certainly an accurate representation of the *munus* given in honour of a member of the Roman elite.

It shows a wealth of detail. There are three gladiators in the bas-relief, but the one on the extreme right is a *murmillo*, so does not concern us here. The two men to the left, who have been identified as *provocatores*, are both wearing the meticulously folded loincloths known as *subligacula* or *subligaria*, with the wide ornate metal belts so typical of southern Italy and gladiators in general; the belts certainly appear to be leather-lined metal, to judge from the incised decoration on them, and the edging of some other material, presumably leather exposed from the fitting on the reverse. The fighter on the right has a type of *manica*; it is on his lower right arm only, and whilst it could be a kind of segmented metal arm-guard, the suggestion of cross-hatching on the guard could be taken to represent quilting or padding.

Two kinds of shields are shown, both in use by legionaries at a time when the convex blunted oval variety (like a rectangle with the corners taken off, and with the characteristic *spina* running the length of it) had not yet given way to the more popular rectangular *scutum*, although the shield of the fighter on the right is partially obscured by his gesture of submission in resting it on the ground; it could conceivably be of the same type as his opponent. Both men have short, straight swords, *gladii*. Each one has a long greave ending above the knee on his leading left leg only, and for body armour is wearing a short breastplate known as

60 Illustration of marble bas-relief dated to the Augustan period around 30 BC, probably showing *provocator*-type gladiators. It was found in the Tiber between Ostia and Rome

a *pectorale* or *cardiophylax*. Looking like a bib, in reality a style similar to the *aegis*, the breastplate of Minerva/Athena, it is held in place by leather straps crossing over the shoulders and fastening at the back.

This chest protector, sometimes decorated as the left hand one is with the traditional Medusa or Gorgon head performing an apotropaeic function, is one of the two identifying elements of the *provocator*. The other is the early 'Imperial Gallic' style helmet, shown in its earliest representation here, a hybrid of Roman and Gallic (Celtic) features, such as the accentuated neck-guard, the wide cheek-pieces, the single feathers in plume-holders at the sides, without the crests associated with other gladiators helmets. This bas-relief depicts a turning point: the old-style gladiators were being joined by fighters like these *provocatores*, with their new helmets clearly modelled on military lines.

But the really big changes were just beginning: the visor, that typically gladiatorial feature of helmets, begins to appear in the archaeological record, other armatures become clearly defined for the first time, and together with the reorganisation of the system under Augustus, the face of gladiatorial combat starts to look familiar to us.

The *provocator* was a class of fighter that carried on in the imperial age and seems to have retained its military nature. The distinctly military armature they sport gives reasonable grounds for thinking that the *provocatores* may actually have been ex-professional soldiers by training.

IMPERIAL *PROVOCATOR*

The *provocator* in the imperial period remained very similar to his republican counterpart. The essential element of the *provocator* was his tradition of reflecting a military origin, but once this *armatura* was added to the gladiatorial categories, its distinct features ceased to move with the times; the connection with the military was forgotten, and the modifications to the equipment reflected the changing fashions in arena combat, and nothing more. The *provocator* in the later imperial period sometimes wore a crescent-shaped short breastplate, rather than a rectangular one, and the open helmet of legionary type became a visored one, as the cheek-pieces were expanded to meet in the middle, then hinged at the sides, and eye-grilles were added to enclose the face (*61*). All other items of equipment remained broadly the same.

A possible example of a plain *provocator* helmet is the Hawkedon, found in Suffolk (*colour plate 15*). It has traces of tinning on the dome, and in its original state was probably quite impressive, though unembellished. Even with a visor, the distinct imperial Gallic style of the helmet is clearly discernible, particularly the deep neck-guard (*61*). By the end of the first century AD, the appearance of the *provocator* was fixed, with very few variations (*62*). This situation applied to all of the classifications of gladiator, and for the next 300 years or so, they practiced a bloody combat sport that had become almost fossilised.

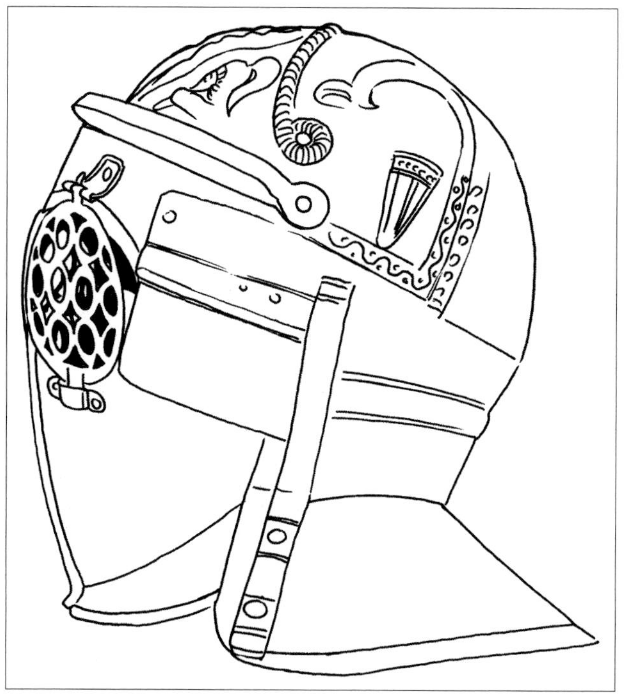

61 Helmet of *provocator*, imperial period

62 Interpretation of a *provocator*

EQUES

Like the *provocator*, the *eques* only ever fought another *eques*. A mounted gladiator equipped with lance, sword and the traditional small round shield of the republican cavalry, the *parma equestris*, he was distinctive for his uncrested round brimmed helmet with its feathers at either side, and for the fact that he did not wear a loincloth unlike the other categories of gladiator. In earlier images of this gladiator, they were shown in scale-armour, though this changed to knee-length tunica in the imperial age.

IMPERIAL *EQUES*

Depictions of later, imperial *equites* usually portray them wearing capacious tunics, sometimes brightly coloured and decorated, with the very typical *clavus*, the two integral woven vertical stripes running the length of the garment from neck to hem (*63*, *colour plate 10*). The two stripes are generally designated in the singular form, *clavus* rather than the plural, *clavi*. The stripes are quite narrow, perhaps an inch wide, and conform to the *angustus clavus*, which members of the

63 Interpretation of the *eques*-type gladiator, with distinctive tunic

equestrian class were allowed to wear, as opposed to the *latus clavus* (3in or 7.5cm wide) reserved for patrician senatorial rank. Perhaps there is symbolism in their clothing that is now lost on us. The *clavus* was a visible sign of class distinction: if the *equites* of the arena were decked out in the insignia of the aristocratic *equites*, perhaps they too enjoyed higher status within the *familia gladiatoria*.

Earlier versions of these gladiators have been represented in scale armour, rather than tunics. The crucial differences were that they never went bare-chested into combat, nor did they wear greaves. Instead, they occasionally had shortened versions of the *fasciae*, the padded wrappings, around their lower legs. As with the republican era *equites*, they carried the distinctively colourful, ringed, medium-sized round shield, the *parma equestris*, probably of layered leather, for lightness. The shield was roughly 2ft (60cm) in diameter. Whether the concentric circles generally shown on the shield form a significant feature of its construction, or a decorated surface (perhaps painted), is hard to tell because the nature of most of the depictions (mosaic) obscures fine detail. The *manica,* the segmented metal arm guard, was worn on the dominant, usually right, arm.

By this time, the helmet of the early *eques* had given way to a visored version, though still without a crest of any kind. External ornamentation of the helmet was restricted to single feathers in the holders at either side of the head (*64*).

64 Equites in combat. *Illustration based on detail of a mosaic in Museo Arquelogico Nacional, Madrid*

When the *equites* entered the arena, it is thought that they started the contest on horseback using lances, or spears, *hastae*, at least 6ft (2m) long, but dismounted at the crucial point of the combat, finishing the fight with swords. It is often said that these swords were *gladii*, which gives more weight to the belief that the swordplay was all done on foot, since the shortness of the reach of the *gladius*, the legionary's sword, makes it an inappropriate weapon for using on horseback. Military cavalry tended to use the *spatha*, the longer slashing sword inherited from the Celtic tradition. As *equites* were generally shown on foot in artistic representations, this has led to confusion over their true character; however, it is thought that the artists were choosing to show the dramatic climax of the combat rather than the initial stages. A late source, the *Origines* of the seventh-century cleric Isidorus of Seville, has an account that tells of the *equites* riding into the arena on white horses, and appearing as the first contest on the programme of the afternoon's events. Though the horses are not often depicted, there is the tantalising possibility that the skeleton of a richly equipped horse found within the *ludus gladiatorius,* the gladiatorial training barracks, at Pompeii, is the mount of an *eques*, as it was found in the vicinity of a large store of gladiatorial equipment, including the *galerus* (tall metal shoulder guard) of a *retiarius*, 15 helmets, some greaves and the remains of two unfortunate gladiators or slaves in leg irons, trapped in a cell.

The usefulness of gladiators who could ride is possibly attested by a reference concerning the acquisition of amber made by Pliny the Elder in his *Naturalis Historia*:

> From Carnuntum in Pannonia to the coast of Germany from which the amber is imported is a distance of about 600 miles – a fact which has only recently been ascertained. And there is still alive a Roman *eques* who was sent there by Julianus, the manager of the gladiatorial exhibitions for Nero, to procure this product. Journeying along the coasts and through markets there, he brought back such great quantities of amber that the nets which are used for holding back the wild beasts and for protecting the podium were studded with amber. The arms too, the litters, and all the equipment of one particular day (of spectacles) were decorated with amber, to vary the display of each separate day. The largest piece of amber that this personage brought to Rome weighed thirteen pounds. (Pliny, *Naturalis Historia* 37. 45-46)

It might be argued that the term *eques* has two meanings, one of which designates the horseman gladiator, and the other, a member of Rome's equestrian order, part of the upper classes; in that sense, it is often translated as knight. When considering the possibility of a member of the aristocracy being sent on an extended errand across dangerous territories, it sounds unlikely in the extreme, given Rome's rigid social structures.

Therefore it seems plausible that it could have been a horseman gladiator who got the commission to travel across Germany, without attracting too much attention; he would certainly have been able to look after himself in the event of trouble. The context of the commission adds to the sense that it was in fact a gladiator who was sent to perform an important task in procuring the amber for decorating Nero's shows. There is no way of knowing which it really was, but it would not be the first time that gladiators with specialist skills were called upon to use them outside the arena; gangs of gladiators were used as bodyguards by the rich, and gladiatorial trainers, *lanistae*, were even called in to train recruits in the army during times of crisis when the intake was massively increased.

Equites were not the only gladiators who fought on horseback. A sub-group of the *equites* were the *andabatae*, heavily armoured fighters, who, according to some literary sources, had the added handicap of visored helmets without eyeholes; an alternative record alleged that they were seated back to front. Either way, they seem to have been a comparative rarity, an exotic rather than everyday performance, with perhaps more comedic value than promise of bloodshed, as they blundered around encased in metal playing a strange mounted version of 'blind man's buff'. Luckily, their horses were not similarly deprived of vision. The Romans were aware of a play called 'The *Andabatae*', mentioned by Varro, which is sadly no longer extant.

VELITES

Taking their name from the lightly armed foot soldiers who were originally the poorest as well as the youngest group in the Roman legion of the second century BC, the *velites* were skirmishers, not heavy infantry. As soldiers, they had carried very short, light javelins, similar to the *pilum*, called *hastae velitaris*, swords, *gladii*, and used a round shield, *parma*, about 3ft (90cm) in diameter. When the army was again restructured in the late republic, the *velites* were abolished and, although there are records of them as gladiators, perhaps former soldiers, as the *provocatores* were, there are no further references to them after the end of the second century BC. In the arena they fought on foot against one another, each *veles* armed with a spear that had a strap or thong, *hasta amentata*. The purpose of the strap may have been two-fold, in that it could guard against accidental loss of weapon, and may have had some use as an aid to hurling the spear itself, as the word *amentare* means to hurl by means of a thong or strap.

IMPERIAL GLADIATORS

Augustus is usually credited with taking all the influence of the gladiatorial games to himself, developing a kind of state monopoly on spectacles, whilst at the same time creating a definitive gladiatorial system. There is evidence, however, from Appian, the second century AD Alexandrian historian, in his *Bella Civilia*, that gladiatorial combats were already taking place in the afternoon as far back as 44 BC. Therefore, it is more realistic to see the control exerted by Augustus over the *munera* as a stage in the evolution of the gladiator shows, a process that was probably not fully realised until the completion of the Flavian amphitheatre in AD 80.

Under Augustus, the circus and especially the arena finally became the outward expressions of sovereignty, over the people and the world under Rome's rule, a vivid realisation of the *imperium* itself. This dominion encompassed not just the citizens and non-citizens, the territories and provinces, but also the natural world wherever Rome put its footprint. It was a showcase for every emperor from Augustus onwards to display in the most graphic ways how comprehensive was Rome's supremacy over the rest of the world.

Gladiatorial combats had become an enduring feature of Roman cultural life, a very potent expression of what it meant to be a Roman, *romanitas*, in the centuries when Rome was consolidating its grip on the rest of Italy; consequently, once Italy was unified under Roman rule, the gladiatorial shows spread outwards through the rapidly growing empire. The combats were exported wherever there was a need to assure the far-flung Roman community that they were participating in the life of Rome; this was particularly true of soldiers posted to the furthest corners of the empire.

In fact, this is demonstrated by the number of amphitheatres built adjacent to military camps and fortresses. The export of *romanitas*, and with it, the gladiatorial combats that were an integral part of its influence, accelerated as the empire expanded. With the spread of amphitheatres in full swing outside Rome itself, their absence from the city itself is all the more striking; the first stone amphitheatre in Rome came about when Titus Statilius Taurus, one of Octavian's (later Augustus) loyal generals sponsored its construction in order to gain political advantage from him. It is in this setting, Statilius' so-called hunting theatre, that the first imperial games were witnessed.

THRAEX (THRACIAN)

This category of gladiator was so popular, it did not disappear or mutate into another named type; however, the *thraex* did acquire new elements as time went on (65). Fashions changed in the arena, but it is possible to recognise the distinct armature of the *thraex*, whatever the date. The emperor Domitian favoured the *thraex,* to the extent that:

> … a chance remark by one citizen, to the effect that a Thracian gladiator might be 'a match for his Gallic opponent, but not for the patron of the games', was enough to have him dragged from his seat and – with a placard tied round his neck reading: 'A Thracian supporter who spoke disloyally' – torn to pieces by dogs in the arena.
> (Suetonius, *de vita Caesarum, Domitianus* 10)

65 Interpretation of imperial period Thracian gladiator (*thraex*)

The *thraex* carried a small square or rectangular shield, of wooden construction, ply with a covering of leather, known as the *parma* or its diminutive, *parmula*; from examples depicted, it appears to have been emphatically convex rather than flat, and tended not to have a boss. From this shield, the *thraeces* got their popular nickname, *parmularii,* just as their opponents with the curved rectilinear shields were called *scutarii*. Because the shield was small, about 24in by 20in, and offered little protection below groin level, the *thraex* wore greaves, *ocreae*, on both legs, which reached up as far as mid-thigh, and is often depicted wearing a form of leg protectors above them, from at least knee to groin, which appear to be padded or quilted fabric wrappings around both legs (*66* and *67*). On the dominant arm a *manica* was worn.

Artistic representations of gladiators tend to show what seem to be non-metallic *manicae*; this is seen more clearly on relief carvings such as those on the tomb of C. Lusius Storax, from Chieti in Italy, where a selection of gladiators are shown in combat. *Manicae* were usually made from padded linen with leather ties; metal plates attached to a backing (usually leather strips) came later, though did not replace the earlier form; they complemented each other.

The most instantly recognisable feature of the *thraex* was his brimmed, crested helmet with its distinctive griffin's head (*68*). In all but a very few depictions of *thraeces*, the griffin is shown on the crest of the helmet, aiding identification. The significance of this particular mythological creature in a gladiatorial context may

66 Reconstruction of an imperial period *thraex*. Helmet discarded, he has won the contest, and will therefore receive the victory palm. Based on *Satornilos* grave, Smyrna, from the second or third century AD. *Reconstruction: Britannia. Photograph: Fraser Gray*

67 Illustration of tombstone of a victorious *thraex*, the grave of *Satornilos*, Smyrna, second or third century AD

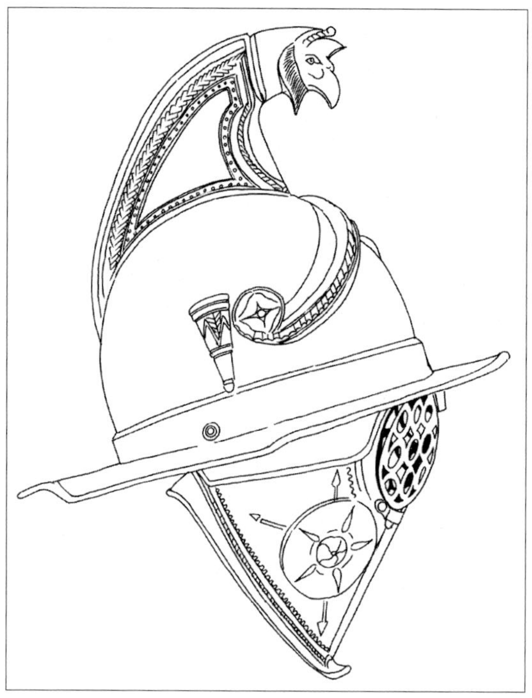

68 Possible Thracian helmet with distinct griffin head on the crest, first century AD. *Based on an example from Pompeii*

stem from its role as a guardian of the dead, or from a reputed association with Nemesis; four griffins were said to draw her chariot. As a symbol, the griffin frequently occurs in Greek and Roman art, and particularly at tombs, as a protector of souls (*69* and *70*). It can be seen on many Roman architectural features, usually in pairs. Herodotus told of griffins that guarded the gold of the Hyperboreans, who incidentally were geographically located near the Carpathian mountains, west of Thrace. Why exactly the creature should be thought appropriate for a Thracian helmet, apart from the link with Nemesis, cultic goddess of the arena, is open to question; there is a suggestion it symbolizes arrogant pride, *superbia*, and that might be thought reason enough for a professional gladiator.

It does, however, have associations with the Underworld, as a protector of tombs as gateways between this world and the next, and it is often used as a decorative motif on funerary monuments and tomdstones.

Often the helmet of the *thraex* is depicted with a plumed crest, and sometimes with single feathers spouting from plume holders at either side of the head; horsehair crests do not occur, having a purely military connotation, perhaps. Equally, there are many representations that have no plumed crest at all, just a curving metal crescent terminating in the griffin's head.

A well-preserved first-century AD wall fresco from Colchester depicts what is probably a *thraex*, to judge from the high leg padding, *fasciae*, and the short, decorated shield (*colour plate 14*). The naively drawn weapon is thin and appears to have a very slight curve, like a *sica*, and the helmet has a plumed crest with

69 Griffin head from the baths of Caracalla, Rome. *Photograph: Pharos Pictures*

70 Griffin head on a relief from the tombs at Ostia. *Photograph: author*

possibly some kind of figurehead (a griffin?) at the terminal point of the crest. The gladiator has a padded armguard, a *manica*, which looks like it is made of fabric to judge from its whiteish colour, on his sword arm, although nothing on his shield arm, and the leg-guards look as if they too might be padded fabric. Over these, he has greaves, *ocreae*, on the lower legs. He is bare-chested and barefoot, and wears a white *subligaria* held in place with a very typical wide gladiator's belt, which has the appearance of being ornamented. Since his plumed crest is white, as is his *subligaria* and shield, it is tempting to think he is wearing some kind of livery or team colour, but this is purely conjecture. He is depicted in the classic defeated pose of appeal, *ad digitum*, with index finger raised to ask for mercy. He has dropped his shield, though not his weapon. Because it is a painting and not a mosaic, the detail is more discernible, and gives a very real impression of what a *thraex* may have looked like.

An ancient Thracian helmet from the fourth century BC found at Kovachevitsa in Bulgaria (ancient Thrace), is in the form of a Phrygian cap; its strongly forward-curving crest looks like an earlier incarnation of the classic Thracian helmet (*56*). Since this was found in the territory of Thrace itself, it is reasonable to suppose that it is in fact an ancestor of the later one, evolving by way of exaggeration of its features – the slight brim becoming much deeper, the crest flattening and lengthening, terminating in the griffin protome.

HOPLOMACHUS

The *hoplomachus* is often confused with the *thraex*, and indeed they have many pieces of equipment in common (*71*). The word comes from the Greek, meaning simply 'armed fighter'. They both had the distinctive forward-curving crested visored helmet, though that of the *hoplomachus* did not have the typical griffin's head on its crest. Both had the same high greaves, and padded leg wrappings, *fasciae*. They even shared the same opponent, the *murmillo*. But whereas the shield, *parmula*, of the *thraex* was small and square or rectangular, that of the *hoplomachus* was round, though still small in size. The shield was always round, convex and made of a single sheet of metal, usually bronze. The thickness of the sheet bronze was an important factor in determining the weight of the shield – too thick, and its defensive qualities would be negated by its unwieldiness.

Pompeii has yielded up a finely decorated example, about 15in in diameter, and weighing nearly 3.5lb (*72*). The rim, or border, running round the shield is at an angle to the convex body, but despite this feature it has the archaic look of the Greek hoplite shield. The shield, again like that of the *thraex*, has no boss, and therefore no hollow area in which the hand can be protected; as the manufacture is all of one piece because it is sheet metal; it is held by means of a strip of copper-alloy (bronze) forming a slightly flattened *omega*, a bridge of bronze through which the forearm can pass, at the centre of the reverse. Usually such a

71 Interpretation of the *hoplomachus* type of gladiator

72 Illustration of metal shield from Pompeii, of the type used by a *hoplomachus*

feature is accompanied by an anchoring second loop for the lower arm or wrist at the edge of the shield, so that the arm can brace the shield without it tipping forward; in addition, to ensure a secure and stable fit on the wearer's arm, some form of padding in a material like felt, leather, fleece, or padded linen would be needed. This would also buffer the effect of heavy blows to the shield, which would otherwise send painful shock energy up the arm. After all, a purely metal shield has a greater deflective property than its wooden counterpart, although the latter has greater powers of shock absorption.

The method of holding the shield also means that the other weapon of the hoplomachus, the sword, or perhaps a longer dagger, like the *pugio*, could be held in the left hand at the same time as the shield, ready for use once the spear was cast or lost.

The *hoplomachus* had only the small round shield to protect his torso, like the *thraex* with his *parmula* (*73*). It is for this reason that the *hoplomachus*, again like the *thraex*, often had the extensive lower body protection in the form of *fasciae*, padded wrappings from thigh to knee, and *ocreae*, longer greaves going past the knees up to mid-thigh (*74*), although in some examples, he wears only one greave. The greaves for all types of gladiator tended to have punched holes to take straps to fasten them to the legs, although some had loops; padding behind the greaves on the lower legs would be essential for comfort, to hold them in position and thus to prevent the lower edges of the greaves from driving into the upper part of the foot, and for shock absorption on the shins (*colour plates 28* and *29*).

Without these defences, their legs would be too vulnerable to attack and the show would be over before it began. This is the reasoning behind most of the gladiatorial armour – it is intended to prolong a fight, rather than have it prematurely terminated by incapacitating, but not necessarily fatal, limb wounds. That the torso itself is bare is part of the jeopardy on display, the better to see the athleticism of the combats, the reality of the wounds and to encourage a target-orientated style of swordsmanship, which would last longer and be more entertaining for the spectators.

Most importantly, the weapon of the *hoplomachus* was not the distinctive curved or angled *sica,* but the short straight-bladed sword, the *gladius*. He is depicted as carrying a spear or lance, in addition to sword and shield, so his hands were full, and we can only guess at the fighting techniques he employed. At some point in the combat, most probably at the start, it seems likely he would have had to cast the spear, as he could not have used it one-handed for the entire combat at the same time as the *gladius*.

The equipment of the *hoplomachus* may have reminded the audiences of a stereotypical Greek warrior, the hoplite, and this may be why he has the name of the Greek infantryman of history, in order to conjure up the sensation of one of Rome's ancient foes, fighting again in the arena.

73 Figure of a *hoplomachus*. *Reconstruction: Britannia. Photograph: Fraser Gray*

74 *Hoplomachus* figurine. *Taken from the Guttmann Collection, with kind permission of Christies Images Ltd*

MURMILLO

The *murmillo* gets his name from the Greek word for a type of fish (*75a* and *colour plate 30*). As many contemporary sources indicated, it was derived from the image of a fish on their helmets, although the archaeological record has no firm evidence to support that assertion. The fish in question was the *mormyros*, or in Latin, *murmo* or *murmuros*, the striped bream, which was very common in the Mediterranean then as now, and best caught by the age-old method of surf-casting, a fishing technique involving casting the net into the surf to trap the fish coming in on the tide. It is in this technique that perhaps a clue to the origin of the *murmillo* may be found, although the usual theory is more to do with the

75a Interpretation of a *murmillo*

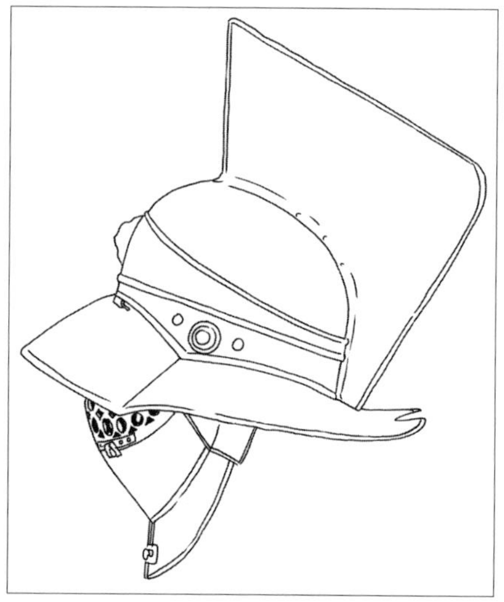

75b Helmet of *murmillo*

reference to a fish motif on his helmet leading to his subsequent association with the *retiarius*, the net and trident fighter. Perhaps an alternative theory could be considered, that the name came some time after an association with the *retiarius* had been established, and that the term *murmillo* 'stuck' after the spectators had called this new prey of the net-fighter after a fish everyone knew was caught only by standing at the edge of the sea and casting the *rete*, the net; it was after all a common Mediterranean fish that everyone would know from the market, rather as cod or haddock would be for us.

However, the pairing of *murmillo* and *retiarius* was quite a late development, and never as fixed as the pairing of *secutor* and *retiarius*, yet the *murmillo* was so-called even when his opponent was the *thraex* or *hoplomachus*, so it would seem the question still stands. One thing is known for certain and that is that the *murmillo* never fought *murmillo*. The search for hard and fast rules in gladiatorial combats is probably futile; we are asking the wrong questions in our quest for order and meaning. All we can do is consider the evidence, and then the possibilities.

The emperor Vespasian's rhetorician, Quintilian, records a sing-song chant supposedly addressed to a *murmillo* by a pursuing *retiarius*: *Non te peto, piscem peto; cur me fugis, Galle?* – 'It's not you I'm after, it's your fish; why are you running away from me, Gaul?'

If there is any historical authenticity at all in this jeering provocation of the heavy-armoured *murmillo*, it reveals two things; firstly, a clever and realistic tactic by the *retiarius* – to exhaust his opponent by baiting him into excessive movement, and secondly, the net-man's reference to the fish emblem on the helmet, identifying the other gladiator as *murmillo*, but calling him 'Gaul'.

Whatever the origin of the term *murmillo*, it is generally believed that they evolved from the earlier category known as the Gaul, or *gallus*, about which little is known. We do know however that the *murmillo* wore a *manica*, an arm guard, on his sword arm.

He carried the large rectangular semi-cylindrical wooden shield very similar in appearance and construction to the legionary *scutum*, and likely to have been decorated with meaningful symbols of *virtus*, fortune and victory. Shield construction of the *scutum* for the Roman legions had basically remained the same since the fourth century BC, when it replaced the round shields previously in use.

Although the shape was modified over time, it had not changed significantly because it was a successful and functional design; this same practical method of construction was used for the large shields of the gladiators. Polybius has an account of the time-honoured method as he observed it in the second century BC:

> It consists of two layers of wood fastened together with bull's-hide glue; the outer surface is then covered first with canvas (or, linen cloth) and then with calfskin. The upper and lower edges are bound with iron to protect the shield both from the cutting strokes of swords and from damage when resting on the ground. In the centre is fixed an iron boss, which deflects direct hits by stones, pikes and heavy missiles. (Polybius, *Historiae* VI. 23)

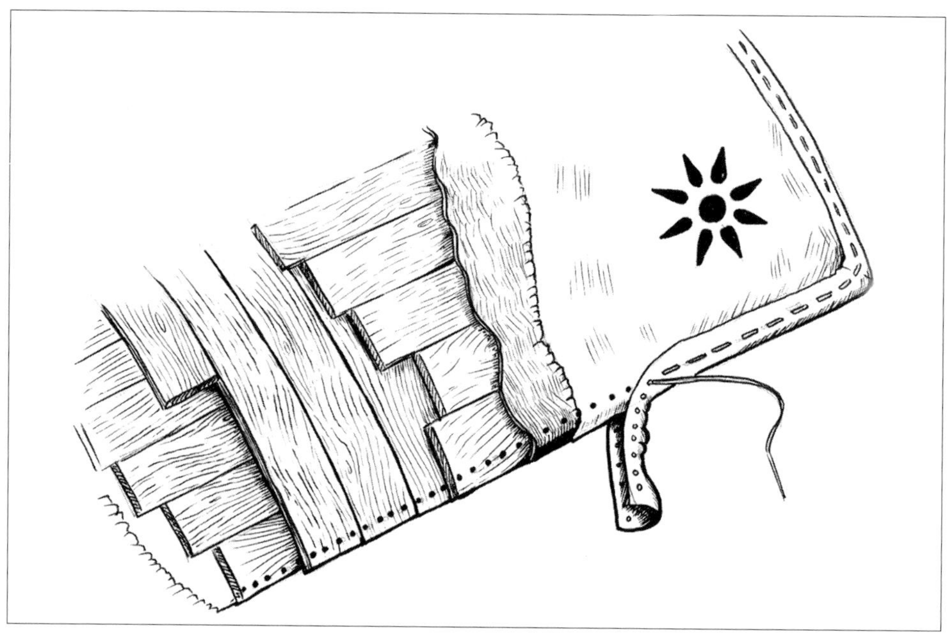

76 Ancient shield construction; in stages, plywood strips, leather and then fabric facing are assembled and then edged with rawhide

77 A modern reconstuction of the *scutum* type of shield. *Courtesy of Jeff Brimble*

Variations on this are few; the metal edging may be copper-alloy (bronze) rather than iron, and instead of the *umbo*, an iron or bronze boss, we sometimes see a long wooden 'barley-corn' shaped reinforcement known as a *spina*. Behind the *umbo* or *spina* a circle was cut out of the wood of the shield, and the transverse handgrip spanned this hole. Though it is not mentioned in Polybius' account, the shield would have been lined (and perhaps even padded on the face) with some organic shock absorber like lambswool felt (*76*). The use of leather to face the shield protects it from wear and tear, almost literally, as it extends the life of the shield by holding the surface together when the strength of the wood is compromised, but before splintering and disintegration set in; it prevents large splinters of wood from flying off the shield after heavy attack from bladed weapons. It is said that the archaic Romans used round ox-hide shields before they borrowed the Greek style, so they would have been well aware of the defensive properties of thick leather.

When reconstructed in this manner, the *scutum* can weigh between 14 and 25lbs (6-10kg), depending on how many layers of plywood and protective surfacing are used. It means that the total weight of the equipment of the *murmillo* was much greater than in the other gladiatorial categories, most of which was due to the heavy shield. The gladiator, however, unlike the soldier, only had to bear the weight for a few minutes, and also unlike the armoured soldier, it might be the only thing standing between his unprotected torso and an early death.

On his left leg was a short greave worn over padding. Unlike the *thraex* or *hoplomachus*, the *murmillo*, having the almost complete cover of the very large shield, the *scutum*, did not need the high, thigh-length greaves that they wore – so long as there was sufficient overlap between the bottom of the shield and the top of the greave, his defence was maintained.

The *murmillo* was armed with the *gladius*, just like the legionary. The early *gladius*, favoured weapon of the republican army, was the *hispaniensis*, the Spanish type, later known as the 'Mainz', and some examples of this sword have waisted blades with a long point, rather than completely straight blade edges; although it was primarily a thrusting, stabbing weapon, we know from Polybius' description that it was used for cutting as well as thrusting, as it was 'sharp on both edges'. Over time, it was replaced by the Pompeii-type *gladius*, with its parallel straight blade edges and shorter point, which was possibly even more efficient at cutting and stabbing. So the *gladius*, in all of its stages of development, should not be pigeonholed as the short stabbing sword of the legionary. In any case, when the word *gladius* is used, it does not necessarily mean the legionary's short sword; it is an all-purpose word for sword. An intriguing detail on the Augustan bas-relief already discussed under the subject of *provocatores* shows not just the aforementioned *provocatores* but also the figure of a defeated *murmillo* to their right; he is bare-chested with a crested, plumed helmet, and a *manica* on his sword arm; his shield, which has been lowered in submission, is rectangular or blunt oval in shape. The shield of his opponent is all that is left of that figure, but it is a much smaller rectangle, marking him almost certainly as a *thraex*; this looks like a typical bout, the classic pairing of *murmillo* and *thraex*. The *murmillo* has definitely surrendered, as he has let his *gladius* drop from his grip; it hangs from some kind of cord or thong attached to his wrist. An example of a *gladius* found at Rheingonheim supports the existence of this feature: it had a silver-plated wooden handle, with a rivet that had at one point had a small ring from a bronze chain.

The bronze helmet of the *murmillo* had a broad brim, with a bulging face-plate that included grillwork eye-pieces (*75b*); its distinctive appearance was partly due to the prominent visor, but also to the angular, sometimes hollow, box crest which was then able to take the insertion of a wooden plume-holder into which a further feathered crest could be fixed. Single plume-holders for feathers were fixed on either side of the bowl (*colour plate 16*). Horsehair crests were an alternative to feathers, *pinnae*, but due to the difficulties in distinguishing feathers from horsehair in the various depictions of helmets, it is impossible to say how common they were.

In common with most of the categories of gladiator, the torso of the *murmillo* was, as we have seen, exposed, and he wore the *subligaria*, the elaborate folded loincloth together with the *balteus*, the ostentatiously wide belt, often highly decorated. A good example of the lavishness of the ornamentation of belts is shown in the bone figure of a *murmillo* gladiator from Lexden, Colchester (*78*).

The *subligaria, subligar* or *subligaculum*, all names for that mysterious complicated loincloth which most gladiators wore, seems to have many variants, if the depictions on reliefs, mosaics, pottery, sculpture, wallpaintings and graffiti are true reflections of the actual situation. The term derives from its parent verb, *subligare*, 'to bind below', and may refer to the fact that in order to secure it, the long piece of material has to be tied around the waist and then pass between the thighs, leaving a section of the cloth to emerge at the front, tucking under the knot at the front waist fastening, and out over the crotch area, like an apron (*79*).

The rear view has often led to it unflatteringly being referred to as a 'nappy', or 'diaper'. Again, our culture does not see such a garment as appropriate male attire; to the Romans, it was quite the reverse. Although total nudity was frowned upon as a suspicious foreign tendency associated with Greek athletes, anyone working in the open air, or exercising, would have worn either an off the shoulder tunic, for ease of movement and to keep cool, or some form of loincloth or kilt tied at the waist, depending on their status and profession. This would have been an everyday sight, particularly in a Mediterranean climate, and entirely appropriate for farmhands, builders, outdoor workers, and gladiators. The Italian custom, regardless of the aberrant behaviour of the few, was always to preserve modesty by covering the genital area.

78 Carved bone figure of a *murmillo* gladiator from Lexden, Colchester. *Illustration: Iain Bell, courtesy of Essex County Council, Historic Environment dept*

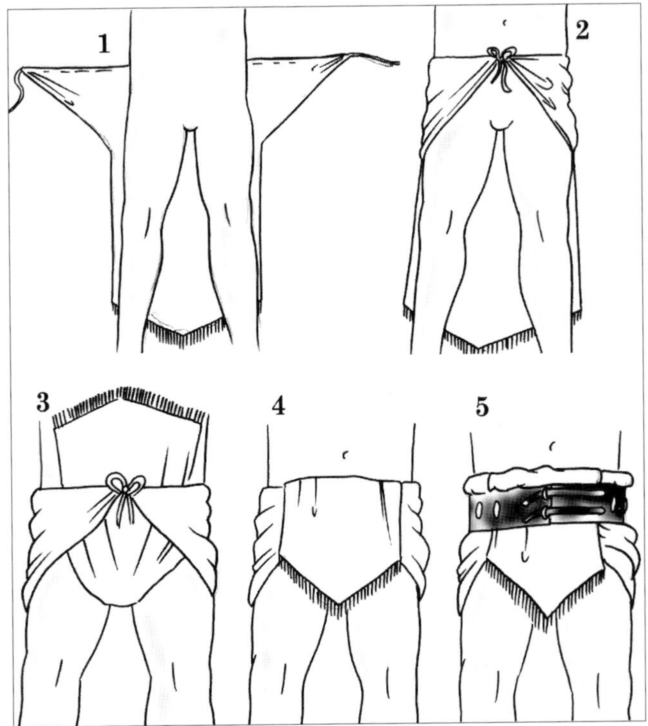

79 Alternative methods of fastening the gladiatorial *subligaria*

Depictions of gladiators show another type of garment for the lower body was a form of kilt, which was basically two semi-circles, formed from a length of cloth strategically arranged at back and front and hitched up at the sides, to make inverted V shapes at the tops of the thighs, and held in position with a belt (*80a* and *80b*). This latter garment inevitably begs the question of how modesty was preserved during strenuous physical encounters; another 'underwear' loincloth, as worn by soldiers under their tunics, might well have been worn. Many representations of gladiators wearing *subligaria* show a decorative exaggerated fringe hanging from the hem of the front 'apron'; perhaps this flashy garment indicates the kind of gladiator we would think of as professional, with an enthusiastic fanbase, a celebrity image to keep up, and some accumulated wealth due to his success in the arena. On the other hand, it could be standard livery for a particularly smart *familia gladiatoria*. We should beware of dressing all gladiators in rags, sweat and desperation, *á la* Hollywood. The true picture has gladiators from the imperial *ludus* in gold-embroidered purple cloaks, ornate helmets, silver weapons, peacock and ostrich feathers at one end of the spectrum, and at the other, shivering wretches straight off the *catasta*, the slave block, clutching rusty swords.

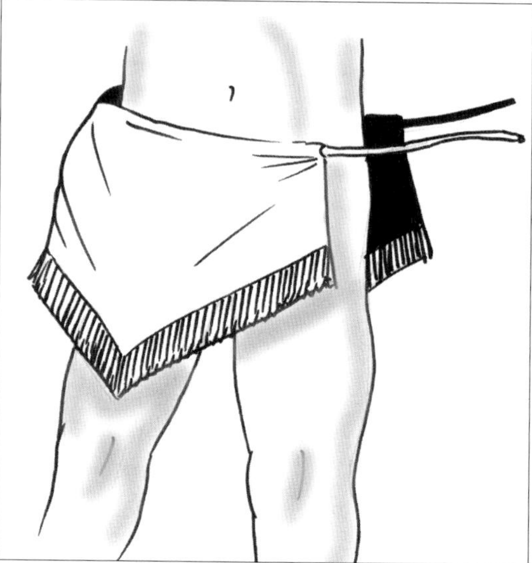

80a Above left Reconstructed gladiatorial *subligaculum* of ornate design, with typical wide belt. *Photograph: Fraser Gray*

80b Above right Possible pattern for *subligaculum*

SECUTOR

It will be obvious by now that any attempt to keep the gladiatorial categories from overlapping each other is doomed to failure. There is much we know about the types of gladiator, but exceptions to the (rather elastic) rule are capable of throwing the definitions, indistinct as they are, into confusion. With that in mind, the first thing to note about the *secutor* is the name: meaning 'chaser, pursuer', it highlights the reason for this particular gladiator's existence. Otherwise known as the *contraretiarius*, the *secutor* fought the *retiarius* (*81*, *colour plates 17* and *18*); it is thought that the category was specially created for that purpose; if that origin is authentic, then there is some justification for thinking that the *secutor* was an offshoot of the *murmillo*.

In a nutshell, the arms and armour of the *secutor* were the same as those of the *murmillo*, and only the form of the helmet differed; it was brimless and had only a low, smooth, featureless crest following the curve of the bowl (*colour plates 19, 20* and *21*). The back of the helmet curled into a small neck-guard (*82*). Unlike other helmets with metal grilles forming the upper half of the visor, the *secutor* helmet enclosed the face completely; the visor had only two small eyeholes, each a scant inch (3cm) in diameter, and although it was hinged to open from the side, it had a catch on the exterior to 'lock' the gladiator in it. Much has been made of the bronze statuette from Arles, in southern France, which features a 'working' visor. Unfortunately, it is not a good example of how the visor actually opened. From the few archaeological finds of this type of helmet, it seems the visor had small hinges on either side in the vicinity of the temples; thus, it would have opened, in a limited way, outwards rather than upwards. However, it does give a good impression of the sinister and anonymous appearance of the *secutor*.

The helmet would have been padded in some way; indeed, in experiments with reconstructions, this style of helmet, more than any other, has been shown to require some form of buffer where the nose meets the metal; this is due to the way the metal follows the face contours more closely, unlike other types. It is this 'snug' fit that made it very claustrophobic to wear, indeed much more so than the other visored types, which were pleasant by comparison. Also, the vision of the gladiator would have been very limited; it must have interfered with peripheral vision to the extent that in order to see something to the right, the head would have to turn to face it. This would obviously be a liability when fighting an agile, fast-moving opponent such as the *retiarius* tended to be. Hearing also would have been somewhat affected due to the close-fitting nature of the helmet.

The limitations of the helm seem specifically designed to make the bout more challenging for both combatants, and therefore more exciting for the crowd. Its smoothness and lack of features meant that the net, once cast, would simply slide off without catching or snagging, which made for a more exciting balance between the two combatants. In experiments with reconstructed equipment, it proved almost impossible to snag the net on the helmet; out of every ten casts,

81 Secutor gladiator

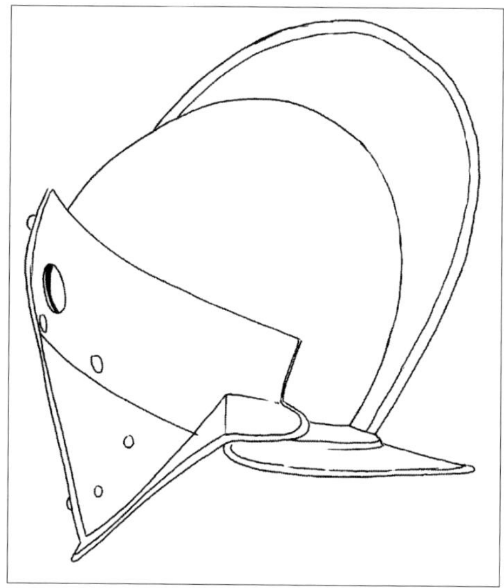

82 Secutor helmet

one or two would initially catch, but of those, only a few would hold long enough to allow the *secutor* to be trapped. Only a damaged or badly maintained helmet might afford the net some purchase, via metal edges or parts standing up from the otherwise smooth surface.

So, although the *secutor* had an exceptionally protective helmet of thicker than average metal, he paid for that with the trade-off loss in vision and hearing, and to some extent breathing capacity.

It would not be impossible for a *retiarius* to get in a fluke blow where the trident prong plunged through the eyehole, but apart from that kind of rarity, the head of the *secutor* was almost too well protected. Aside from its practical functions, the look of the helmet was important as it echoed the fish theme by having the appearance of something that might be seen on a fishmonger's slab. Its smooth streamlined form, complete with fin-like crest, particularly in a shiny metal finish, had a strong resemblance to a fish head – like the bream or *mormyros*.

An exotic permutation of the *secutor* was the *scissor*, which appeared in the eastern empire (*83*). The helmet was exactly the same as that of the *secutor*, and short greaves were worn, but a coat of scale or ringmail was worn as body armour. The *scissor* carried a *gladius* but not a shield; instead of the shield, his left arm had a *manica* terminating in a hollow metal tube into which his forearm and hand fitted. At the end of this bizarre device was a small crescent-shaped blade affixed by a metal shank to the main body of the tube. Like the *secutor*, the *scissor* fought the *retiarius*, with the lunate blade presumably being used to attack and defend, perhaps even to cut through the net in the event of entanglement.

83 An exotic and rare permutation of the *secutor* was the *scissor* gladiator. *Based on the research of Marcus Junkelmann*

RETIARIUS

Of all the gladiator categories, the most instantly recognisable is that of the *retiarius*, the net and trident fighter, named after the net he used, *rete* (*84a*). Until halfway through the first century AD, there is no record, whether pictorial, literary, or archaeological, of this type of gladiator. After that point, the traditional pairing of *retiarius* and *secutor* starts to appear regularly, quickly becoming one of the most popular and enduring of the arena combats. From this, it is fair to assume that the *secutor* was invented at the same time as the *retiarius*, in order to create an exciting and novel combat; nothing like it can be detected at any earlier point in the historical record.

The reason for the comparatively sudden appearance of this type of fighter cannot even be guessed at, and the usual sources are silent on the subject. All other categories of gladiator have an originating connection, however weak, with military or martial activities; the *retiarius*, with his obvious fishing and sea-related equipment, does not follow that pattern. The best we can do is to agree that the Roman appetite for watching new and inventive ways of killing may have inspired this innovation (*84b*). That it was a success is beyond doubt; the *retiarius* and his opponent, the *secutor*, persisted as a pairing until the gladiatorial spectacles were themselves abolished.

The equipment of the *retiarius* is what distinguishes him so obviously from all the rest. There is never any ambiguity about the identity of a net-fighter. Above

84a Retiarius gladiator

84b Illustration of tomb relief, showing a *retiarius* engaging a *secutor* gladiator from the top of a *pons*, or bridge, erected in the arena

all, he carried the trident, known usually as the *fuscina* or, less often, *tridens*; it was a weapon used by no other category of gladiator. The trident was peculiar to the *retiarius*, as was the net he used. So many depictions of the *retiarius* show him holding the trident with both hands, with the left arm (as that is usually the leading arm for right-handers) forward and the right arm back at an angle, ready to thrust, that this is possibly the textbook stance for trident fighting. His body armour consisted solely of a high metal shoulder-guard, the *galerus*, on his left, or leading, shoulder, overlapping and affixed to the top edge of a *manica* protecting the left arm (*85* and *86*). Of course, this presupposes that the *retiarius* was right-handed, and that he would therefore cast his net with his right hand, while gripping his trident and dagger in the left hand. However, in a fragment of relief, one of the very few representations of this gladiator to actually show him with a net (from Chester, Cheshire, and now in Saffron Walden Museum), he is holding it in his left hand (*colour plate 23*). What is more, the *galerus* and *manica* are on his right shoulder and arm, and he grips the trident in his right hand. This complete reversal of his weapons and armour seems to show a left-handed *retiarius*. The style of the relief is quite unsophisticated, yet it conveys quite unequivocally the standard appearance of the retiarius: bareheaded, bare upper torso, *subligaria*, *galerus*, *manica*, *fuscina*, *rete*.

There is one aberrant depiction of a gladiator with trident and shield; it is a poorly executed graffito from a wall in Pompeii, and it is clearly not a *retiarius*, because the fighter appears to be helmeted, yet he carries what seems to be a trident. This combination, if accurately represented, must have been difficult to manage, to say the least, since the trident requires two hands on the shaft for maximum impact. For that reason, it would be better to treat the graffito as an interesting conundrum, nothing more.

With no helmet, greaves or shield, the standard was much less weighed down than the heavily armoured gladiators, and also *retiarius* he had no means of disguise. It is precisely this high visibility that made it such a scandal to become a *retiarius*, more so than any other gladiator. As a rule, the less concealed the gladiator's face and body were, the lower his status. The net fighter was not regarded in such high esteem as his helmeted, more warlike colleagues; his status was at the bottom of the gladiatorial pecking order. This is made clear in the contemptuous tone of the poet Juvenal's satirical dig at a young nobleman of the aristocratic Gracchi family, who was *dedecus Urbis*, 'the disgrace of Rome', because he deliberately chose to be a gladiator, and a *retiarius* to boot:

> Beyond this, what is there, except the gladiatorial school? And that's where you've got the disgrace of Rome: a Gracchus fighting, but not in a murmillo's gear, and not with shield or curving blade. He rejects that sort of get-up, you see: look, he's brandishing a trident. Once he has poised his right hand and cast the trailing net without success, he raises his bare face to the spectators and runs off, highly recognisable, all through the arena. There is no mistaking his tunic, ... (Juvenal, *Satirae* VIII 199-208)

85 Left Bronze *galerus*, or shoulder-guard, from Pompeii

86 Below *Retiarius*, watched by centurion, turns the *galerus* towards his opponent to deflect a blow. *Reconstruction: Britannia and Roman Military Research Society. Photograph: Fraser Gray*

In the next line there is also a reference to his shoulder-guard having decorative fastenings: *de faucibus aurea cum se porrigat, et longo iactetur spira galero* – 'extending from his neck, the twisted golden cord streaming out behind his tall shoulder-guard'. All in all, this young Gracchus was making an aristocratic spectacle of himself, dressed as a *retiarius* with an eye-catching *ensemble*. Nonetheless, it just increased the sense of scandal, because not only was he a *retiarius*, but an amateur one at that, indicated by the tunic he wore; tunics were definitely out for professionals – they invariably had bare torsos. In another satire, Juvenal conveys the sense of scorn directed at *retiarii* generally, and draws a distinction between the ones who wore tunics, indicating their amateur status, and professionals:

> Then there's the fact that the nets aren't kept alongside the tunics of disgrace, and that the shoulder-guards and the trident of the gladiator who fights naked are not stored in the same locker. Such souls are relegated to the lowest section of the school and in their prison they have different chains. (Juvenal, *Satirae* VI 354-358)

So not only was Gracchus a despised and lowly gladiator, he had made it 10 times worse by parading the fact of his voluntary fall from high society to arena – he showed his face. And he wore a tunic, one of the 'tunics of disgrace', which identified him as being in the ranks of the lowest of the low, quite literally. To be a *retiarius* meant even your equipment was despised; it seems the *lanista* would make a point of storing the equipment of the gladiators in different places, according to their status. The *retiarius* was given the poorest living quarters, but this would not have troubled rich boy Gracchus, as he was fighting as a free man, a volunteer, not a slave, and therefore probably billeted in luxury accommodation elsewhere.

There is a faint suggestion that the wearing of a tunic, to be one of the *tunicati*, implied some kind of effeminacy, which was deplored, at least by the social commentators – but then, with few exceptions, they were observing the vulgar world from a lofty, usually aristocratic standpoint, where 'the good old days' had been replaced by a rapidly degenerating society. In their view, anyway: what the ordinary Roman in the street thought about the *retiarius* was obvious from the longevity and popularity of that style of fighter.

Some depictions of the net-fighter show him in an off-the-shoulder tunic instead of *subligaria*. Regardless of how, or whether, his body was clothed, the item of armour he always wore was the *galerus* (*85*). This was made from sheet metal, usually bronze, and was fixed by straps to the *manica* worn on the upper arm, and possibly anchored by a further leather strap passing across the upper torso. The guard plate of the *galerus* extended upwards from the shoulder, to a height of approximately 6in (15cm), although this varies slightly in the known examples. A *galerus,* one of three found in the gladiator barracks at Pompeii, has significant decorative emblems on it, a crab, an anchor, and a dolphin entwined with a trident, all connected to the fisherman background of the *retiarius*.

Other examples of the *galerus* are plainer; some, seen in mosaics and reliefs, seem too tall to be practical, but that is probably due to artistic exaggeration. The main property of the *galerus* was that it was like having a little shield strapped to your shoulder, leaving the hands free to wield the trident, net, and long knife or dagger (*86*); the dagger was the *pugio* that every *retiarius* carried as an extra weapon and for emergencies, like cutting the net free of the trident if it should inadvertently get entangled in the mesh. There is a graceful example of a *pugio* found at Pompeii, with an iron blade of which the tang runs the full length of the grip; the grip is of bone with a pommel and guard of ivory. This is a weapon of prestige, not the dagger of a *tiro retiarius*. Wearing the *galerus*, with the head tucked in, and shoulder turned side on, the otherwise vulnerable *retiarius* could improve his defences. The *galerus* was light to wear, about 1lb (1.1-1.2kg) or so in weight, so it did not impede movement at all, and mobility was the *retiarius*' main advantage.

The net of the *retiarius* is rarely shown, perhaps because of the artistic difficulty in depicting its mesh. The impression given by the few existing representations is that it was a round net, *rete* or *iaculum* (from the Latin *iactare*, to throw, cast, fling), which is the most workable shape, judging from experiments. The edges were weighted with lead pellets, pebbles, amber maybe, or even as in one famous combat in the presence of the emperor, pieces of gold. In a reconstruction of such a net, it was found that the key factors influencing the efficacy of the net were shape, in that a circular net was better for coverage of the opponent once cast, and weight and density of the cord used. The size of the mesh was of secondary importance, although larger mesh was obviously more entangling. An alternative to weights around the net's circumference is a heavier grade of rope or cord edging it; this has the advantage of easier maintenance, as the individual weights have the tendency to fall off occasionally.

From experiments, it seems likely that the technique of the *retiarius* was as follows: he would hold the net ready in his right hand (assuming that was the dominant hand), taking care not to let the net trail and get caught in the trident, by dipping the prongs down while he then cast the net underarm. The net itself is shown in some depictions as having a loop to attach it to the wrist, so it can be retrieved easily, and not become a liability, trip-hazard or opportunity for the other fighter.

The trident itself was a formidable weapon in skilled hands. The prongs were closer together than is commonly imagined; it was presumably based on some form of actual fishing trident, *fuscina*, in which case the prongs would have been close enough to ensure all three could make contact somewhere along the length of a medium sized fish. An early Etruscan fishing scene shows a trident in use from the side of a small boat. There is evidence for a spear being substituted for the trident on occasion; again, spear fishing was doubtless a common activity among the fishing fraternity.

As an addition to the *pugio*, secondary weapon of the *retiarius*, there is evidence for an unusual four-pronged weapon on a tomb-relief from Romania. A *retiarius* holds the un-named weapon in his right hand, and trident and *pugio* in his left (*87* and *88*). On the tombstone only three long prongs are visible, but this may be due to the artistic difficulty in representing three-dimensional perspective. Until recently, archaeologists had held the view that this weapon was a fanciful creation by the sculptor; an alternative theory was that it had some unknown religious significance.

87 *Retiarius* holding an unusual four-pronged weapon on a tomb relief from Romania. *Reproduced with kind permission and assistance of Marcus Junkelmann*

88 Detail of the mystery pronged weapon

In 1993 an exciting series of discoveries was made at Ephesus, in Turkey, when, in the course of an entirely different archaeological survey, a cemetery for gladiators was found to be nestling under an overgrown orchard. Within this cemetery, many tombstones with epitaphs were revealed, showing that many of the burials were of gladiators.

When the bones were removed for analysis, they had evidence of many old wounds, some fatal, some not. One bone in particular proved to be vital in the interpretation of the mystery weapon (*89*). When Professor Karl Grossschmidt, the expert anthropologist, was examining a femur bone of a particular skeleton, he noted that there were four odd looking marks in a square pattern. It is believed that the marks in the bone were the result of an injury sustained during combat, particularly as that part of the body would not have been well protected. Because of the distinctive pattern of the injury, there is strong evidence to believe that this particular, non-fatal wound was inflicted by the mystery four-pronged weapon.

When Tim Noyes, an ancient blade specialist and reconstruction armourer, was approached about the possibility of recreating this weapon, his first reaction on examining the depiction on the tombstone was that it represented some form of sword trapper and breaker, for defence rather than attack. However, after looking at the bone injury, he realised that the four prongs would have been too close to trap any blade; therefore, the purpose of the weapon must have been primarily offensive.

89 Femur bone of a skeleton from the Ephesus gladiator cemetery, with four distinct indentations in a square pattern, possibly caused by a four-pronged weapon displayed on the Romanian tomb relief (*87*). *After Professor Karl Grossschmidt, University of Vienna*

In other reconstructions, the prongs have been round-section for their entire length, but his reconstruction used four square-section prongs, rounded and sharpened only at the tips (*90*). His argument for this method is that ancient processes would have meant that square forged prongs would have been consistently stronger and easier to produce than their round counterparts before the advent of oil tempering. An additional advantage of this method of manufacture is that the four square bars used to make the prongs can be heated in a forge and twisted to form a once-piece handle and tang, which gives the weapon greater resistance to breaking (*91*).

The reconstruction has longer prongs than that pictured on the Romanian tombstone; the reasoning behind this decision is that the damage on the femur bone as shown could only be caused by a blow of very great force; the longer prongs deliver this type of impact because they enable the gladiator to put more weight behind the thrust. In the absence of any actual artefact to refer to, the construction of the hilt relied upon the depiction on the tombstone. Obviously square, and held at an angle, the hilt seemed to be a flattened box shape, so the reconstruction used a bronze holder to contain a wooden insert through which the prongs would pass, increasing its stability and strength (*92* and *93*).

The mystery weapon, as depicted, has shorter prongs, but in the overall context of the style of the tombstone, it is clear that the sculptor was not recreating his subject to natural proportions, for example the entire trident shaft looks too thick to be useable.

90 Metal rods at initial stage of manufacture for armourer Tim Noyes' interpretation of the mystery weapon known in his workshop as the 'Ephesian Teeth'

91 Twisting the rods to form the basic weapon

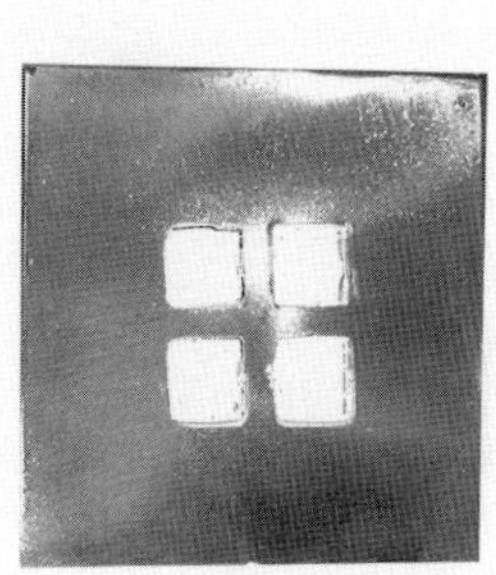

92 Components of the mystery weapon

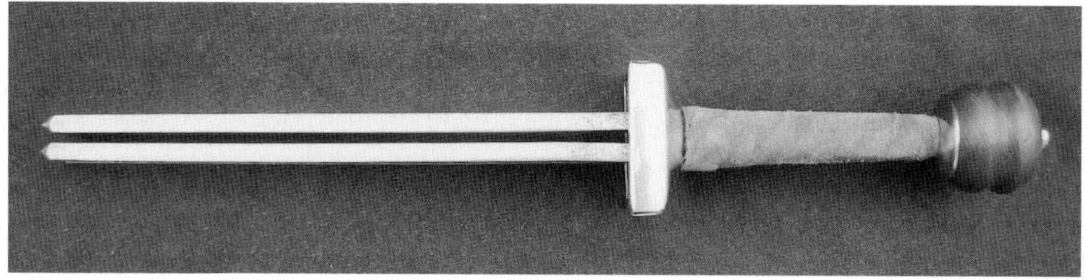

93 The finished weapon. The armourer concluded that although the four puncture wounds could have been caused by rounded points, ancient metal production and hardening techniques meant that square section prongs were easier to produce and harden

How widespread the occurrence of this unknown weapon was, we do not know, but it is indicative of more than purely local use that the only two potential proofs of its existence lie hundreds of miles apart (*94*).

The *retiarius* was always paired with the *secutor*, his 'pursuer' or 'chaser'; only much later in the imperial period did the *murmillo* become his adversary. A little-known variant of the *retiarius* was the *laquearius*, who had all of the equipment of the *retiarius*, but with a rope lasso instead of a net, though it has been thought that the lasso man might have been a light entertainer, a novelty act, like the *paegniarius*.

PAEGNIARIUS

The *paegniarii* seem to have been comedy fighters, whose combats did not involve sharp weapons and were played strictly for laughs. They have an ancient pedigree, more related to the Atellan farces from which they seem to have strayed. They would presumably have been deployed in the intervals between more bloodthirsty parts of the programme, at lunchtime perhaps, to hold the crowd's interest and to provide light relief.

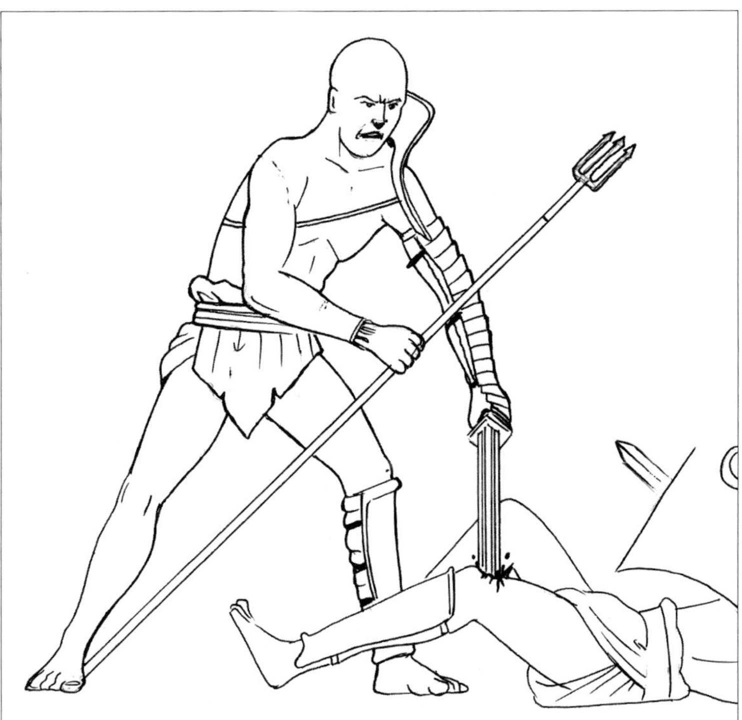

94 *Retiarius* using the four-pronged 'Ephesian Teeth'

A variant on the usual *paegniarius* was offered by Caligula, who, as Suetonius relates, 'would stage comic duels between respectable householders who happened to be physically disabled in some way or other'. In depictions of *paegniarii*, they do not wear armour, and they carry only non-lethal weapons, like whips and sticks. So the knockabout contests they performed would not have presented much danger to life and limb, as is indicated by the inscription on the grave of the *paegniarius* Secundus; it proudly states he was attached to the *familia* at the *Ludus Magnus*, the great imperial gladiator training school next to the Colosseum, that it was the *familia* who had set up the memorial, and that he lived to the ripe old age of *annis XCVIII, mensibu(s) VIII, diebus XVIII.*

CRUPELLARIUS

This was an extremely heavily armed gladiator originating in Gaul, a type first mentioned by the first century AD historian, Tacitus (95). In an account of the revolt of Julius Florus and Julius Sacrovir in AD 21, the *crupellarii*, heavily-armoured Gallic gladiators fought against the Roman legionaries. Tacitus gives a colourful account of the outcome:

95 Interpretation of a *crupellarius*, a heavily-armed gladiator originating in Gaul

> There was also a party of slaves training to be gladiators. Completely encased in iron in the national fashion, these *crupellarii*, as they were called, were too clumsy for offensive purposes but impregnable in defence … the infantry made a frontal attack. The Gallic flanks were driven in. The iron-clad contingent caused some delay as their casing resisted javelins and swords. However the Romans used axes and mattocks and struck at their plating and its wearers like men demolishing a wall. Others knocked down the immobile gladiators with poles or pitchforks, and, lacking the power to rise, they were left for dead. (Tacitus, *Annales* III. 43)

Gladiators with that amount of heavy armour were unknown elsewhere in the Roman empire, but a small figurine found at Versigny, France, fitting the description of a *crupellarius*, shows a 'robotic' looking gladiator clad almost entirely in plate armour from head to foot (*96*). The helmet has a perforated bucket appearance, and it is not difficult to imagine the Roman legionaries being impressed by their adversaries' defences. A theory advanced by M.C. Bishop and J.C.N. Coulston is that this gallic armour composed of articulated iron strips could have been the forerunner of the so-called *lorica segmentata* of the early Imperial Roman infantryman, yet another example of Roman military borrowing and adaptation.

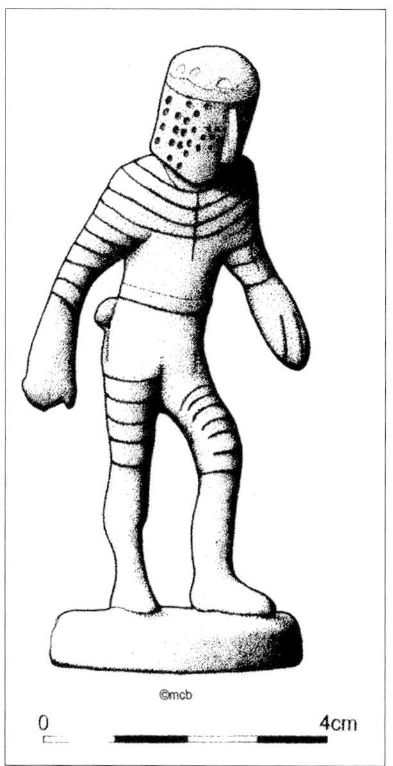

96 Small figurine found at Versigny, France, fitting the description of a *crupellarius*. *Reproduced with kind permission of M. Bishop*

GLADIATRIX

The subject of female gladiators has always aroused strong emotions; then as now, they have been seen as aberrations or novelties (*97*). There are a few references to women fighters in the literary sources, and some evidence from inscriptions on monuments. From these pieces of evidence, the existence of the *gladiatrix* as an authentic gladiatorial category rather than a fevered fantasy can be established; however, proof of existence is not the same as a guarantee of frequency of occurrence. Juvenal gives a scathing picture of the wannabe *gladiatrix*:

> Everyone knows about the purple wraps and the women's wrestling floors. And everyone's seen the battered training post, hacked away by her repeated sword thrusts and bashed by her shield. The lady goes through all the drill, absolutely qualified for the trumpet at the festival of Flora. Unless, of course, in her heart she's planning something more and is practising for the real arena. What sense of modesty can you find in a woman wearing a helmet, who runs away from her own gender? It's violence she likes. All the same, she wouldn't want to be a man – after all, the pleasure we experience is so little in comparison! What a fine sight it would be if there were an auction of your wife's things – her sword belt and her arm protectors and her crests and the half-size shin guard for her left leg! Or, if it's a different kind of battle that she fights, you'll be in bliss as your girl sells off her greaves! Yet

97 Gladiatrix. Still picture from Channel 4's *Gladiator Girl (director: J. Freeston), YAP. Subject: Mandy Turner, Britannia*

> these are women who break out into a sweat in the thinnest wrap and whose delicate skin is chafed by the finest wisp of silk. Hark at her roaring while she drives home the thrusts she's been taught. Hark at the weight of the helmet that has her wilting, at the size and the thickness of the bandages that surround her knees – and then have a laugh when she takes off her armour to pick up the chamber pot. (Juvenal, *Satirae* VI 246-264)

The woman so unkindly described by Juvenal was obviously 'playing at it', and he makes the point that she was practising at the training post, the *palus*, using a wooden sword, *rudis*, and perhaps had some ambition to go into the arena with real weapons, although from his account of the soft life she normally led, it would seem that she was just a lady of means with a new-found enthusiasm for the world of the gladiator.

An example of a wooden sword that has amazingly survived nearly two thousand years was found during excavations at the Flavian timber fort at Carlisle, which was established in AD 72 or 73 (*25*). The sword is dated not later than AD 83 or 84, and is made of oak. Its shape replicates a *gladius*, and the sword measures about 22in (572mm) from pommel to tip. It has a semi-circular pommel, and the overall width of the sword tapers gradually down to the point. Although this was found in a military context, there is no reason to think it is not typical of practice swords in general. Because it was found in a gatehouse of the fort, the possibility of it being a child's toy sword is remote, and indeed its size, which mirrors that of the real *gladius*, makes that very unlikely. A replica made from naturally dried Roman oak from the same fort was too hard to shape accurately with a knife. The *rudis* needed to be robust to stand up to repeated impacts. Juvenal's *gladiatrix* may well have wielded something similar at the practice *palus*.

In general, Rome was not in favour of female gladiators, because they offended the strong Roman sense of propriety – by entering the arena, that bastion of hyper-masculine, not to mention military, virtue, they were in the wrong place, almost insultingly so. Nero, ever the exception in terms of Roman propriety, enjoyed watching the *gladiatrices*, and even made some of the wives of the aristocracy take up weapons and fight each other. But this did nothing to increase general acceptance. As a rule, the business of the arena did not create equality as we might think of it; instead, it positively thrived on the promotion of inequality – of skill, defences, height, and of course, strength.

Yet the prevailing attitude of the public was that it was somehow shocking, if undoubtedly thrilling, to see a woman fight as a *gladiatrix* (*98* and *99*). In the arena, the chaos and disorder of the world was put to rights with displays of criminals executed, animals (and hence nature) conquered, wrongs repaid, death called up to order. It was a microcosm of the *imperium*; if women entered the arena to fight as a man would fight, rather than simply to be executed in a beast spectacle or by fire or sword, or by some other ingenious and hideous method, it was a challenge to the order of things. Which is not to say it didn't happen – it did, but not frequently enough for it to be classified as part of the regular spectacle.

To judge from the evidence, which is thin, it is unlikely that most people in the provinces ever saw women fight; if they did, it might be as a peculiarity of a particular area with an unusual supply of suitable women combatants; equally, it might be a once in a lifetime occurrence, a genuine novelty.

The likelihood of seeing the *gladiatrix* would depend on their availability, and it is fair to say that, if they were used on as regular a basis as men, one might expect to find inscriptions or other epigraphical evidence advertising their impending performance occurring as frequently in the archaeological evidence as do those of their male counterparts. No such confirmation is seen. Indeed, their comparative rarity is indicated by the proud boast of the Ostian *editor*, on a municipal inscription, '*Qui primus omnium ab urbe condita ludus cum ...or et mulieres ad ferrum dedit*' – 'who was the first of all since Rome was founded to make women fight', (88.2 [1976], 612) recorded in a collection of inscriptions from Ostia by the French School at Rome.

In his 'Book of the Shows', *Liber de Spectaculis*, the poet Martial provides invaluable background information to the spectacles presented in the recently

98 Rome's fascination with women warriors from classical myth to the Renaissance provided inspiration for the appearance of the reconstructed *gladiatrix*. As the exposed breasts shown on this wounded Amazon might offend a modern audience, shaped female breastplates are often worn as a creative alternative in reconstructions

99 Protective female breastplate. *Subject: Mandy Turner, Britannia*

completed Colosseum (Flavian amphitheatre) by the emperor Titus. He seems to confirm the appearance of women in the arena in two epigrams:

> It is not enough that warrior Mars serves you in unconquered arms, Caesar. Venus herself serves you too. Illustrious fame used to sing of the lion laid low in Nemea's spacious vale, Hercules' work. Let ancient testimony be silent, for after your shows, Caesar, we have now seen such things done by women's valour. (Martial, *Liber de Spectaculis* 7,8)

Yet though they were often despised, laughed at, or treated as exotic novelties, like the dwarfs the emperor Domitian once pitted against them, it is clear from Martial's words that women were capable of evoking admiration for their courage and skill in the arena, however infrequent such bouts might have been.

Another example of a woman fighting in the arena comes from Juvenal again (*Satirae* I, 22-23), when he mentions how 'Mevia shoots the Tuscan boar, holding the hunting spears with one breast bared!' Here, he is referring to a woman *venatrix*, a wild-beast hunter who is portraying herself in a disgraceful manner, as a bare-breasted Amazon in a *venatio*. In this depiction, we see again the Roman taste for myth in the arena, in the well-used format of the Amazon. The emperor Commodus had an obsession with gladiators and Amazons, and extended that obsession to his mistress:

> He was called Amazonius because of his passion for his concubine Marcia, whom he loved to have depicted as an Amazon, and for whose sake he even wished to enter the Roman arena in Amazon's dress. (*Scriptores Historiae Augustae*, Commodus 12.1)

There will always be an anxious debate over the ability of women fighters, especially in a professional situation such as serving in frontline combat and this confirms one of mankind's most enduring, if discriminatory, beliefs – women are not physically capable of summoning up the aggression or the brute strength needed for hand to hand fighting.

Admiral Sir Michael Boyce (former Chief of Defence staff) stated in 2001 that he believed aggressiveness is not a 'natural female trait' His comments came at a time when the British Army had just carried out an assessment of the feasibility of women serving in frontline infantry and tank units. Admiral Boyce acknowledged that some women may be able to meet the physical demands of frontline operations, but he questioned whether they could cope in close combat: 'Fighting in a ship or in an aeroplane is a lot different from having to take it hand-to-hand to the enemy. They are not required to close with the enemy and eyeball them and be very aggressive.'

This is not an isolated viewpoint. Our culture finds it surprising, shocking even, that women should fight, should seek to fight, and even be good at it. Yet there are now developments in admitting women to one of the most physically challenging arms of all the armed forces, the Parachute Regiment; a woman lieutenant in the Royal Logistic Corps has recently been accepted to undertake their gruelling training course in an attempt to become the first female to join. She will compete alongside men in a twenty-mile march carrying a 35lb pack and rifle, an aerial obstacle course and a boxing match. The fact that this item made its way into the newspapers and other media indicates that it is still newsworthy when a woman attempts to compete with men in the physical arena. We do not share the Roman opinion that this is scandalous, quite the reverse, but we do share their sense of the novelty of the event; otherwise, it would not have generated column inches or airtime.

Of course, there have always women who have been shining examples of successful combativeness, but they are too few to provide an antidote to the cultural taboo. Such a prejudice had its counterpart in ancient Rome, where the audience in the amphitheatre watching a female gladiator enjoyed a similar mixture of scandalised fascination. It is important to understand that the rarity and novelty of women gladiators, or *gladiatrices*, gave them a greater entertainment value. Added to that, the social shock of seeing a woman, particularly if she was high class, voluntarily fighting in the arena, cannot be over emphasised.

Gladiators were the lowest of the low, *aut perditi homines aut barbari*, 'either abandoned men or barbarians', as Cicero put it, so for noblewomen to join their ranks must have been a double scandal.

Evidence for the existence of female gladiators comes mainly from Roman writers. Suetonius tells of the extravagant entertainments laid on by Domitian: gladiatorial shows by torchlight in which women as well as men took part.

The poet and satirist, Martial, who enjoyed the patronage of Domitian, flattered him shamelessly by praising a contest he gave in which women were pitted against dwarfs. It was apparently a big hit with the general populace. The historian Cassius Dio tells how Nero aimed to impress the visiting Parthian king Triades by having his freedman Patrobius arrange an expensive show at Puteoli in AD 66, which consisted entirely of Ethiopians, male and female, young and old. In that show, the performers were probably not gladiators, however, but prisoners of war.

Also during the reign of Nero, we hear from Tacitus that Roman women of high status, as well as male senators, fought at the Emperor's command at Rome in AD 63:

> The same year witnessed gladiatorial displays on a no less magnificent scale than before, but exceeding all precedent in the number of distinguished women and senators disgracing themselves in the arena. (Tacitus, *Annales* XV 29)

Petronius, one of Nero's favourite writers, has one of his guests at his 'Trimalchio's Banquet' talking about a show in which there will be a woman who fights in a chariot (*essedaria*). This is a type of *gladiatrix* for which there is no pictorial evidence, only literary references. Indeed, there is not one depiction of a chariot in the context of the arena whether driven by female (*essedaria*) or male (*essedarius*), yet they are mentioned quite frequently, particularly on inscriptions, where the contrasting fortunes of two male *essedarii* make it clear that chariot-fighting was just as demanding as combat on foot. One, Caius Iulius Iucundus was an *essedarius* who died aged 25 years old, the other, Maximus Iulianus, was also an *essedarius*, who had fought 40 times, and had won the laurel crown of victory, the *corona*, 36 times (*CIL*,VI 4335, *CIL*,VI 33952).

Taking account of all of the references to *gladiatrices*, it is clear that women in gladiatorial shows did not come from one specific social group. The provenance of *gladiatrices*, as with their male counterparts, was diverse and unhindered by status, for as previously discussed, they could be slave or free, rich or poor, prisoner of war or volunteers. Obviously, in the case of slaves, they had no choice in the matter. A slave of either sex on the auction block, the *catasta*, who looked a good prospect for the arena, who perhaps possessed special combat skills, or whose appearance was unusual or outstanding in some respect, might well find themselves purchased and added to a troupe of gladiators.

For the free man (or woman) to fight as a gladiator was the ultimate humiliation, a social death and doubly so for the woman, whose motivation for such an apparently insane plunge into the gutter can only be guessed at. As mentioned above, the writer Juvenal leaves us in no doubt how worthy of scorn and ridicule he considered them to be, although we must be careful not to assume that his contempt was shared by the entire populace. He was, after all, a satirist, highlighting the extremes in the society he observed.

Quite apart from the obvious disdain Juvenal conveys for this type of woman, his withering scorn fortuitously carries a wealth of incidental detail about the gladiatorial equipment often worn by them. Of most importance is the reference to the wearing of a heavy helmet, *galea*, with plumes, as the theory has been advanced that, of all varieties of fighter, that of *gladiatrix* is the least likely to hide her gender by concealing the face, of course, there are other ways that an audience can tell, but it seems a waste of the shock value not to draw attention to the female identity in this way.

This seems to be borne out by the first- or second-century AD stone relief carving, from Halicarnassus (modern Bodrum, Turkey), now in the British Museum, of two female gladiators in combat, in a face-to-face stance like male fighters (*100*). The Greek inscription tells us they are called Amazonia and Achilleia (probably stage names), that they had been granted honourable release from the arena (*missio*), and probably gained their freedom in the process, in view of the commemorative plaque. This implies that they had given crowd-pleasing performances on a number of occasions, demonstrating the clear advantage of being a rare and luxurious novelty on the day's programme of events. After all, what *lanista* in his right mind would permit and encourage the killing of a major asset?

It would seem that women fighters could, by virtue of their skill, courage and sheer novelty value, survive long enough to gain their freedom and glowing

100 Relief carving, from Halicarnassus (modern Bodrum, Turkey), now in the British Museum, of two female gladiators in combat. The Greek inscription tells us they are called Amazonia and Achilleia, and that they received their freedom

tributes in stone. In the case of Achillea and her fellow *gladiatrix* Amazonia they received the unquantifiable gift of freedom.

As the celebratory inscription gives no clue as to their country (or countries) of origin, and their names have obviously been chosen as suitably heroic and mythical, these women could have been born anywhere within the Roman empire. That they were slaves is certain, for they received their freedom as a reward, yet there is no way of knowing by what tortuous route they arrived in the arena.

It is possible that they were amongst prisoners of war taken captive during one of Rome's many campaigns; perhaps they came from proud people with a warrior tradition, such as the Dacians, whose later defeat and subsequent enslavement is portrayed on Trajan's column.

Romans were very familiar with stories about the mythical Amazons from epics like the *Iliad*, and they enjoyed watching gladiatorial combats dressed up as myths. It does not take too great a leap of imagination to see how the two female gladiators could have been promoted as re-enacting one of the many ancient conflicts from legend, hence their stage names.

On their travels, it is likely that the *gladiatrices* encountered shrines to Nemesis, often located within the confines of the arena itself, wherever their precarious, involuntary profession took them. Nemesis had started as a deity of fate, possibly originating at an ancient site of her cult, Rhamnous in Greece. Like the Greek Furies, the Erinyes, she was not an avenger at first, but simply an unbiased agent of fortune, suddenly swooping down with outstretched wings to dispense death indiscriminately. In this aspect, she has similarities to the Etruscan Vanth, the beautiful winged woman who is depicted as present at the death of a person, ready to take his soul to the nether world.

As an agent of death and chance, Nemesis came to be associated with the amphitheatre, and in this way, as they spread throughout the Roman Empire, so her cult was transmitted.

As Nemesis/Fortuna, a conflation of the Greek deity of fate and retribution with the Roman goddess Fortuna, *Deae Nemesis sive Fortunae*, she was perceived not as a vengeance-bringer, but as the power of destiny and changing fortune, *Nemesis id est vis quaedam Fortunae*, a suitable goddess to placate, as you passed the small shrine or *nemeseum* usually placed within the amphitheatre grounds. She was more properly a deity of the amphitheatre, and her cult was not confined to gladiators. Anyone with an interest in the events connected with the amphitheatre, administrators and soldiers, businessmen and magistrates, as well as gladiators and slaves, would have been attracted to the worship of Nemesis. Magistrates particularly, with their official duty to present games at sometimes great financial risk to themselves, would welcome her protection as Fortuna. Acknowledging her political importance, Claudius even put her on his coinage.

Also known as Adrasteia, or Adraste, her symbols were the wheel and the tiller, attributes of the force of changing directions, her companion the snake; among her epithets were 'avenger, punisher', 'majestic, glorious', 'holy', 'she who watches the things of the earth' and 'from her, no-one can escape'. As the Greek playwright Aeschylus notes in *Prometheus Bound*: 'Wise are those who bow down before Adrasteia'.

Some further items provide evidence for the existence of female gladiators. One is the afore-mentioned inscription from the Roman port at Ostia, in which the *editor* (the person providing and paying for the games) boasts that he 'was the first of all, since Rome was founded to make women fight'. Another, a shard of Italian red-ware pottery (possibly Samian) found in Leicester, with a small hole drilled in it, so it can be worn around the neck, has a simple message scratched onto it: VERECUNDA LUDIA: LUCIUS GLADIATOR. This means 'Verecunda the dancer, or actress [or perhaps woman gladiator, since that is an alternative translation of *ludia*] and Lucius the gladiator.

It has been suggested that perhaps Verecunda and Lucius both belonged to the same troupe of gladiators, *familia gladiatoria*, who travelled round the province of Britannia, and perhaps even further afield, although the alternative, more prosaic translation of *ludia* might be 'gladiator's girlfriend', 'moll', or even 'prostitute'.

In conclusion, if indeed the prohibition of an activity can be taken as positive proof that it existed, then the ban imposed by Septimius Severus in AD 200 on appearances by women in the circus or arena certainly shows that *gladiatrices*, as well as female athletes generally, had become numerous or visible enough to attract official disapproval. An earlier decree of the senate that had become law in AD 19, prohibited free women under the age of 20 from contracting themselves as *gladiatrices* (*auctoratae*), as well as free males under 25, unless they had the emperor's consent. All of this legislation from the first through to the third century AD goes towards establishing that women gladiators had a recognisable presence in the arena.

Despite the obvious overreaction inherent in the scathing words of Juvenal, it was inevitable that the notoriety of the *gladiatrix* really would, in the end, become an intolerable reproach to the public face of Rome.

Having explored the evidence, it is unsatisfactory to be forced to conclude that there is not enough information to build a vivid, detailed picture of what an average *gladiatrix* would have worn, what weapons she would have employed, what was her background and how she was trained.

However, common sense dictates that there was no such thing as an average *gladiatrix* – her rarity ensured that. Despite the lack of evidence, the stone relief of Achilleia and Amazonia is our best opportunity to build up a picture of the *gladiatrix*, though it is only ever going to be a picture based on two individuals. To carry that over to all *gladiatrices* would be misleading and dangerous, in the same way that it would be a mistake to lay down hard and fast rules for each gladiatorial category.

In terms of Amazonia and Achilleia, we can see that they wield short swords, *gladii*, and carry large rectangular shields, *scuta*. They both appear to be wearing some kind of belted kilt or loincloth, *subligaculum*, with the front 'apron' part of the material that seems to be hanging down.

Close inspection of the relief seems to suggest that they may be bare-breasted, which if true would have been an expected advertisement of their gender though impractical and uncomfortable in the arena, even in the guise of a myth re-enactment.

They seem to have padded bindings or a segmented arm guard, on their arms, like the *manicae* so often seen on gladiators as depicted in mosaics, and there is what appears to be a helmet at the feet of each woman: it is impossible to positively identify the objects as helmets, but in the context, there seems no better explanation. In view of the shape of the shields, and the fact that like is fighting like, these two women may in fact be *provocatrices*, though that itself may be a definition too far; the fact they are both female may be all that 'like versus like' implies in this case.

Juvenal supports the sense we get from all the evidence that women used the same equipment as men, but to return from proof to supposition, it is important to consider the grave finds unearthed in 1996 at a Roman cemetery on the south bank of the River Thames, in what is now Southwark, analysis by archaeologists at the Museum of London have identified a fragment of the pelvic bone of a young woman in her twenties.

Buried with her was a dish decorated with the image of a fallen gladiator, as well as other vessels with symbols possibly associated with the arena, including three lamps with images of the Egyptian jackal-headed god Anubis, who was associated with the Roman god Mercury. This latter deity had a ritualistic representation in the arena as the conductor of souls, that is, escorting the dead out of the Porta Libitinaria, the gate of death through which the victims were taken out for disposal.

The grave contained evidence of an exotic and high-status feast, with dates, almonds, figs and a dove. Remains of stone-pine cones had been burned as incense; stone-pines were associated with immortality, and were often grown around amphitheatres.

The best we can say when considering the significance of these items in a gladiatorial context, is that the woman was given a wealthy burial, and could as easily have been an enthusiastic fan of gladiators as a *gladiatrix* herself. The fact that London had its own seven thousand-seat amphitheatre within walking distance of the cemetery where she was buried merely adds to the speculation.

MANICAE

When examining evidence for this type of arm guard, it should be borne in mind that the artistic depictions of *manicae* range from straightforwardly identifiable as fabric, or downright ambiguous – in these cases, the surface appearance of the material of which the *manica* is composed gives the impression of either metal plates, boiled leather or some kind of padded fabric. So it is therefore very important to look carefully at the medium in which the *manica* is portrayed, as well as the context.

When the depiction shows very thin dark lines (possible strapping or thonging), between each lightly coloured segment, defining and emphasising the bulge of each segment, and particularly when those lines dangle from the arm, it is safe to say that we are looking at a form of padded soft organic material *manica* (linen, canvas, leather) of conventional and early type.

However, in some examples of represented *manicae*, identification is not so clear-cut. In cases where the gladiator is clearly wearing some form of arm defence, such as several figures on the Zliten mosaic from Libya, or the figurine of a *secutor* from Arles, it is by no means so simple to pick out the nature of the construction of the *manicae* (*101*). Particularly where mosaics are used to show gladiatorial combat, the differences in colour tone are marked, and there is some reason to suspect that the *manicae* are composed of metal rather than fabric or leather. Equally, it is not unreasonable to suppose that armour in military use could make the transfer to the arena or vice versa (*colour plate 25*).

One possible visual indicator of a metal *manica* is a strap, like a baldric, that runs around the body trunk, passing under the other (shield) arm. Modern reconstructions show that an unsecured metal *manica*, without additional body strapping to anchor it, slips too easily off the arm due to its own weight; on the other hand, a padded fabric *manica* stays up of its own accord, needing no extra fastening other than the thonging which ties it onto the arm (*102*).

101 Figurine of a *secutor* from Arles showing *manica*

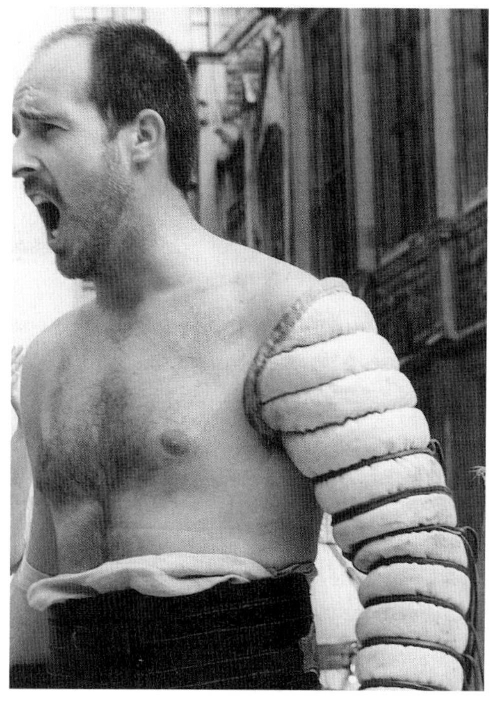

102 Padded limb protection. *Reconstruction: Britannia, I. Weston and I. Burridge. Photograph: Fraser Gray*

Even with the addition of a strap to keep it in place, modern metal *manica* reconstructions have shown that the *manica* can still rotate, become loose and slipping on the arm; one solution has been to introduce small metal discs or plates onto the anchoring belt exactly where it is fastened to the *manica* (*colour plate 21*).

This not only stabilises its movement, but also adds some extra protection to the body at the upper chest and shoulderblade. This solution is possibly depicted in the fourth century AD mosaic from Torre Nova on the Via Casilina, which is now in the Villa Borghese at Rome, and on the Piddington knife, both of which represent gladiators with something resembling this feature (*colour plates 19 and 22*). The Villa Borghese mosaic shows scenes from the arena, with several types of gladiator depicted. One in particular, a *retiarius* called Meleager, though his name is abbreviated to Melea in the mosaic, wears a fine example of a *manica* that is not only held in place by a body strap, but sports a large circular disc roughly where the strap meets the *manica*. Unless this is meant to represent some extremely ornate decoration, it appears to show the kind of anchoring, reinforcing feature needed to secure the *manica*. Presumably, it would have been made of metal, possibly with padding on the reverse.

In the summer of 2002, excavators led by Roy and Diana Friendship-Taylor discovered a third-century AD penknife at Piddington (*colour plate 19*). It has an iron blade folded into a copper-alloy (bronze) handle, which depicts a fully-armoured *secutor*, and is around 3in (70mm) high. The helmet quite clearly shows the fin-shaped crest and wide neck guard of the *secutor*. His sword arm and leading leg are protected by what appears to be *manica* and *fasciae*, and he is armed with a *gladius* and a *scutum*. The most curious element of the Piddington figure is a large disc roughly in the area of the right nipple adjacent to the *manica* of his sword arm.

It has been suggested that the disc is a curious opening in a smooth breastplate, but this is unlikely as this classification of gladiator (even in the provinces) is normally bare-chested, and to provide a gladiator with a breastplate with one small area exposed seems nonsensical. It is more likely to represent a disc stabiliser/strap reinforcer, and this feature is sited in exactly the same place as that of Meleager the *retiarius* in the Villa Borghese mosaic. The figure is very stylised, and this may explain why the Roman craftsman omitted to depict a strap, although this is conjectural.

The arm guards used by the gladiators were of two kinds, padded organic material, such as strong linen or leather, and metal. Although there is no precise date for the adoption of *manicae* of overlapping metal plates, it seems to have come into use somewhat later than the leather fastened, padded guards of linen stuffed with wadding. In fact, they tended to complement each other, as it would have been impossible to wear the metal *manica* without a layer of padding under it, to prevent chafing and hold it securely on the arm (*103*).

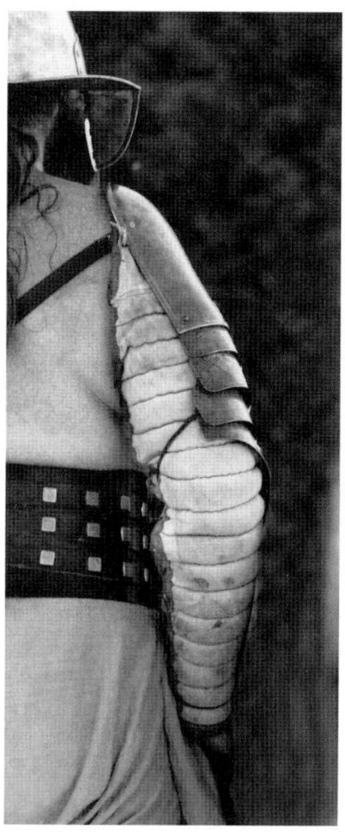

103 Padded limb protection used in conjunction with metal limb armour. *Photograph: Simon Barnes*

It has often been thought that the technology for the manufacture of the metal plates out of which the *manica* may have been constructed was not available at the time of the late republic and early empire; yet there appear to be examples of something resembling segmented metal arm guards at quite early dates. For instance, there is the curious example of the *crupellarius*, a type of gladiator/soldier used by the Gauls in an uprising against the Romans in AD 21 (*95* and *96*). Turning first to the literary source of evidence, Tacitus says that 'they were completely encased in iron', and when describing what methods the Romans had to use in order to attack them, he also says, '... the Romans struck at their plating and its wearers like men demolishing a wall'; this seems to suggest that the plating was rigid and substantial. The very word 'plating' indicates that we are not dealing with armour of metal scales or ringmail. Secondly, there is a fortuitous find from Versigny in France, which corroborates this description in every detail.

As previously mentioned in the text, this find is a bronze figurine about 4in (10cm) tall, and it quite clearly shows something which can only be banded or segmented armour protecting arms and legs. The very nature of the configuration of the armour, where it covers the torso and limbs without any join being apparent, is highly suggestive of metal rather than padded fabric. Even allowing for extreme artistic licence, this figurine seems to show a type of armour similar in principle to that of the *crupellarius* described by Tacitus.

The fact that the *crupellarius* was a Gaulish warrior in a battle near Augustodunum (Autun, eastern France), and the figurine was also found in France, at Versigny, is not conclusive evidence that they represent the same category; however, it is possible to infer from the fact that the two pieces of evidence have great similarities, that the existence of large metal plates for arm (and leg) defences at an early date in the imperial era is at least plausible, and should therefore not be automatically ruled out.

Many scholars are of the firm opinion that segmented metal armour is first encountered in the period of the Dacian wars (AD 101–106) when it was possibly developed as an answer to the *falx* wielding Dacian tribes. There is evidence for the use of this weapon by the nomadic tribespeople of Dacia; it appears on the Adamklissi memorial monument and on the pedestal of Trajan's Column in Rome. It caused such concern because of its devastating effect on the legionary armour that substantial modifications were made to the standard version to protect soldiers facing the *falx* in any future battle. *Falces* come in a bewildering variety of sizes; they were not produced to standard sizes as they were made at different locations by individual craftsmen throughout the Dacian territories. They have some aspects in common with the weapons of the Thracians, the *sicae* and *macheirai*, and in fact the Thracians used the *falx* as well. The special offensive value of the longer *falx* was that it could be used when fighting from the nomads' open-topped wagons, as it had a long reach. The extended length of the handle seems to point towards a two-handed use of the weapon, and if used in this fashion, the hooked end could have great penetrative power, because the massive energy concentrated at the tip would enable the point to penetrate armour.

If the Romans felt vulnerable against such a weapon, then it is highly likely they would have been prompted by their losses to develop a defence. There has been much speculation as to the exact nature of *manicae*, as they had to protect the arm, without affecting its flexibility. Modern reconstructions prior to 2001 have been inconclusive, despite various theories as to its construction. Fragmentary finds of limb defences (*lames*) at Newstead and Carnuntum had already given some insight into Roman plate armour for arms and legs, but had not provided enough information to form a view as to how this type of armour was constructed.

The problem had always literally hinged on the elbow joint; in order to fully protect the arm by enclosing it in what amounted to a flexible 'tube' composed of metal segments, the ability to fully bend the arm was lost, an acute angle of the arm being vital for combat. This problem was avoided if it could be shown that an early form of coutre plate (as in the medieval armour component allowing full elbow movement) was employed. Some have thought the *retiarius* figure on the Chester relief carving (in Saffron Walden museum) shows a faint impression of what could be a type of coutre plate at the elbow of the *manica* below the *galerus* being worn on the right shoulder and arm (*colour plate 24*). However, it seems more likely that the area of the elbow in question has either been rendered inaccurately, or left unfinished. Because of the naive style of the carving, it is impossible to draw a firm conclusion, but it does not sufficiently support the coutre plate theory.

However, we are on firmer ground with the find in January of 2001, when a significant discovery was made at the Roman fort at Carlisle, Cumbria, one that would throw light on the confusion surrounding Roman plate armour. Headed by archaeologist Mike McCarthy, the excavation yielded a large amount of fragmentary Roman armour, which was passed to Thom Richardson, Keeper of Armour and Oriental Collections at the Royal Armouries at Leeds for analysis and identification. The site was waterlogged and therefore some organic material had been found still in its military context. Three large and two small groupings of fragmentary armour were X-rayed and assessed. The smaller groups were identified as scale armour. However, the larger clusters are of great interest in the debate about *manica*, as they appear to consist of the extensive remains of laminated limb defences (*104* and *105*). This type of armour, which is popularly known as segmented, is rarely depicted, and is principally seen on the metopes, the set of carvings from Trajan's monument at Adamklissi, previously mentioned above. These show legionaries who wear scale armour and laminated (strips of metal, *laminae*) defences for the right (sword) arm, fighting Dacians who are wielding the bill-like *falx*. As we have seen, the *falx* was a vicious weapon against which the Roman infantry of Trajan's army had inadequate defences.

The plates found at Carlisle were identified as iron, and in one of the clusters, there are enough of them to completely cover the length of the arm from just below the shoulder to the wrist at least, with a cluster of smaller plates that could have intended to cover the hand. It has been estimated as having been nearly 24in (600mm) long in its original condition, meaning that it would have easily reached from the upper arm just below the shoulder down to the hand, partially covering it.

Of the three larger fragments, therefore, only one seems to comprise a complete *manica*; the other two appear to be the two halves of a single *manica*, but this cannot be assumed. Whatever their provenance, they share some features with the complete set, inasmuch as they are of the same conformation, with larger plates at the top, decreasing in width down the arm, so that although the upper arm is semi-enveloped, the lower arm is protected by smaller plates, matching the narrower curve of the forearm. One fragmentary upper arm piece has two surviving copper-alloy ring fittings; the complete *manica* has one remaining copper-alloy hook, reminiscent of hook fittings found on surviving *lorica segmentata*. In addition, all the individual plates have copper-alloy rivets, indicating that they were joined together, probably by means of leather strips. Importantly, the *manica* plates 'underlap', rather than overlap; overlapping plates deflect downward-glancing blows whereas underlapping plates provide better defence when the arm is committed to a thrust.

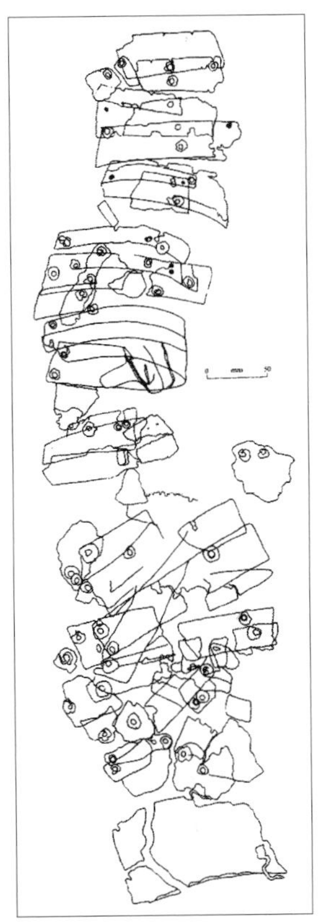

104 Right Line drawing of the Carlisle *manica*. *Courtesy of Royal Armouries, Leeds*

105 Below X-ray of *manica* from Carlisle. *Courtesy of Royal Armouries, Leeds*

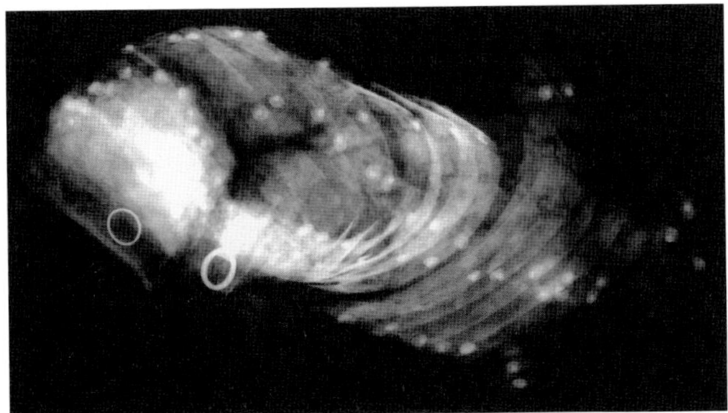

106 Michael Hardy in his workshop

This supports the conclusions of specialist Roman armourer, Michael Hardy, whose reconstruction of the Carlisle arm-guard (*106*, *colour plates 25a* and *b*) demonstrates that, because the arm twists as it thrusts, only the area of the arm thus exposed to the opponent's weapon (for instance, Dacian *falx* on campaign, or indeed *sica*, *fuscina* or *gladius* in the arena) needs protection. Because this is only a partial covering of the arm, it is still fully flexible, avoiding the need for a special elbow component.

Interestingly, there is a sculpture of an armoured figure from a museum collection at Alba Iulia, Romania, with a strange mixture of equipment that has so far defied positive identification (*107*); it has been variously suggested that the figure is a soldier, a representation of the god Mars, or a gladiator. An analysis by J.C.N. Coulston brought the problem into focus: the sculpture appears to show a *manica* worn on the right arm, and a composite breastplate of metal strips (*lorica segmentata*) and scale; it is a full-length figure, though headless, wearing a tunic down to just above the knee; the less damaged leg is clearly bare; the torso has three horizontal bands, possibly indicating some form of *lorica segmentata*, with added scale sections on the shoulders. The sculpture, of uncertain date somewhere between the second and fourth century, was at first thought to be that of a gladiator, due to the large curved rectangular shield, though opinion

107 The *Alba Iulia* figure from Romania. Soldier or gladiator? *With kind permission of M. Bishop*

moved away from that theory towards the military explanation, when it was noticed that he wore a sword scabbard on his left hip; this not only dated the sculpture more closely to the second or third century AD, but also poured cold water on the gladiator theory, since gladiators are not depicted with sword scabbards, as a general rule.

Gladiator or soldier, or even deity, the important feature of the sculpture for the purposes of investigating the construction of *manica* is the clearly defined arm-guard on the undamaged upper arm section. This is similar to the examples shown on the Adamklissi metopes, and has parallels with the *manicae* of gladiators. To all intents and purposes, the *manica* is constructed in the same way, whoever is wearing it.

Unfortunately, the sculpture has lost its head, so identification is virtually impossible. Its high-status appearance makes it unlikely to have been a gladiatorial tombstone, yet the suspicion still lingers. It is an enigmatic piece, but as a further example of a *manica*, military or gladiatorial, it is of some value. The very fact that there has been continuing and unresolved doubt over its subject just goes to show how close the two killing professions could be.

Ironically, actual finds of segmented metal limb defences are rare, but those that do occur tend to be found in a military context. Finds of this type that could be positively identified as gladiatorial are to be hoped for, but have not materialised, despite the afore-mentioned pictorial sources showing gladiators wearing something resembling metal *manicae* in mosaics, sculpture, pottery and frescoes. Perhaps due to the nature of their profession, these depictions occur far more frequently than contemporary representations of soldiers.

Of all the types of evidence to support the existence, and method of construction of metal *manica*, the Carlisle Roman fort archaeological discovery is the main contributor to the meagre fund of information about this undeniably misunderstood piece of defensive armour. The Carlisle fragments have provided many answers to the question of metal laminated limb construction and solutions to the problem of reconstructing arm defences in a military and gladiatorial setting.

Whether made of metal or padded linen, there are references to makers of these armguards (*manicarii*) on the staff of the gladiator training schools. One such inscription, which lists the four divisions or classes (*decuriae*) of fighters in the imperial *ludus* of the emperor Commodus, gives the name of one Demosthenes, *manicarius*, in the second d*ecuria* (CIL VI 631, ILS 5084). The fact that the *ludus* kept a specialist worker whose sole responsibility was the manufacture, repair and alteration of *manicae* gives an idea of how common they were.

In the late second and early third century AD, provincial depictions of gladiators became more widespread, and in the north-west regions glass cylindrical drinking cups with gladiatorial scenes were produced and distributed around the North Sea. One such cup was found at Vindolanda on Hadrian's Wall, in all probability the prized possession of a soldier based there (*colour plate 26*). It is very fine, with enamelled decoration that has remained bright and clear, showing the true colour and dynamism of the gladiatorial contest. It was obviously painted by someone who had witnessed at firsthand gladiators fighting, because the detail is superb. It shows not only a pair of gladiators, but also the officiating umpire or referee and his assistant, the *summa* and *secunda rudis*. Both officials hold sticks (the *rudis*) to keep order, and both wear the typical loose fitting off-white tunics with the red *clavus* (stripes) on each. The figure in the centre is a heavily armed *secutor*, and thanks to the exquisite detail on this cup, it is possible to distinguish the dark-coloured outer arm-guard from the one worn under it. The *secutor* is wearing what looks like a padded linen *manica* underneath a *manica* made of some dark material, which from the colour can only be metal, since it matches the colour used to depict the helmet, outer leg greave and weapon. The two *manicae* extend from the upper arm down past the elbow. It is possible to make out the rolls of fabric on the arm so characteristic of the padded *manica*. The *secutor* is bare-chested, wears a wide belt, some form of loincloth or *subligaculum*, possibly fringed, and carries a semi-cylindrical shield, the *scutum*, with a metal boss and decoration. On his left leg he has padded *fasciae*, over which is worn a short greave, or *ocrea*. The helmet is perfectly plain, with no crest or features.

His opponent, the *retiarius*, is bare-headed, carries a downward pointing trident, together with a clearly visible *pugio* in his left hand. He also is bare-chested, wears a loincloth, possibly fringed, and above all, he is wearing a *galerus* and *manica* on the left shoulder and arm. Again, the colour of the armour, contrasted with the flesh tones of the body, leaves no doubt that this is metal. The *manica* seems to go right down the arm, even covering the hand. This cup is a superb piece of evidence for the existence of metal *manicae*, with the accurate representation of colour contrast and equipment detail making identification more definite, and providing yet another piece in the jigsaw puzzle of gladiatorial armour.

GALEA, CASSIS

Thanks to the 15 complete helmets found at the gladiatorial training barracks at Pompeii, the development of the gladiatorial helmet can be much more easily traced, although there are still appreciable gaps in our knowledge. Since eleven out of the fifteen are lavishly decorated and embossed, they have been seen by some scholars as purely parade helmets, for use in the *pompa*, the traditional procession with which all *munera* began (*colour plate 27*). The argument for that view rests on three points: it was too heavy, too expensive and too vulnerable to damage.

However, all three points can be challenged: the weight of a gladiatorial helmet was indeed about double that of a standard infantry helmet, on average about 9lb (4kg), though some could be less than that, depending on the design and decorative features. But the gladiator was wearing the helmet for a much shorter time, say no more than 10–15 minutes at most, whereas the soldier had to keep his helmet on for possibly hours at a time, with strenuous activity continuing meanwhile. Also, the gladiator put on his helmet at the last moment before entering the arena, and, if he survived, took it off straight after. The effort required is not superhuman; provided the helmet is a good fit, and suitably padded, the exertion is not too great. As for the charge that the helmet was too expensive to be risked in actual combat, the whole point of the *munera* was that they should be spectacular, and therefore that the equipment should be eye-catching and flamboyant; in any case, the helmets themselves were rarely the target for sword blows, as that would have been an unnecessary risk of the blade, which was far more important to the outcome of the contest than the integrity of the helmet. On the other hand, swords that bounced off the edges of shields could be accidentally driven up into the face of an opponent, or even thrust at the visor in order to intimidate or distract. The only weapon that might have been deliberately thrust at the helmeted head with the aim of inflicting injury is the trident, used by *retiarius* against *secutor*, but as the latter's helmet made a virtue of its featurelessness and simplicity, this does not assist the argument about embellishment. The trident could not usually catch any part of the helmet's surface as it was smooth; the *secutor* helmet was thicker than the others, the extra metal protecting against the force of the powerful impact that a trident, correctly used, could inflict.

In addition, it was very often just the domes and crests that were embellished and decorated; the visors (face-plates) tend to be plain and unadorned, with standard components such as hinges and eye-grilles, which are secured with minimal rivets and fastenings, indicating that damage could be repaired quickly (*colour plate 16*). This does not point towards parade use only; by the all-pervasive practicality of the construction, these helmets can be identified as for actual use in the arena, despite their apparent richness.

Lastly, the embellishment adds to rather than detracts from the strength of the structure; if the embossing of helmets had weakened them, then we would not expect to see it at all in the practical military application for instance, of the deeply embossed dome eyebrows of the imperial Gallic type 'A' legionary helmet of the first-century AD, and the deep boss and punched decoration on the dome and neck-guard of the auxiliary cavalry type 'B' from Witcham Gravel, Ely, Cambridgeshire, also first-century AD. Both of these helmets are contemporaneous with the Pompeian gladiatorial helmets, and they have elements of decoration that, if that were a compromising issue, one would not expect to see in a military context. We can conclude that decoration would not have weakened the helmets to any significant degree.

Placing the Pompeian helmets in context, by virtue of the fact that they have effectively been frozen in time, they conveniently showcase the development of the brimmed gladiatorial helmet. The common factor uniting the late republican/early imperial period helmets of this type is that they all have a flatter, more horizontal brim (*108*). This style can be clearly seen in depictions from that period, for instance in the tomb relief of C. Lusius Storax (Chieti Museum) in which all the various gladiators, whatever their category, have more or less horizontal brims on their helmets. As the first century AD gave way to the second, brimmed helmets of a modified type, also found at Pompeii, begin to occur more frequently, both in archaeological examples and in artistic depictions. The development from the horizontal or flatter brim is seen in the way that the brim starts to dip around either side of the faceplate, to form a slight arch. This creates a 'floppy hat' appearance, but also has the effect of pulling down the neckguard to become more protective at the back (*109*). In time, in helmets not seen in the Pompeii finds, but present in other helmet finds of the second and third centuries, such as the Berlin *murmillo galea*, this curvature, or dipping, is exaggerated to such a degree that the brim disappears, mutating into a complete arch, or 'bonnet' effect, with a wide neck-guard meeting the back of the *galea* at an acute angle (*110*). This progression of flat, then curved, to arched brim, in three stages, can be clearly followed. An intriguing possibility is that we are not the only ones to notice the evolution of the helmet brim. Approximately one year after the eruption of Vesuvius buried and consequently preserved the helmets at Pompeii, the poet Martial celebrated the inauguration of the Flavian amphitheatre (better known to us as the Colosseum), with the publication of his *Liber de Spectaculis* (Book of the Shows). In this, he writes, using his sharp observational powers, of a particular gladiator who was what we would call a good all-rounder. It was quite unusual for one fighter to possess so many skills of differing types of gladiatorial combat; nevertheless, this paragon actually existed, and was certainly not a figment of Martial's imagination:

> Hermes, favourite fighter of the age;
> Hermes, skilled in all weaponry;
> Hermes, gladiator and trainer both;
> Hermes, tempest and tremor of his school;
> Hermes, who (but none other) makes Helius afraid;
> Hermes, before whom (but none other) Advolans falls;
> Hermes, taught to win without wounding;
> Hermes, himself his own substitute;

108 Opposite top Horizontal brimmed gladiatorial helmet of the early first century AD

109 Opposite middle By the late first century the brim starts to warp and fold downwards. Could this be the languid/drooping style of helmet '*casside languida*' mentioned by contemporary poet Martial?

110 Opposite bottom By the late second and early third century the brim seems to have warped and dropped further into a classic bonnet shape

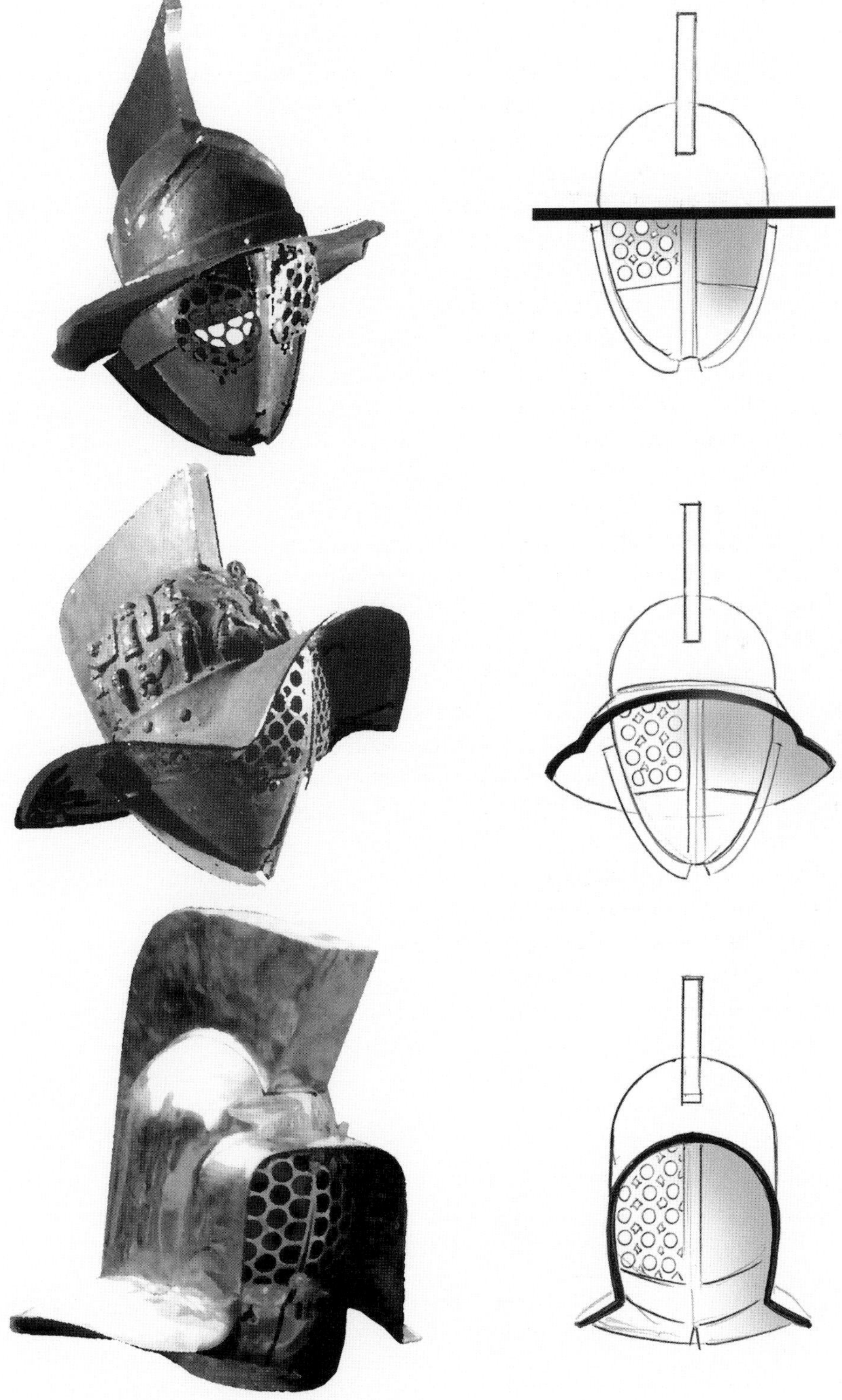

Hermes, goldmine of seat-mongers;
Hermes, darling and distress of gladiators' women;
Hermes, proud with battling spear;
Hermes, menacing with marine trident;
Hermes, formidable in drooping helmet;
Hermes, glory of Mars universal;
Hermes, all things in one and thrice unique.
(Martial, *Liber de Spectaculis* 5.24)

In this tribute to a great gladiator, Martial gives away some interesting information, probably unintentionally. The key phrase of interest for the purpose of highlighting the actual historical process of helmet development is one which is thought either corrupt in its meaning, or just impossible to interpret. That phrase is *casside languida timendus* – 'formidable in drooping helmet'. The word *languida* to describe his helmet has been the source of much head-scratching; it carries a meaning of fatigued, weary, drooping, and that seems a strange epithet to apply to an inanimate object like a metal helmet. Some have seen in this description the implication that the helmet, being heavy, causes weariness, and thus the adjective is transferred.

There is another possible explanation for the choice of this particular word by Martial, and that is that the helmet he saw Hermes wearing in the arena was one of the transitional, newer models of helmet, with the second stage 'drooping' brim, which ties in well with the archaeological evidence from Pompeii and the many depictions in Roman art and souvenirs of this time. In this case, the 'drooping helmet' may be a description of its actual physical appearance of the brim.

The visor, or faceplates, evolved alongside, and as a result of, the changing shape of the brim. Each half of the visor was hinged at the side, opening outwards; it is this method that indicates that the visor had its beginnings in enlarged cheek-pieces, as they grew in size over time, to meet in the middle and eventually to cover the face entirely.

FROM POMPEII TO SUFFOLK: A HOMEGROWN CURIOSITY

A significant discovery was unearthed in April 1965. A copper alloy (bronze) helmet was brought to the surface by ploughing on a farm in Hawkedon, Suffolk (*colour plate 15*). The helmet has been tentatively dated to the first century AD. It has an exceptionally wide neck-guard and has been calculated as being more than twice the weight of surviving first-century AD legionary helmets, making it an unlikely military find. It stands comparison with a more richly embellished *provocator* gladiator helmet found in Pompeii, with which it shares many similar features, notably the overall shape and proportions (*111*).

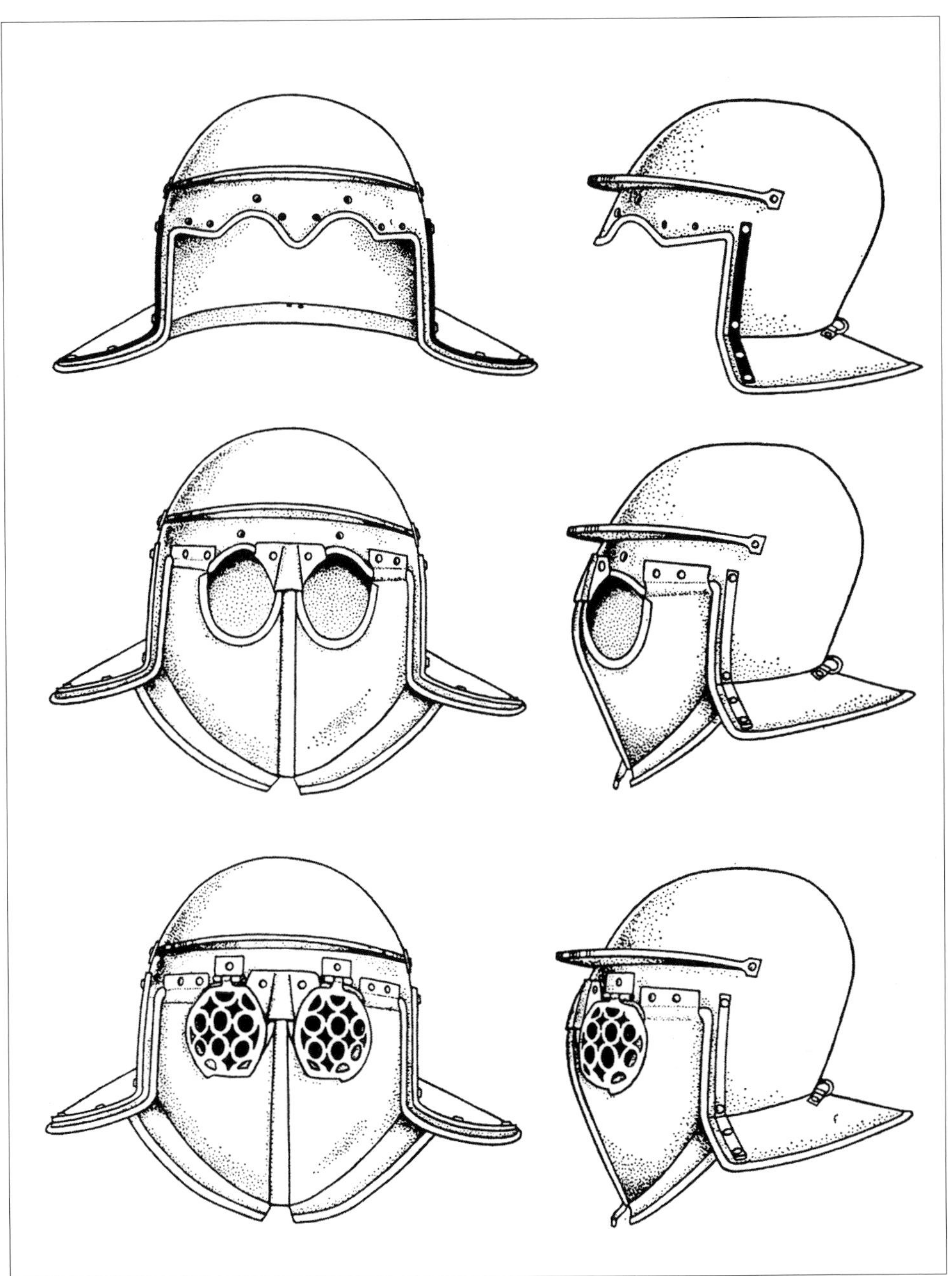

111 The Hawkedon Helmet from Suffolk. *After conjectural images by P. Compton*

Despite the excellent quality of manufacture of this helmet, it is not as fine an example as its surviving cousins in Italy, mainly because it is plain and unadorned. But it appears to share a common ancestry. Perhaps it was manufactured in the same workshop supplying Pompeii and even Rome's arenas, but destined as it was for a distant province, ornament was judged unnecessary – utilitarian function and ease of production were perhaps more important than form; after all, it was only for Britannia.

The Hawkedon helmet weighs 2,280gm without the missing face-plate. This may have been lost when the helmet suffered most of its initial damage; there is some speculation that the remote location of this find, far from any recorded major Romano-British settlement (the closest being Colchester) was due to its being caught up in the Boudican revolt, possibly worn by a rebel in defence or just taken as booty. Despite being made of copper alloy, traces of tin coating remain on its surface. Modern armourers who have attempted this tinning process on military reconstructions have shown that this finish resembles polished silver. This must have provided a striking and brilliant contrast to the blood and sand of a provincial arena.

The helmet dome and neck-guard are of one-piece construction that must have involved considerable time and expertise to produce. The neck-guard has a stamped panel with the fragmentary word '…OS', perhaps part of the name of the *lanista* who owned this helmet and all the equipment that went with running a *familia gladiatoria*. The whole piece appears to have been hammered out of one thick bronze sheet, not a job for an amateur. The hand-cut edge was once covered in copper alloy binding, some of which was lost, but a sizeable portion remains. Worthy of note are the counter-sunk holes around the eye area and a prominent domed rivet projecting from one of these holes.

With the absence of a faceplate we can only guess at the Hawkedon helmet's appearance. Comparisons have been made with its more embellished 'sister helmet' in Pompeii and with that in mind, using the rivet configuration and arch over either eye, a convincing reconstruction drawing was made (*British Museum Quarterly*, vol. XXXIII Number 3-4 K.S. Painter, linework P. Compton).

The conjectural illustrations in this paper have striking similarities to the type of helmet worn by the later imperial *provocator* classification of gladiators.
The Hawkedon helmet provides a solid reminder that the games of death were not just being played out in the heart of the Roman Empire.

FOOTWEAR

Just about every fighter had bare feet – they were fighting on sand, and sandals or boots with leather soles, with or without hobnails, *caligae*, would be treacherous. The safest footwear would have been no footwear at all, and this is borne out by the majority of representations of gladiators, whatever their category. The exception to this would have been the *equites*, who are often depicted wearing some form of shoe or low boot, which might have been made from some robust material like thick felt to retain grip on the floor of the area. Sometimes gladiators are shown wearing coverings of what looks like linen padding or leather gaiters which extend down the leg and over the top of the foot, to cushion it from chafing and rubbing by the bottom edge of the greave. However, this does not go around the foot to enclose it or cover the sole.

A recent analysis by Professor Karl Grossschmidt of the University of Vienna of a number of skeletons from a recently discovered gladiators' graveyard in Ephesus, Turkey, found that the bones of the hands and feet indicated that they had been extremely over-developed; they had odd-looking swellings in particular areas due to constant strain. This was attributed in part to the gladiators having habitually walked and trained barefoot on the sand of the arena, causing their feet to develop an abnormal bone structure. Marks on the bones indicated that their tendons had been bigger than average, in the same way as tennis champions' racket arms are often slightly longer and thicker than their other arm. In the light of this new evidence and the existing pictorial proof, it seems safe to say that, as a rule, gladiators were barefoot.

7

TIMOR MORTIS, AMOR MORTIS: ATTITUDES TO GLADIATORS AND THE GAMES

How the gladiator was viewed within Roman society is not a question with one answer. That society had Seneca, Pliny and Cicero, with all their intellectual baggage at one end of the spectrum; at the other, the anonymous graffiti artist who scratched an informal portrait of a *retiarius* called Vindocomus, complete with *galerus*, *manica*, *fuscina*, and next to his name, the mark known as *theta nigrum*, the black *theta* (*theta* for *thanatos*, the Greek word for death) signifying that he had perished, on a piece of stone at the Colosseum (*113*). Was this a fan of Vindocomus, recording his death as a tribute to a personal favourite of the arena, or a supporter of the man who killed him, crowing over the defeat of a disliked gladiator?

There are several such casual inscriptions from the Colosseum and elsewhere, particularly at Pompeii; graffiti presumably inspired by the afternoon's events. The straightforward hero-worship or scornful mockery presented in that kind of inscription, like its football supporters' spraycan graffiti counterpart today is unmistakeable. A good example of this type of uncomplicated admiration is seen in the scratched, almost childlike images of the *thraex* Hilarus being defeated by the *murmillo* Attilius (*112*). Dated to AD 60 in Pompeii, it seems fresher than a great deal of modern graffiti, and it shows us that the combats were not merely the preserve of the rich and influential; the man in the street who did this piece of instant art had obviously witnessed the fight he depicted. Not for him the modern preoccupation with the name of his hero or team loyalties in giant letters on a wall: he wanted to record an important moment that he had seen with his own eyes.

Less straightforward, however, are the other manifestations of interest in gladiators, which tend to reflect Rome's ambivalence towards them. It is an oversimplification to see the gladiator only in terms of modern celebrities such as footballers, boxers, Hollywood action heroes, but there are some similarities.

112 Graffito of *thraex* Hilarus losing to the *murmillo* Attilus

113 Graffito of defeated *retiarius*, Vindocomus. The '*theta*' symbol (from the Greek word for death – *thanatos*) after his name indicates that he was killed

These are more to do with the reactions of the crowd and their sometimes fanatical hero-worship of the giants of the football pitch, boxing ring, multiplex. These larger than life stars have their acolytes, fanclubs, souvenir industries, and they command huge sums of money for every appearance they make. This has the effect of making them even more desirable; they are unreachable, like gods, and yet we can watch them perform. Each successful appearance feeds their fame, with many thousands (millions, if television is included) of eyes devouring their every move. This is the power of the spectacle as experienced in the Colosseum. It is exhilarating to be the centre of attention, to hold the gaze of the crowd; how much more so when that crowd is 50,000-strong.

That just two men fighting in the sand could be the focus of so many people's attention is the ultimate description of the arena dynamic, and it is echoed today in society's appetite for 'battles of the giants', when two superstars of the world of sport are pitted against each other. Boxing particularly meets this criterion of the one on one combat, as the intimacy of the struggle for supremacy is played out.

This is why people watch street-fights, car crashes, televised and dramatised warfare. They are mesmerised by the unfolding violence, and yet although it satisfies some dark human need, it is never enough. Death, danger, courage and fear make an intoxicating formula, one that reached its apogee in the arena.

Nowadays, we do not normally carry our intoxication to the ultimate level, by demanding blood, but then again, we can have all the blood we want, provided we suspend our credibility and let the special effects convince us.

The software that makes it possible for us to not only watch appalling violence in surgical detail but also to take part in risk-free blood-letting, is able to produce visceral effects on the human frame that would seem to be of a similar quality to those evoked by actual experience. The difference must only be one of degree. In a litigious, risk-averse society, more and more people seek the freedom to dice with death, but do not have the means to satisfy this longing. The bull-running in Pamplona is an example of the urge to place oneself deliberately in harm's way in order to enhance the feeling of being alive, but these outlets are few and far between, and disappearing fast. If asked, the software games player would probably like the facility to switch to 'real', if ever such an add-on could be devised in the drive for virtual reality. But then, it wouldn't be virtual, just real. This vital distinction is what made the gladiators compulsive viewing.

The closest thing we have to a gladiator in our midst in the modern world is the bullfighter, the cultural inheritor of the arena tradition. The aficionados of bullfighting do not call it a sport; rather, it is a spectacle in which the animal's fate is certain, so the interest for the audience lies in the dance of death between the bull and the fighter, specifically the skill and courage, sheer *machismo*, demonstrated by the matador in the face of extreme peril (*114*). It is plain that the *corrida* has qualities that cannot be found elsewhere in the modern world. The mixture of thrilling jeopardy, danger and fear, pain and courage, is typical of the gladiatorial combat, and for the spectators, the effect of such a performance is probably the same. Daniel Hannan, writing bullfight reviews for the *Spectator*, describes the effect:

> To watch such a performance is not so much thrilling as draining. It is like the final act of *Tristan and Isolde*, crescendo after crescendo until you feel you can take no more; and then, when the blade plunges, a sense of almost unbearable poignancy.

That is surely a near-perfect description of the Colosseum spectators' experience, with the same sense of poignancy noticed by the Roman writers who watched the spectacles and commented on them. As Seneca remarked, in his *Naturales Quaestiones*: 'Death summons us all indiscriminately. Take courage from this despair'.

We spend vast amounts of newsprint and airtime discussing the physiques of our modern heroes, analysing their motivation and their performances, as if we can somehow discover the secret of the excitement they generate, participating vicariously in their adventures. They move dynamically; we watch passively. If they fail, we turn on them and rip them apart, metaphorically, via the media. This

114 Female bullfighter Sanda Moscoso stares defiantly at the bull that gored her thigh during Spain's first six woman bullfight in 2005. This bloody sport played out on the sand is one of the many surviving legacies of the Roman arena. *Photo: courtesy of EPA/VILLAR LÓPEZ*

contract between the spectator and the performer is one the gladiator knew well. He lived and died by it.

To the Romans, the gladiator was a symbol of more than just death-defying skill and courage. By the very nature of his powerful oath, the *sacramentum* (to be burned, chained, beaten with rods, and killed by the sword), he represented a state of hopelessness in which he was free of the normal sexual constraints.

Gladiators were thought to be licentious and sensual precisely because their bodies were not their own, but were disposed of by their owners for pleasure and profit; they were seen only as beasts to be used for entertainment. Because of this narrow focus of physicality, by which the gladiators were trained to ignore hardship, pain and fear, they lived in a realm unlike anything else in the Roman world.

For Romans of all classes, the gladiator was imbued with powerful metaphorical significance, a fact exploited by many writers: the Stoic writer Seneca the Younger would often use the gladiator to illustrate philosophical issues, for instance he spoke of the folly of failing to make plans at the right time; *gladiator in arena consilium caput* – the gladiator is making his plan in the arena, *i.e.* too late.

Quite apart from their training in violence, this imperturbability in the face of death must have been unsettling for any normal Roman in their company, and of course, the alien is always attractive. To call it despair makes it sound as if the gladiators were enervated by their hopeless position, but in fact it is that very despair which energises the gladiator. Seneca's philosophy of life had a decidedly gladiatorial flavour: *Qui mori didicit, servire dedidicit* – 'He who has learned how to die has learned how not to be a slave' (*Epistulae* 26.10).

More than any other profession in Rome, that of the gladiator certainly did teach him how to die; it was inherent in the terrible oath he had sworn, in which the prospect of dishonouring himself by avoidance of pain and death was worse than death itself. In his compendium, *Noctes Atticae*, Aulus Gellius, the second-century AD lawyer, reported on the gladiator who could laugh while having his wound probed at knifepoint. This is an illustration of the extreme fortitude, verging on masochism, produced by the gladiator's training. It was a sign of the fierce indifference to personal suffering in which a gladiator rejoiced, a significant factor, again recognised by Seneca as a key element in all important conflicts, physical or philosophical:

> Warriors glory in their wounds; they rejoice to display their flowing blood... The man who returns from battle unhurt may have fought as well, but he who returns wounded is held in higher esteem. (Seneca, *De Providentia* 4.4)

As a Stoic, Seneca often spoke approvingly of the gladiator's ability to disregard his pain, describing the *gladiatores fortissimi* thus:

> Among the gladiators of the greatest fortitude, one suppresses any sign of his wounds and digs in his heels. The other, regarding the clamouring people, signifies to them that his wound is nothing and that he will not tolerate any intercession. (Seneca, *De Constantia Sapientis* 16.2)

However, once he had entered the ranks of the living dead, *vis mortua* in Cicero's description, no wanton act of cruelty, no extreme of brutality or excess of licentiousness was enough to condemn him. Abandoning the normal world of life and hope, he lived in the harsh world of the gladiator, ruled by violent force and the demands of the present moment only. St Augustine compared the gladiator's spirit to that of the sinner who was, 'already despairing of himself, already having the spirit of a gladiator, *gladiatorio animo*, and thus able to do whatever he wills, since of necessity he must be condemned' (*Enarrationes in Psalmos*, 70.1).

VENUS AND MARS: '*FERRUM EST QUOD AMANT*'

The gladiator was a by-word for raw unbridled sexuality, and this earned him a different kind of admiration from the hero worship of the arena fans. The graffiti on the walls of the gladiatorial barracks in Pompeii spells out the sexual prowess of at least two of the gladiators there; Crescens the *retiarius* is *puellarum dominus* ('master of the girls'), *puparum nocturnarum dominus et medicus* ('lord of the maidens, giving them their nightly medicine), and Celadus the *thraex* is *suspirium et decus puellarum* (the girls' hero who makes them all sigh) – (*CIL* 4.8916, 4.4353, 4.4289, 4.4342, 4.4345, 4.4356).

From the context of these pieces of graffiti, they look suspiciously like boasts made by Crescens and his fellow gladiator, Celadus, rather than the scrawled devotion of their female fans, but either way, they show us the pitch of adoration that gladiators could inspire, and the extent of their 'pulling power'; in another fragment of possible self-promotion, Celadus is called 'thrice victor and thrice crowned the girls' heartthrob', thus connecting his success in the arena with his success in the *cubiculum*, or more likely, the *cella*, his room at the barracks.

Gladiators were the ultimate 'bit of rough', and it wasn't just the impressionable young girls who sighed after them. Juvenal reserves his most strident disapproval for the type of upper-class woman who deserts everything just to run off with a gladiator:

> Eppia, the senator's wife, accompanied a troop of gladiators to Pharos and the Nile.... Oblivious of her home and husband and sister, she disregarded her fatherland and shamelessly deserted her wailing children...But what were the good looks and youthfulness that enthralled Eppia and set her on fire? What did she see in him to make her put up with being called a gladiator's groupie? After all, her darling Sergius had already started shaving his throat and with his gashed arm had hopes of retirement. Besides, his face was really disfigured: there was a furrow chafed by his helmet, an enormous lump right on his nose, and the nasty condition of a constantly weeping eye. But he was a gladiator.... That's what she preferred to her sons and her fatherland, to her sister and her husband. It's the steel that they're in love with. (Juvenal, *Satirae* VI 83-112)

Ferrum est quod amant – Juvenal's rant ends with a very perceptive judgment. The sword, *ferrum*, meaning literally 'iron', another way of saying *gladius*, is what these women love. Predictably, *gladius* was slang for 'penis', as was the equivalent Greek term, *machaera*, but in his overheated tirade Juvenal seems to be saying that it is the sexual magnetism of the gladiator himself, no matter how beaten up and disfigured he might be, that these high-class women fall for, though of course the double meaning would not be lost on his readership. The disgraced Eppia may well have had more than one counterpart in real life. In Petronius' *Satyricon*, the slave-woman Chrysis gives a cynical description of the type:

> Some women get heated up over the absolute dregs and can't feel any passion unless they see slaves or bare-legged messengers. The arena sets some of them on heat, or a mule-driver covered in dust, or actors displayed on the stage. She jumps across the first fourteen seats from the orchestra and looks for something to love among the lowest of the low....I have

never yet gone to bed with a slave, and heaven forbid I should ever see a lover of mine crucified. That's for ladies who kiss the whipmarks. (Petronius, *Satyricon* 126)

The ex-gladiator Encolpius, to whom she is speaking, was surprised 'at such contrasting sexual desires', and thought it 'very strange that the maid should cultivate the superior outlook of a lady, and the lady the low taste of a maid.' It is precisely this kind of reversal that titillated the dulled sensual impulses of the Roman aristocracy, although, as with all jaded and depraved appetites, the solution never lay in more novelty, spectacles, cruelty – that just exacerbated the problem. As Livy put it in the preface to his history, *Ab Urbe Condita*, 'Of late, wealth has brought us avarice, and abundant pleasures, yearning – amidst both excess and the desire to perish and destroy all things.' The pursuit of ultimate sensation would only lead to one thing, the lust for death, *libido moriendi*, a craving that Seneca warned against as 'that emotion, which has taken possession of so many.'

Gladiator fever could afflict even the very highest echelons of society, with both men and women playing at being gladiators, though not always in the arena. Gladiators were often rumoured to have illegitimately fathered men of high status, like the consul under Claudius, Curtius Rufus and Nero's Praetorian Prefect, Nymphidius Sabinus. Of the former, Tacitus wrote of 'his inglorious birth' and that 'some said Curtius Rufus was a gladiator's son. I do not want to lie about his origin but would be embarrassed to tell the truth....' The most extreme example of this kind of gossip, true or not, is the story, reported in the dubious *Scriptores Historiae Augustae*, about the supposed father of the emperor Commodus:

Some say, and this seems plausible, that Commodus Antoninus his son and successor was not begotten by him but from an adulterous union, and they embroider such a tale with a story current among the common people. Allegedly Faustina, Pius' daughter and Marcus' wife, had once seen gladiators pass by and was inflamed with passion for one of them. While troubled by a long illness she confessed to her husband about her passion. When Marcus had related this to the Chaldaeans (astrologers), it was their advice that the gladiator be killed and that Faustina should wash herself from beneath in his blood and in this state lie with her husband. When this had been done the passion was indeed abated, but Commodus was born a gladiator not a *princeps*; for as emperor he put on nearly a thousand gladiatorial fights, with the people looking on. (*Scriptores Historiae Augustae, Life of Marcus Aurelius*)

This story may well have been constructed by some well-meaning Roman spin-doctor in order to explain Commodus' obsession with gladiators, and how much of it is based on fact is impossible to say. Faustina caught a glimpse of a gladiator in the *pompa*, the gladiatorial procession, as it passed by, and was immediately enthralled by this face in the crowd; that detail seems plausible enough.

The fact that commentators felt the need to attribute Commodus' own obsession to his mother's earlier one with an anonymous gladiator shows to what lengths the Roman people would go in order to explain his aberrant behaviour. By blaming it either on the unknown gladiator who supposedly fathered him, or to exposure to 'gladiator madness' in his mother's womb, it appears that the writer was trying to avoid the nationally embarrassing conclusion that a past emperor, even a reviled one like Commodus, could have freely chosen to be a gladiator, and most scandalously of all, 'with the people looking on'. It was bad enough that he had practiced the gladiator's art, but to make an exhibition of himself in that role, to show himself in the arena under the gaze of his subjects – that was the true disgrace. St Paul, in his first letter to the Christians at Corinth, uses that same theme of public exhibition in comparing his mission to the trials of the arena; he likens God to the *editor* of the games, placing them in the *pompa* to parade before men:

> I sometimes think that God means us, the messengers, to appear last in the procession of mankind, like the men who are to die in the arena. For indeed we are made a public spectacle before the angels of Heaven and the eyes of men. We are looked upon as fools, for Christ's sake....
> (1 *Corinthians* 4.9, translated by J.B. Phillips)

On a practical level, gladiator's blood was thought to have other useful properties, such as curing epilepsy. It also formed part of an ancient marriage ritual whose true meaning had been lost over the centuries: the bride's hair was parted by the point of a spear that had been stuck into a dead gladiator. Whether the spear actually had human blood on it at the time is not clear. The writer Festus had several explanations for the ritual, the first one advancing the gladiator connection:

> The head of the bride used to be dressed with the celibate spear which had been planted in the body of a gladiator thrown aside and killed, so that in the same way the spear had been joined with the gladiator's body, the bride would be joined with her husband.... (Festus 55.3)

Plutarch was more puzzled as to the origin of the custom: 'Why do they part the hair of brides with the point of a spear?' According to Pliny the Elder, a spear that had killed had the power of a charm or talisman, symbolising new life (as a reversal of its power to take life) and therefore guarding against difficulties in labour and childbirth:

> It is said that difficult labour ends in delivery at once, if over the house where is the lying-in woman there be thrown a stone or a missile that has killed with one stroke three living creatures – a human being, a boar and a bear. A successful result is more likely if a light-

cavalry spear is used, pulled out from a human body without the ground being touched (…*evulsa corpori hominis, si terram non attigerit*). (Pliny, *Historia Naturalis* 28.33–34)

So, when people looked at gladiators, they were seeing a complicated picture, not just purveyors of raw, animalistic aggression, masculine strength, and unchecked sexuality, but also the epitome of despair and hopelessness, despised untouchables, yet bringers of cures for some ills at least.

The story of the emperor's wife who fell for a gladiator may be nothing but fantasy, or it may have elements of truth, now long since indistinguishable from the fictions. Even if the rumours were true, Faustina was not the only empress to succumb to the attractions of the gladiator; Messalina, the nymphomaniac third wife of the emperor Claudius, certainly did have sexual relations with one gladiator at least, according to Cassius Dio. This particular paramour was called Sabinus, the former prefect of Claudius' German bodyguard, and he had been defeated in the arena. Claudius and the rest of the spectators were eager to see him die in gladiatorial combat, but Messalina successfully pleaded with Claudius for Sabinus' life to be spared. Messalina is not a typical illustration of the sexual magnetism of gladiators, since she was completely undiscriminating in her choice of lovers, and even had her own well-used cubicle in a brothel. And it looks like Sabinus was 'volunteered' for the arena, possibly by the jealous Claudius.

Predictably, the unidentified rich woman whose remains were found in the gladiator barracks at Pompeii has been labelled as the sort of upperclass Roman matron who preferred the rough sexual favours of gladiators. This find very conveniently seemed to confirm the cliché of the lady descending into the gutter (in this case the barracks) in search of sexual satisfaction.

The circumstantial evidence seems damning: the skeleton of a woman bedecked with fine jewellery, including an emerald necklace, gold armbands, rings, jewel casket containing a cameo, was found in a small cell with the skeletons of at least 18 men. The cell had also been used to store weapons and other gladiatorial equipment, which were found wrapped in fine cloth in wooden boxes. But was this really a gladiator 'groupie'? A few of the men could not have escaped even if there had been a way to avoid the choking rain of ash – they were in leg-irons, trapped in the barrack-room that would become their tomb. It seems an odd kind of orgy, conducted in ever-worsening conditions – near darkness under the inescapable cloud of ash, pumice bombardment, noxious fumes and rapidly reducing oxygen levels would not have contributed to a party atmosphere.

The rich woman was found entwined with what has been thought to be her gladiator lover of the moment, as if we imagine they were caught in the act as the lava burst through the door. In fact, all of the occupants of that cell died either at the point when the roof collapsed under the weight of the ash and pumice deposits raining down on it for hour after hour, or later, when the volcano's superheated pyroclastic flow of ash and gases surged over the city, annihilating any remaining survivors.

What she was doing at the barracks in the first place we shall never know; the most likely scenario is that she was fleeing from the city with at least one other person, and that because they were beaten down by a solid rain of pumice and overwhelmed by the blizzard of sodden ash-flakes that turned to grey soup in the lungs, they sought shelter in the nearest building: the *quadriporticus* behind the Large Theatre that had been converted into gladiatorial barracks after the earthquake of AD 62.

The total darkness that settled over the city, the constant noise of explosions, and the unremitting hailstorm of rock triggered a terrible panic, and when people became aware that it was falling and settling at a rate of about five to six inches an hour without abating, that would have been enough to make any remaining inhabitants run for their lives.

The modern world's first assumption that this notorious discovery was an adulterous assignation between a wealthy Roman matron and her bit of gladiatorial rough trade, fitted the stereotype we hold so dear, that of the prodigious sexuality of the gladiator. The fact that even today the image of the gladiator exudes sexual as well as physical menace speaks volumes for the persistence of his reputation as nocturnal athlete as well as bloody killer. For the Romans too, the gladiator carried a powerful sexual charge, amplified by his close acquaintance with sudden and violent death. Here we part company with the ancient spectators; for this element of the thrill, most of us have no direct experience to draw upon, and even if we did, the direct link between eroticism and violence has been intentionally weakened by the dominant culture of the West. It is now a subtext, lurking underneath the mass-produced violence of the blockbuster movie.

Modern society has had to find its surrogate gladiators in unlikely places; with the absolute prohibition on actual bloodshed that we take as a mark of civilisation, the CGI experts and software producers have stepped forward with cyber-reality in which no-one is harmed, but the player's adrenaline is still boosted by the gratuitous use of prodigious amounts of blood, gore, and astounding physical violence dealt out by and to unlimited protagonists.

The sword is still what they love, but the violence it represents has become dislocated from any redeeming exemplary quality, let alone any erotic charge. Unlike the Romans, we tend to glorify physical aggression for its own sake, finding no valuable lessons for society within the framework of single combat, with the arguable exception of the soldier's conduct on the battlefield. Even there, the virtuous emphasis tends to rest on heroic acts of rescue rather than on successful enemy engagements.

The gladiator is, as ever, exiled to the boundaries of polite society.

MEMENTO MORI

The whole point of professional gladiators was that they should not, and usually did not, fear death. Yet we will never recover the thoughts and emotions of the gladiator just before he walks out onto the sand. As Dr John Morris once said, we have an archaeology of things, not of thoughts.

The things which Romans had in their homes to remind them of the spectacles often surface as archaeological finds, such as the souvenir oil-lamps, glassware, vases, bone- and ivory-handled folding knives, amulets and votive objects in the shape of swords, intaglio and metal rings, terracotta figures, mosaics – all of them depicting elements of the arena or gladiators in various poses, but particularly fighting, falling, pleading for *missio* at the moment of truth (*115, 116* and *colour plate 33*). We would find it strange to decorate our homes with images of death, slaughter and the dramas leading up to it, yet the Romans obviously treasured these items, to judge from the contexts in which they were found.

These are not isolated finds; the Roman world was full of these gladiator-themed products. Bearing in mind the contempt in which gladiators were held socially, it seems odd that houseroom was given to so many items connected with the arena. So often do these items occur in the archaeological record that it is hard to escape the conclusion that gladiatorial souvenirs, trinkets and arena-themed decorations were as common in everyday Roman life as *Star Wars*, Manchester United, WWF and TV spin-offs are today. Pliny mentions the case of a freedman of Nero who, when putting on a gladiatorial show at Antium, arranged for paintings containing lifelike portraits of all the gladiators to be displayed in the public porticoes. He goes on to say that portraits of gladiators have for generations held the public's interest, and that it was Gaius Terentius Lucanus who first commissioned pictures of gladiator shows and then had them publicly exhibited. Given the fact that these pictures would need to be portable, it seems likely they were painted, as was Nero's giant 120ft portrait, on linen,

115 Colchester vase. *Exploded view: N. Nethercoat*

116 Small clay figure, souvenir of the *munera*

using the four main pigments, white, yellow, red, and black. These were the cultural forerunners of our billboards and hoardings, plastered with pictures of Beckham.

To get an idea of the scale and degree of celebrity enjoyed by the most famous gladiators, we need only turn to one specific product, and that is glassware. Very few named gladiators are known to history, and where they are identified, it is often because they appear on a particular type of blue-green mould-blown glass beaker, which appeared in the western provinces towards the end of the first century AD. Research carried out by Roman glass experts, Mark Taylor and David Hill, has established that this drinking vessel design was so popular that it has left more surviving examples (mainly fragmentary) than any other type of circus beaker. In addition, the popularity of this mass-produced item was confirmed by the existence of 'pirated' poor imitations.

There are about eight or nine different types of beaker, and the same 15 or so gladiator names, stage names rather than real names, crop up again and again on them. Four pairs of these are particularly well represented, and they are obviously big stars of the arena from Italy, renowned throughout the empire. The names on the glass cups help to date them very precisely, something quite unusual in archaeological terms (*117*).

At least three of these names were so famous that they are mentioned in Roman literature, one, Spiculus (Spike or Sting), a *murmillo*, being a favourite of Nero, on whom he bestowed riches, property and land. It was that very same Spiculus who was called for by Nero, in vain, when, in his last desperate hours, the emperor could not summon the courage to end his own life.

Of the rest of the pairs, Calamus (Arrow), Cocumbus and Petraites (The Rock), were also *murmillones*, (though Cocumbus may be a misreading, and thus a repeat of Columbus), and their opponents, Columbus (Dove), Hories, Prudes (Careful) and Proculus (Hammer), were *thraeces*. Columbus, Proculus and Petraites were especially well-known stars in Italy, and the glass cups apparently celebrate their most memorable fights in Rome. Petraites was such a household name that he got a mention in the 'Trimalchio's Feast' section of Petronius' *Satyricon*, when Trimalchio boasted of the heavy cups he owned depicting fights between Hermeros and Petraites.

Some of these famous names even appear in graffiti scrawled on the walls of Pompeii. The distribution of the cups is empire-wide, and as they are often found at the site of military settlements in the provinces, no doubt they were personal souvenirs of soldiers reminding them of combats they had actually seen and the stars they supported.

Taking sponsorship a stage further than is customary nowadays, there is evidence that army units themselves owned troupes of gladiators; an inscription from the lower Rhine mentions a gladiator named Ursarius of the XXXth legion. The link between gladiators and the military is a strong one. For example, one of the Colchester beakers depicting gladiatorial combat names a *retiarius* as

117 Exploded view of 'gladiator' glass beaker. *Reproduced with kind permission of Roman glass specialists David Hill and Mark Taylor*

Valentinus of the XXXth legion. Since this legion was based at Xanten on the Rhine, both the gladiator Valentinus and the cup, or just the cup, must have been taken to Colchester. Either way, the military connection is established beyond doubt. There is no modern parallel for this type of military patronage, but when we remember that the arenas sprang up in the provinces to bolster and cultivate Roman identity, it is perfectly logical that the soldiers serving in far-flung regions would want their own amphitheatre, their little bit of Rome. These provincial amphitheatres often were associated with the military fortresses that first enforced the *imperium*. For soldiers with spare cash, and very little to spend it on out in the sticks, the investment of a *familia gladiatoria* must have been an attractive proposition, a project to pass the time, have a bet on, and stave off homesickness. Above all, it would have demonstrated how men should die in the service of Rome, whether in the field or the arena. For the audience, it would be a salutary lesson in the implacability of the Roman character.

To take our culture with us these days requires only small handheld objects like CDs, radios, MP3s and cellphones. Yet the fact that it can be so easily transported exposes it to the diluting effect of globalisation, until we begin to wonder exactly what our culture consists of – not the sort of question that would even have occurred to the Romans.

But we still borrow from them, sometimes in unexpected ways. This is illustrated in the recent case of an unpleasant 'gladiator' game in a young offenders' institution, where officers deliberately paired prisoners in cells in the hope of provoking assaults, (one big, one small, one black, one white) and then placed bets on how long it would take before an attack was made by one or the other. This was actually called 'the gladiator game' by inmates and officers alike. It is interesting that the gladiator is thought to be the best vehicle for something so dishonourable; this is just another way in which the modern world has hijacked the image of the gladiator. Almost everything that is commonly assumed about the gladiator today comes from two main sources, and it is fortunate that they both have the power to transcend our assumptions. I refer of course to the films, *Spartacus* and *Gladiator*, both of which have contributed immensely to the continued interest in the arena. Certainly, there are inaccuracies in both, but neither claimed to be an historical dissertation. They have done a service by rejuvenating the flagging interest in the classical world, and in the case of *Gladiator*, by reviving the previously unpopular epic. In the adulation that Russell Crowe received from both men and women for his role as the hero Maximus, is it reasonable to suggest that it has faint parallels with the adulation of the authentic gladiator?

Just as we have DVDs, magazines,   s and posters of great sporting events to remind us of glorious victories (Bobby Moore holding the World Cup aloft in that famous 1966 pose springs to mind), so too must the mobile population of the Roman empire have spread its mementoes of the giants of the arena across the provinces. We can replay the crucial moments, the exciting twists and turns of fate that make spectating so riveting; equally, the Romans had their own visual aids, intricate mosaics depicting bout after bout, victory palm-decorated samian ware for the table, gladiator-clad oil-lamps of bronze, terracotta, silver and bronze rings with incised palm motifs .... Who is to say that they were less effective at recalling the atmosphere of a show than our own coldly efficient media?

TURPISSIMUM AUCTORAMENTUM

The terrible solemnity of the oath by which a gladiator bound himself to his profession has no equivalent in our world. It implies a belief that to desecrate the oath by breaking the terms of its contract was to bring down the worst of fates, dishonour and damnation of memory, upon oneself. There was nothing given in return, no balancing benefit if the oath were upheld, only the satisfaction of honour itself. By contrast, the soldier's oath, the *devotio*, at least brought personal glory and reputation as part of its fulfilment. The gladiator who bound himself by the oath, at the start of his new life, however long or short that might be, had no choice but to honour it; Seneca calls the oath ' the most loathsome of contracts', *turpissimum auctoramentum*, and 'the most powerful bond', *maximum vinculum*. The oath, *sacramentum*, became a binding contract, *auctoramentum gladiatorum*, which the gladiator placed upon himself.

He was an outsider in every sense of the word, inhabiting the very edges of society, with only his fellow gladiators for company. This isolation from the respectable every day world, as if he were diseased, made him even more feared and avoided. He was a practitioner of an occupation so vile that to be called a gladiator (as Mark Antony was by Caesar), was an actual insult. Yet people were ambivalent in their attitudes to gladiators – they loved what they despised, they glorified what disgusted them, to paraphrase Tertullian. Nowhere is the mechanism by which this occurs seen more clearly than in the account of Saint Augustine's pupil, Alypius:

> He went to Rome ahead of me to study law and there, strange to relate, he became obsessed with an extraordinary craving for gladiatorial shows. At first he detested these displays and refused to attend them. But one day during the season for this cruel and bloodthirsty sport he happened to meet some friends and fellow-students returning from their dinner. In a friendly way they brushed aside his resistance and his stubborn protests and carried him off to the arena.
>
> 'You may drag me there bodily,' he protested, 'but do you imagine that you can make me watch the show and give my mind to it? I shall be there, but it will be just as if I were not present, and I shall prove myself stronger than you or the games.'
>
> He did not manage to deter them by what he said, and perhaps the very reason why they took him with them was to discover whether he would be as good as his word. When they arrived at the arena, the place was seething with the lust for cruelty. They found seats as

> best they could and Alypius shut his eyes tightly, determined to have nothing to do with these atrocities. If only he had closed his ears as well! For an incident in the fight drew a great roar from the crowd, and this thrilled him so deeply that he could not contain his curiosity. Whatever had caused the uproar, he was confident that, if he saw it, he would find it repulsive and remain master of himself. So he opened his eyes, and his soul was stabbed with a wound more deadly than any which the gladiator, whom he was so anxious to see, had received in his body. He fell, and fell more pitifully than the man whose fall had drawn the roar of excitement from the crowd. The din had pierced his ears and forced him to open his eyes, laying his soul open to receive the wound which struck it down...When he saw the blood, it was as though he had drunk a deep draught of savage passion. Instead of turning away, he fixed his eyes upon the scene and drank in all its frenzy, unaware of what he was doing. He revelled in the wickedness of the fighting and was drunk with the fascination of bloodshed. He was no longer the man who had come to the arena, but simply one of the crowd which he had joined, a fit companion for the friends who had brought him.
>
> Need I say more? He watched and cheered and grew hot with excitement, and when he left the arena, he carried with him a diseased mind which would leave him no peace until he came back again....
>
> (St Augustine, *Confessiones* VI.8)

In the case of the gladiator, there is no question about his *infamia*, his social degradation. But yet he was the keeper of his own honour, unlike the unfortunate Alypius, Augustine's pupil. Alypius was unable to help himself, and his position was one of uncontrollable appetites and emotions; he could not resist his own weakness. After all, he had been forewarned about the dangers of getting sucked into that strange bloody world. He knew what to expect, but was unable to stop himself. By contrast, the German prisoners of war, in the following passage, who probably weren't even proper gladiators, but *noxii* who were condemned *ad bestias*, found the strength of mind in terrible circumstances to free themselves and choose the time and place of their own deaths, rather than be torn apart for entertainment. They showed that they were not under the fear of death, whereas Alypius was in thrall to the very sound and sight of it. Seneca talks admiringly of the bravery of the Germans, as well he might; it was a feat he would have been glad to emulate in their position. This extraordinary switching of positions gives the condemned, the lost and the disgraced the opportunity to overcome in the midst of their despair in a way that mere onlookers can never do:

> There is no reason why you should think that only famous men have had the strength necessary to break the chains of human bondage.... Men of the lowliest rank have escaped to safety from their own heroic impulse. Even when they were not allowed to die at a time convenient to them, even when they were not allowed a real choice in the means of their death, they snatched whatever opportunity was at hand and by sheer force made for themselves lethal weapons from objects which are not by nature harmful. Recently, for example, a German who was destined to be one of the wild animal fighters at a public

entertainment was preparing for the morning show. He withdrew from the rest for a moment, to relieve himself (he was given no other opportunity to withdraw without a guard). There, in the toilet area he found a wooden stick with a sponge attached to the end (it was used for wiping away the excrement).

He stuffed the whole thing down his throat and choked to death.... Though apparently without any resources he devised both a method and a means of death. From his example you, too, can learn that the only thing that makes us hesitate to die is the lack of will... Recently, again, when a man was being carted off under close guard to the morning show, he pretended to not his head in sleep. Then he lowered his head until he had stuck it between the spokes of the cartwheel, and remained calmly in his seat until his neck was broken by the turning wheel. And so, he used the very vehicle which was carrying him to escape it.'

(Seneca, *Epistulae* 70.19-21,23)

The contrast between St Augustine's pupil, Alypius, powerless to prevent his own mental slavery, and the German prisoners, who took the only way out to freedom via self-inflicted physical death, could not be greater. Alypius' downfall came in through his ears; the roar of the crowd was irresistible. Anyone who has been in a large audience in a stadium knows the intoxicating feeling of being part of something greater than the self that thunderous cheering *en masse* can induce. It is clear that the Romans understood only too well that the power of the spectacle was experienced not only with the eyes, and that the fear of death and the love of death were two sides of the same coin needed to pay the ferryman. This is not to suggest that the Roman spectators had some special insight into the games. Doubtless there were plenty of people who regarded it as crude entertainment, a diversion, and no more than that, just as there are audiences now who see all forms of dramatic presentation, from Shakespeare to soap, as part of the same utilitarian package, for consumption and amusement, not moral uplift. However, it is very plain that the emotional transaction between gladiator and spectator exploits far more than a desire to entertain and be entertained, and that is as true today as it was at the height of the Colosseum's fame.

The decline of the gladiatorial spectacle was gradual, influenced by the immense financial burdens it placed on the state, and also by the changing climate of opinion over the centuries, as the Christian perspective took hold under the emperor Constantine. First to go were actors, excommunicated in AD 314 after bishops campaigned against their lewd performances. Gladiators carried on, although Constantine abolished the penalty of sending criminals to the arena in AD 325. This was the beginning of the end, however, and in AD 404 the emperor Honorius banned gladiatorial spectacles altogether. The last recorded show in the Colosseum took place in AD 523, but it starred only beasts, not humans.

8

GLADIATORS IN THE TWENTY-FIRST CENTURY: RECONSTRUCTING THE SPECTACLE

The first thing to be said about any modern attempt at recreating a spectacle is that the motive for doing it at all must be very clearly defined right from the start because the subject matter is very delicate. There is a very fine line to tread between authenticity and bad taste, particularly when the subject of the recreation is bloody murder, whichever way you look at it.

The recreated event in question, namely the gladiatorial games as seen at the London amphitheatre, *c.*AD 90, aims to follow in the footsteps of games over 1900 years old; obviously, no-one can know what the experience of attending those games was like, and because the spectators cannot be made to order, the sensibilities of a twenty-first century audience have to be accommodated, because in one important respect, the shows then and now have the same challenge: to attract and to keep the attention of the audience.

It goes without saying that killing anything is out of the question, and so it should be.

However, if that leg of the show is kicked away, what remains but a ghastly parody? How is it possible to compromise on the essential ingredient of any self-respecting gladiatorial show, *i.e.* blood?

This is the true challenge, but it becomes easier when it is remembered that the reaction of the spectators is all; if they can be brought to a state of willing disbelief, then the rest is comparatively easy. More than any other type of re-enactment, the gladiator show depends utterly on its audience, and there is a symbiotic exchange between performers and crowd, while the spectacle unrolls itself. The spectators have to take part, just as their counterparts did, 2000 years ago.

THE 'GLADIATOR' EFFECT: TO WIN THE CROWD

Gladiators started to appear all over Europe in the wake of Sir Ridley Scott's epic. A chord was struck with the viewing public, who found that they had been transported back to second century AD Rome without the aid of a time machine. The film was the first to tackle a Roman theme for 35 years, and it succeeded spectacularly, to use an entirely appropriate word. Suddenly, gladiator fever was rife in the province of Britannia once more.

Societies attempting to recreate history, whether it takes place on or off the battlefield, have to ask themselves what response they are looking for in the target audience. Most re-enactment groups are striving to recreate an authenticity of period that enables the audience, however large or small it might be, to step back into the past. This is where the recreation of gladiatorial spectacle really comes into its own. For an authentic taste of the arena, the spectators are at the heart of the matter; they drive the event forward, and therefore their interest and engagement is the engine for the entire event. Moreover, this seemed to be an ideal format for an informal experiment in human nature. Therefore, when the Museum of London under the leadership of Simon Thurley approached Britannia with a view to providing two gladiatorial *spectacula*, the only possible response was eager acceptance. The events would be in celebration of the Museum's 25th birthday, and to coincide with the opening of the new viewing gallery for the original London amphitheatrical remains, several feet below ground level at the Guildhall, where a shrine to one of the gladiator's favourite deities, Hercules, had been found in 1988, at the entrance to the arena. As a bonus, the remains of the 'gladiatrix' found at Southwark were receiving interest, and it seemed the time was ripe to bring gladiators back to Londinium.

AN AMPHITHEATRE IN THE GUILDHALL YARD

The first decision to be made in recreating this kind of spectacle is how far to go in bringing authenticity to an ancient entertainment whose central element was the unavoidably deliberate bloodshed. The decision was taken that the integrity of the original events that occurred at the Guildhall in the middle to late first century AD should be respected; otherwise, the exercise was a pointless reconfiguration of history.

Two approaches were broadly possible; one would have to take what was termed the 'Carry on Cleo' route, and ignore the serious ritual aspects in favour of broadbrush parody, relying on exaggerated fake violence to signal the underlying pacific intentions of the show, so as not to upset modern sensibilities; the other would seek to create the same atmosphere that would have been generated at the original shows by means of realistic portrayal of death. Disclaimers would be necessary to ensure that everyone was aware that, although it was not real, we would be seeking a real response, with all the potential negative audience reaction that might entail.

On the history side of things, the overall time period of the portrayal had to be carefully considered; a British based society such as Britannia would be best placed to recreate the dynamic Flavian period of the late first and early second centuries when so much of Londinium was still in the making. The context of these games could not possibly put them at the heart of the empire; rather, it was a challenge to envisage what a province like Britannia might have had in the way of spectacle at that time, given that resources were much more limited, climate was less than kind, and certainly not Mediterranean. In addition, visits from any passing imperial dignitary, let alone the emperor, were few and far between.

The reign of Domitian was settled on, partly because that coincided with a fresh building phase of the London amphitheatre, and partly because by that time, the gladiatorial categories and the conventions of the arena were well known cultural exports disseminated throughout the empire. Hundreds of amphitheatres across Europe and North Africa recreated in lesser scale what the Colosseum achieved at Rome. The souvenirs, the armour and weapons, the written sources – all have rich seams deposited at about this time. In short, the public would be given the 'archetypal Roman gladiators' they would expect to see. The essence of gladiators, after all, is the opposite of dry history, so pleasing the twenty-first-century mob was the primary aim.

The plan was to try to present a display of gladiators much as they would have been shown at the London amphitheatre, but more than that, to put the games into an authentic framework, relying on written reports of the programme of events to place the spectacle before the crowd in its entirety; the idea was not just to present a few gladiators fighting, but to give the audience the unsettling feeling that for a moment, time might have slipped. That, after all, is what motivates people to visit ancient sites, to read history and immerse themselves in the fine detail. I do not believe they act out of simple self-improvement, to acquire historical knowledge for its own sake, although that is a welcome side effect; I believe they are seeking to confront the truths of the past in order to feel the closeness of the long dead. If that sounds strange, it is just another way of saying that because we are human we are always interested in other humans, dead or alive. The Romans hold great fascination for the people of this island; we know we were conquered, but we don't feel as if we were. We look around for traces of the people who lived here in order to see how much like us they were. The vehicle of the games was an ideal opportunity to see how much like the Romans we really are.

Preparing the overall design, a provincial look was required, and gladiators in plainer armour (colour plate 32) that had been subject to constant use, wear and repair in the very unforgiving climate of Britain. Not the finely embossed and polished armour of the examples found in Pompeii for the *familiae gladiatoriae* that travelled round the cold and rainy province, working the circuit and getting short-notice contracts; this called for the battered, serviceable and dignified look of the Hawkedon helmet, with the idea that no doubt, once in a blue moon, the stars of the gladiatorial world might fetch up on these shores, and fortunate souls would catch their performances and remember them for the rest of their lives – but less stellar gladiators would be the regular entertainment, the reliable sign of fully paid-up Roman citizenship.

Fabrics were carefully chosen to reflect this approach; vegetable dyed wools and linens were used, the idea of using exotic animal pelts like leopard and lion were rejected as unrealistic, and not just for the avoidance of controversy. Where required indigenous looking furs and pelts from sources such as antique shops were used.

Damaged armour was repaired after each show, in the manner that many original examples had been in a metal-poor pre-industrial society, with whatever authentic materials (rivets and copper alloy patches) could be used.

Despite the less forgiving climate of Britain compared to Rome or its Mediterranean environs, the indications are that the climate was slightly warmer, so wherever possible the principle of exposed flesh and partial armouring was retained to re-enforce the image of the gladiator. Early attempts of combining full wool tunics and long breeches with many types of gladiatorial armour just did not sit well presentationally, or indeed reflect any known representations of the genre in Britain or abroad.

Looking at the show as a whole, not just the gladiators, it was essential to have an infrastructure in place, just as the original would have done. The London amphitheatre might not have been built in magnificent stone (its later incarnation, after the early first century fire that destroyed it, was timber and stone), but it was an imposing structure, fully capable of housing several thousand people at its height. To recreate that space, bleachers were laid on in the large open expanse of the Guildhall, enough to seat 1200 spectators per show, with further space for standing room only tickets. The elliptical shape of the arena was impossible to create with bleachers, but the key point was that the seating should be in the round.

An amphitheatre is nothing else but a fully enclosed arena (*118*). The experience of the audience would stand or fall on their sense of being focused on the arena; that could only happen if the spectators surrounded the event. Just as with bullfighting, whatever might be thought of the animal welfare issue, the audience needs to be conscious of itself. So much rides on the responses of the crowd, that quite literally the show cannot proceed if they are not fully able to function as a body. For that to happen, they must see and be seen. They need to be able to see what is going on in the arena without distraction or impediment, and equally, they have to be aware of each other. Nothing contributes to an authentic festival atmosphere more than the sense that people have come in the expectation of amusement and entertainment in the company of their peers. It's reminiscent of Saturday afternoon football, but with ritual elements that have

118 A small provincial amphitheatre, typical of those found in Britain. *Reproduced courtesy of The Lunt Roman Fort, Baginton*

disappeared from our public lives. So the tiers of wooden seating go a long way towards achieving the very first goal of any recreation of a spectacle—the audience's sense of itself was vitally important to the success of the enterprise (*119* and *120*).

Next, the set dressing needs to convey the spectrum of activities that would have been taking place at the amphitheatre. A team of *libitinarii* had the responsibility for making sure that everything in the arena was in order, from the flooring (unfortunately, sand coloured matting was the closest central London could get to the sand of the arena), to the clearance of debris (shields shattering, swords snapping, blood flowing), and the supply of clean water for the gladiators between bouts.

In addition, once the show was under way, theirs would be the responsibility for clearing the human debris, stretchering off the dead and injured gladiators. They were under the control of the 'referee', the *summa rudis*, with his staff of authority, the official whose job it is to ensure the smooth running of the combats, to judge when the fight should be temporarily halted if equipment comes adrift, or a gladiator fails to observe the procedures of the arena, such as deferring to the editor in the question of whether the defeated opponent should be despatched. He has a second, the *secunda rudis*, because it is sometimes hard

119 Audience participation at a modern re-enactment event is vital. *Reconstruction: Britannia, Dr Simon Thurley and the Museum of London. Photograph: Fraser Gray*

120 The Guildhall yard played host to over 6,000 strong audiences in its first gladiatorial games in over 1600 years. Here, the crowd shows its support for a beaten gladiator by much hand-waving and chants of '*mitte!*' *Reconstruction: Britannia, Dr Simon Thurley and the Museum of London. Photograph: Fraser Gray*

work watching everything that goes on, and keeping on top of the fast moving combat.

Other essential ingredients for the right atmosphere include the arena musicians (*121*). No water-organ here, this was just the province of Britannia, after all, but nevertheless, each bout was announced by the *tibia* and *tubae*; of course, the *pompa* which preceded the show was headed by an array of musicians. It is vital to have all of the sensory prompts in place, and none more so than those of the ear. One of the most moving moments of the spectacle came when the *tubae* blared out over the city of London. We later heard from many members of the audience purchasing last minute tickets that they had felt almost summoned to investigate from as far away as Holborn and the Bank of England by the eerie and poignant call of the *tubae* and the sound of 1500 people shouting for blood, sounds last heard over 1600 years ago. When the roars of the crowd as they got into the spirit of the enterprise were added to this historical cocktail, it was, shameful to admit, curiously addictive for the performers. When the stamping of

121 A re-enactment of the games isn't just about the gladiators. Musicians, priestesses and an imperial party all add to the spectacle. *Reconstruction*: *Britannia, David and Valerie Marshall, Lee Gillett* (Praecones Britanniae). *Photograph: Fraser Gray*

thousands of feet on the wood of the bleachers started up, the thunder recalled Oliver Reed's ecstatic comparison with the god of storms in the film *Gladiator*, the sound rising over the arena and making hairs stand up on the backs of many necks.

There is no point in denying it; it had a naked power, and the gladiators responded to that. The audience was able to look around and be transported, if they wished – priestesses sat in reserved places, having presided over dedications to Nemesis Fortuna Londoniensis, ritual figures of Charun and Mercury waited in the shadows with mallet and hot iron, traders hawked trinkets around the amphitheatre, souvenir *tesserae*, amulets, wooden swords for children, rose petals for those wishing to express their appreciation of particular fighters, and prostitutes and beggars for local colour. Over all wafted the spicy pungency of Roman sausages and flat breads for those in the audience who needed to keep their strength up for the afternoon show. Between shows, street music floated over the scene, the crowds lingered, and it was suddenly very easy to conjure up Roman Londinium.

A QUESTION OF BLOOD

The real dilemma of the modern reconstruction of gladiators is whether to show blood. As the decision had been taken to stay as close to the original as possible, the delivery of what would amount to copious quantities of blood was a technical issue surmounted by behind the scenes special effects experts. The deal was that we would ask the spectators to believe what they saw only inasmuch as they were convinced by it; in return, they would have to accept that no attempt would be made to disguise the fact that the whole show was about killing. They would have to go away and ponder their motives and sensations afterwards, though it has to be said that very many people who were in those original audiences have reassured us that it was the right decision to take. No one likes to feel patronised, and there would have been a danger of parody or worse if the blood and killing had been replaced by something softer. In effect, we were inviting the audience to see what their personal reactions would have been if they had been present at the original Guildhall amphitheatre.

Despite the cultural conditioning that we all supposedly carry around, it appeared surprisingly easy for the audience to accept the bloodletting, and to go further by positively supporting it. The trick was not to overdo the blood; if too many throats are cut, albeit by the magic of special effects to pump the arterial blood over several feet if it calls for it, then the audience does seem to suffer a form of callousing of the sensitivity. The drama of the human struggle for survival, and its undoubted poignancy, is central to the arena performances. The blood is a way of emphasising both the depth of that drama, and that it is serious, not slapstick. It would be entirely undesirable to treat the project as a comedy. What we never lose sight of, particularly when performing at actual amphitheatres, is that countless people and animals died where we are just pretending.

If all of this sounds unduly pretentious, it is worth bearing in mind that analysis of this kind of event is bound to dwell on the dynamics of the visceral response. There is no point being coy about what is on offer; it is an attempt to elicit the same feelings as would have been experienced by our Roman counterparts. The arena provided a theatrical experience par excellence, but with depths of meaning that are lost on us. We are not Romans, but we are humans, as they were, and therefore we can get some way into the heart of the games. That is all we are claiming.

Looking around the amphitheatre during a particularly dramatic combat, which resulted in a gladiator's death, the shouting, screaming and stamping (*120*) was deafening. I personally felt I had stumbled upon some modern yet arcane equivalent of the anthropological discovery. It came to me then, watching the crowds pelting the unpopular winner with bottles (plastic, luckily), coins (copper, unfortunately), boiled sweets, and general fruit, that the human being acting collectively is not modern at all. Perhaps the parallels with football supporters are justified, but there was an edge to the calls for '*iugula*' that seemed to hark back to the original inhabitants of Londinium.

There was one further essential element, and that was the *editor*, the eminence paying for our entertainment. Although it was a departure from strictly accurate history, there was a need to have a presiding authority, and Domitian, the twisted and pathologically disturbed emperor fitted the bill. Encouraged in this choice by the client, Domitian has become a runaway success, a counterpoint to the drama of the arena. Purists may disapprove, but it was felt that since Domitian did travel around his empire, there was no reason to suppose he might not have called in on Britannia at some unrecorded point in time. It gave the perfect balance to the proceedings, and enabled an accompanying imperial guard of several tough Roman legionaries to impose the feeling that Rome was not so far away.

The emperor's entourage, his secretary, his wife, personal slaves with wine, fruit, peacock-feather fans – all were present. The *pulvinar*, the imperial box, was absolutely a prerequisite for Domitian's despotic tendencies to be showcased. It is impossible to act the mad, perverted tyrant when seated cheek by jowl with the plebs, modern or ancient. Distance is all. The emperor arrived by chariot; in other shows, he has since been conveyed by slave-borne litter. The important thing is that he should not walk very far. Once he is ensconced in the imperial box, the focus for the audience's entreaties is in place.

Because this was at heart a theatrical performance, toga-wearing masters of ceremonies playing local dignitaries were on hand to explain to the spectators their role in the afternoon's drama. Taking them through their basic Latin of '*iugula*', and '*mitte*', explaining the protocols, and delivering a dedication to the goddess Nemesis and to the emperor in Latin was another doorway opening into the past.

When the intention is to arouse the audience's atravistic tendencies by brutal slaughter, there has to be a format. In this case, as well as the fake blood convincingly delivered, there was the need to get the audience to support the gladiators. In the London of the first century, the crowd would have had the opportunity to peruse the programme and choose their favourites, to catch up with fighters they had seen before: we could not reproduce that. So, once again, in the service of a greater good, history and recreation briefly parted company. To induce the audience's sympathies and support, the gladiators were introduced as two troupes, not one, with the home team and its banner in opposition to the northern interlopers; again, comparisons with football supporters are unavoidable.

The gladiators themselves were given names and background stories, some were condemned criminals, some were army mutineers, some were captured beyond the borders of the Roman empire and were imported as commodities; some had simply enlisted to pay off debts or to grab glory in the arena. All were recruited in the knowledge that they were to go out and entertain and thrill, in equal measure, preferably without lifting the veil on the artifice. Interestingly, when something is simulated, it can often run into the same difficulties as the original article. This was definitely the case with the combats, as individual egos vied for the best audience reactions, as undoubtedly their Roman counterparts would have done.

For the manager, the difficulty was always in matching the pairs for the best possible fight. Combined with the need to spare more fighters than were killed, and plan the surprise pairings so that the audience got the variety it craved, it was a reflection, however pale, of the concerns of the *procurator familiae gladiatorium*. The rhythm of the show was all important, no embarrassing pauses or stumbles could be permitted.

On a technical note, fighting on sand in another arena recently, proved the thesis of Professor Grossschmidt in respect of the excessive overdevelopment of the musculature of the feet that inevitably comes with regular exercise on that surface. The entire troupe came home more exhausted than usual and with sore feet, and no doubt over time they would have developed the distinctive muscle bands and wear and tear associated with fighting on sand.

The feedback from the background stories from the public, in particular parents, teachers and children who were watching, was very positive, as it demonstrated that the show had helped to illustrate the bigger picture of not only how Rome functioned as a slave-based society and economy outside the arena, but how many people came to be standing in the sand in such a desperate and dramatic situation in the first place.

We had decided to introduce female gladiators for educational, as well as theatrical reasons; this became especially relevant when the announcement was made about the discovery and controversial pronouncement of the Southwark 'gladiatrix'.

London's appetite for gladiators showed itself to be as strong as ever when more than 6000 people came to watch the first Roman games to be staged (albeit re-enacted) for at least 1600 years in London. After the show, over-excited children were taking anything they could lay their hands on as souvenirs – bits of palm branches, matting, even shield fragments and pieces of the coloured sashes worn by the gladiators.

What started as an experiment has now become a regular fixture, and once again the *familia gladiatoria* plies its bloodstained trade round the province, proving that gladiator fever has never really gone away.

BIBLIOGRAPHY

ABBREVIATIONS

CIL *Corpus Inscriptionum Latinarum* (Berlin 1869-)
ILS *Inscriptions Latinae Selectae*, ed. H. Dessau (Berlin 1892-1914)
JRS *Journal of Roman Studies*
LCL Loeb Classical Library

ANCIENT TEXTS

Apuleius, *Metamorphoses*, otherwise known as *The Golden Ass*, trans. R.Graves, Penguin Books, London 1950

Athenaeus, *Deipnosophiston*, trans. G.B. Gulick, LCL, Harvard University Press, 1927-1941

St Augustine, *City of God*, trans. H. Bettenson, Penguin Books, London 1984

—, *Confessions*, trans. R.S. Pine-Coffin, Penguin Books, London 1961

Cicero, *Tusculanae Disputationes*, trans. J.E. King, LCL, Harvard University Press 1927

—, *De Officiis*, trans. W.Miller, LCL, Harvard University Press 1913

—, *Philippicae*, trans. C.A.Ker, LCL, Harvard University Press 1938

Cassius Dio, *Roman History*, trans. E. Cary, LCL, Harvard University Press 1914-1927

Herodotus, *The Histories*, trans. Aubrey de Selincourt 1954, rev. ed. J.M. Marincola Penguin Books, London 1996

Homer, *The Iliad*, trans. E.V.Rieu, Penguin Books, London 1950

—, *The Iliad: A New Prose Translation*, trans. M. Hammond, Penguin Books, London 1987

—, *The Odyssey*, trans. R. Fitzgerald, William Heinemann Ltd 1962

Horace, *Satires and Epistles*, trans. N. Rudd, Penguin Books, London 1973

Josephus, *The Jewish War*, trans. G.M. Williamson, rev. M. Smallwood, Penguin Books, London 1981

Juvenal and Persius, *Satires*, ed. and trans. S. Morton Braund, LCL, Harvard University Press 2004

Juvenal, *The Sixteen Satires*, trans. P. Green, Penguin Books, London 1998

Livy, *Ab Urbe Condita Libri* or *A History of Rome*, trans. H. Bettenson, Aubrey de Selincourt, Penguin Books, London

Martial, *Epigrams*, trans. D.R. Shackleton Bailey, LCL, Harvard University Press 2003

Petronius, *The Satyricon and The Fragments*, trans. J. Sullivan, Penguin Books, London 1965

Pliny the Elder, *Natural History: A Selection*, trans. J.F.Healy, Penguin Books, London 1991

Pliny the Younger, *Letters*, trans. B. Radice, Penguin Books, London 1969

Plutarch, *The Fall of the Roman Republic*, trans. R. Warner, Penguin Books, London 1958, rev. 1972

—, *Vitae*, trans. B. Perrin, LCL, Harvard University Press 1914-1926
Polybius, *Historiae*, trans. W.R. Paton, LCL, Harvard University Press 1922-1927
Scriptores Historiae Augustae, or *Lives of the Later Caesars*, trans. A. Birley, Penguin Books, London 1976
Seneca, *Moral Essays/Epistulae Morales*, trans. J.W. Basore, LCL, Harvard University Press 1928-1935
—, *Epistulae*, trans. R. Campbell, Penguin Books, London 1969
Strabo, *Geographica*, trans. H.L. Jones, LCL, Harvard University Press 1923-1932
Suetonius, *The Twelve Caesars*, trans. R. Graves, Penguin Books, London 1957, revised 1979
Tacitus, *The Annals of Imperial Rome*, trans. M.Grant, Penguin Books 1956, revised 1989
—, *Histories*, trans. C.H. Moore, LCL, Harvard University Press 1939
—, *The Agricola and The Germania*, trans. H. Mattingley, revised S.A. Handford, Penguin Books, London 1970
—, Tertullian, *De Spectaculis/On Spectacles*, trans. T.R.Glover, LCL, Harvard University Press 1931
Varro, *De Lingua Latina/On the Latin Language*, trans. R.G.Kent, LCL, Harvard University Press 1938
Vegetius, *Epitoma Rei Militaris/Epitome of Military Science,* trans. N.P. Milner Liverpool University Press 1993
Virgil, *The Aeneid*, trans. C. Day Lewis, World's Classics, Oxford University Press 1952

SECONDARY TEXTS

Adams, J.N., *The Latin Sexual Vocabulary* (Gerald Duckworth & Co. Ltd. 1982)
Adkins, Lesley and Roy A., *Dictionary of Roman Religion* (Facts on File Inc., New York 1996)
Aldrete, Gregory S., *Daily Life in the Roman City: Rome, Pompeii and Ostia* (Greenwood Publishing Group 2004)
Augenti, Domenico, *Spettacoli del Colosseo: nelle cronache degli antichi* (L'Erma di Bretschneider, Roma 2001)
Auguet, Roland, *Cruelty and Civilization: The Roman Games* (Routledge 1972)
Balsdon, J.P.V.D., *Life and Leisure in Ancient Rome* (Phoenix Press 1969)
Barton, Carlin A., *The Sorrows of the Ancient Romans: The Gladiator and the Monster* (Princeton University Press, third reprint 1996)
Beare, W., *The Roman Stage* (Methuen & Co. Ltd., London 1950)
Bishop, M.C. and Coulston, J.C.N., *Roman Military Equipment* (B.T. Batsford Ltd, London 1993)
Bomgardner, D.L., *The story of the Roman Amphitheatre* (Routledge 2002)
Boardman, John Griffin, Jasper and Murray, Oswyn, *The Oxford History of the Classical World* (Oxford University Press 1986)
Carcopino, J., *Daily Life in Ancient Rome* (Penguin Books, London 1991)
Connolly, Peter, *Greece and Rome at War* (Greenhill Books London 1998)
—, *Colosseum, Rome's Arena of Death* (BBC Books 2003)
Cruse, Audrey, *Roman Medicine* (Tempus Publishing Ltd 2004)
Duncan-Jones, Richard, *The Economy of the Roman Empire: Quantitative Studies* (Cambridge University Press 1974)
Freeman, Charles, *Egypt, Greece and Rome: Civilizations of the Ancient Mediterranean* (Oxford University Press 2004)
Futrell, Alison, *Blood in the arena: the spectacle of Roman power* (University of Texas Press 1997)
Gardner, Jane F., *Roman Myths* (British Museum Press 1993)
Grant, Michael, *Gladiators* (Weidenfeld and Nicolson, London 1967)
—, *The History of Rome* (Weidenfeld and Nicolson, London 1978)
—, *Myths of the Greeks and Romans* (Weidenfeld and Nicolson, London 1989)
Hopkins, K. *A World Full of Gods: Pagans, Jews and Christians in the Roman Empire* (Phoenix 1999)
Hopkins, Keith and Beard, Mary, *The Colosseum* (Profile Books 2005)
Jackson, Ralph *Doctors and Diseases in the Roman Empire* (British Museum Press 1988)

James, Dominic, *Romans and Christians* (Tempus Publishing Ltd 2002)
Janson, Tore *A Natural History of Latin,* English translation by Merethe Damsgard Sorensen and Nigel Vincent (Oxford University Press 2004)
Jones, A.H.M., *The Roman Economy: Studies in Ancient Economic and Administrative History* edited by P.A. Brunt (Oxford Basil Blackwell 1974)
Jones, Peter & Sidwell, Keith (eds), *The World of Rome* (Cambridge University Press 1997)
Junkelmann, Marcus, *Das Spiel mit dem Tod: So kampften Roms Gladiatoren* (Philipp Von Zabern 2000)
Kohne, Eckart & Ewigleben, Cornelia (eds), *Gladiators and Caesars,* English translation by Ralph Jackson (British Museum Press, October 2000)
Kyle, Donald G., *Spectacles of Death in Ancient Rome* (Routledge 1998)
La Regina, Adriano(ed.), *Sangue e Arena* (Electa, Roma 2001)
Leighton, Robert, *Tarquinia: An Etruscan City* (Gerald Duckworth & Co.Ltd 2004)
Mancioli, Danila, *Vita e Costumi dei Romani antichi: Giochi e Spettacoli* (Museo Della Civilta Romana, Edizioni Quasar di Severino Tognon, Roma 1987)
Mellersh, H.E.L., *Chronology of the Ancient World 10,000BC- AD 799* (Helicon 1976)
Museum Ephesos Publication, *Gladiatoren in Ephesos: Tod am Nachmittag* (Wien 2002)
Ogilvie, R.M. *The Romans and their Gods* (Pimlico 2000)
Paoli, Ugo Enrico, *Rome: Its People, Life and Customs* (first published as *Vita Romana* in 1940, English Language edition Bristol Classical Press 1999)
Plass, Paul, *The Game of Death in Ancient Rome: Arena Sport and Political Suicide* (University of Wisconsin Press, Madison, Wisconsin 1995)
Price, Simon and Kearns, Emily, (eds), *The Oxford Dictionary of Classical Myth & Religion* (Oxford University Press 2003)
Rajak, Tessa, *Josephus: The Historian and His Society* (Gerald Duckworth & Co. Ltd 1983)
Sabbatini Tumolesi, Patrizia, *Epigrafia anfitreale dell'Occidente Romano: 1. Roma* (Edizioni Quasar di Severino Tognon, Roma 1988)
Salisbury, Joyce E., *Perpetua's Passion: The Death and Memory of a young Roman Woman* (Routledge, New York 1997)
Sebesta, Judith Lynn & Bonfante, Larissa (eds) *The World of Roman Costume* (University of Wisconsin Press, Madison, Wisconsin 1994)
Sekunda, N. and Northwood, S. *Early Roman Armies* (Osprey – Men at Arms 282 1995)
Shelton, Jo-Ann, *As the Romans Did: A Sourcebook in Roman History* (Oxford University Press 1988)
Vismara, Cinzia, *Vita e Costumi dei Romani antichi: il supplizio come spettacolo* (Museo Della Civilta Romana, Edizioni Quasar di Severino Tognon, Roma 1990)
Webber, Christopher, *The Thracians 700 BC-AD 46* (Osprey Men-At-Arms 360 2001)
Wiedemann, Thomas, *Emperors and Gladiators* (Routledge 1992)
—, Greek and Roman Slavery (Routledge 1981 reprint 1983)
Winkler, Martin M., (ed.), *Gladiator: Film and History* (Blackwell Publishing, Oxford 2004)
Wiseman, T.P., *The Myths of Rome* (University of Exeter Press 2004)
Wistrand, Magnus, *Entertainment and Violence in Ancient Rome: The Attitudes of Roman Writers of the First Century AD* (Acta Universitas Gothoburgensis 1992)

PAPERS AND SPECIALIST MATERIAL

Antiquity Volume 62, Number 237, Dec 1988, Archaeology and the Etruscan Countryside: Graeme Barker (P 772-785) ISSN 0003-598X
Arma Volume 7 No.s 1 &2 1995 ISSN 0960-9172 (P13-17) The Sculpture of an Armoured Figure at Alba Iulia, Romania J.C.N. Coulston
British Museum Quarterly Volume XXXIII Number 3-4 A Roman Bronze Helmet from Hawkedon, Suffolk K.S. Painter 1969
Christie's Catalogues: The Art of Warfare The Axel Guttmann Collection Parts 1 & 2 6 November 2002 (Christies International Media Division 2002) www.christies.com

Current Archaeology (Number 186,Volume 16 No. 6 June 2003) *Gladiator's Cups* Jennifer Price and *Sex And the Cemetary; New Light on glass vessels in Romano-British Graves* Hilary Cool (Friary Press Dorchester)

Journal of Roman Military Equipment Studies Volume 1 1990 MC Bishop ISSN 0961-3684

Journal of Roman Military Equipment Studies Volume 11 Re-enactment As Research 2000 Edited by A.T. Croom & W.B. Griffiths ISSN 0961-3684

Royal Armouries Yearbook Volume 6 2001 (P186-189) Preliminary Thoughts on the Roman armour from Carlisle: Thom Richardson) ISSN 1366 3925

ARTICLES

Ancient Rome – where life was sheep: Crowds at the Colosseum were far more likely to see a farm animal put to death than a lion – or a Christian. Mary Beard *The Times Weekend Review* February 26 2005

Inmate died in a game of prison gladiators. Article by Crime Reporter Richard Edwards, *Evening Standard*, 3 March 2005

PICTURE CREDITS AND CONTACTS

Marcus Junkelmann (author of *Das Spiel mit dem Tod*) & in association with:
Rheinisches Landesmuseum Trier, Treves, Deutschland
Archäologoischer Park Carnuntum, Petronell, Niederösterreich
www.junkelmann.de

Etruscan Tomb Pictures: Misha Nedeljkovich
Associate Professor, College of Journalism and Mass Communication
The University of Oklahoma, 395 W. Lindsey Gaylord Hall 3520B
Norman, Oklahoma 73019-2051 USA

Sarcophagus information:
John-Michael H. Warner, Visual and Performing Arts
The University of Colorado, 1420 Austin Bluffs Parkway
Colorado Springs, CO 80933-7150 (719) 262-4062 (voicemail)
(719) 262-4066, fax)
jmwarner@uccs.edu

Retiarius image: Carolyn Wingfield (Curator)
Saffron Walden Museum (copyright holder)
Saffron Walden Museum, Museum Street, Saffron Walden
Essex CB10 1JL 01799 510333

Guttmann Collection Images: Christies www.christies.com
Christie's Images
1 Langley Lane, Vauxhall, London. SW8 1TJ
Tel: + 44 (0)20 7389 2420 Fax: + 44 (0)20 7582 5632

Additional Guttmann photographs: Guttmann Collection, Photograph © David S. Michaels
Legion Six Historical Foundation, Los Angeles, CA
www.legionsix.org

Piddington Knife:
Roy (& Liz) Friendship-Taylor M.Phil., MAAIS., AIFA
UNAS (Upper Nene Archaeological Society)
members.aol.comunarchsoc/unashome.htm
(Replica Piddington Knife Nodge Nolan)

Roman gladiator glass cup drawing and information (specialists in Roman glass and Roman glass reproduction)
Mark Taylor and David Hill
www.romanglassmakers.co.uk

Gladiator glass copyright: Vindolanda Trust, Chesterholm Museum, Bardon Mill, Hexham, Northumberland, NE47 7JN
Vindolanda Tel: 01434-344-277, Fax: 01434-344-060
www.vindolanda.com

Health Sciences Library, University of Virginia (Roman surgical instruments)
Joan Echtenkamp Klein, Assistant Director for Historical Collections and
Services, for kind permission to reproduce the images: jre@virginia.edu.

Colchester Castle Museum (Colchester Thracian fresco)
Colchester Museums, Museum Resource Centre,
14 Ryegate Road, Colchester, Essex, CO1 1YG
http://www.colchestermuseums.org.uk
Images: mei.boatman@colchester.gov.uk

Royal Armouries, Armouries Drive, Leeds LS10 1LT
(Manicae information and images)
http://www.royalarmouries.org/

Bullfight Image EPA
picture.purchase@epa-photos.com

Other images
www.pharospictures.co.uk

RECONSTRUCTION GROUPS FEATURED

Britannia first/second-century gladiatorial re-enactment and fourth/sixth-century AD combat
www.durolitum.co.uk

Matt Bunker (Medicus Matt – supplier of Roman surgical pictures).
ERA fifth/sixth-century living history and gladiatorial re-enactment and ancient
surgery displays. www.erauk.org

Ludus Gladiatorius is a group that seeks to recreate the professional gladiatorial games
and their history from AD 100-200. www.ludus.org.uk

OTHER RELEVANT SOCIETIES

The Ermine Street Guard: the first Roman re-enactment society founded in 1972
http://www.esg.ndirect.co.uk/

Legio XIV Gemina RMRS
http://www.romanarmy.net/

The Colchester Roman Society
http://www.romanauxilia.com/crswebsite/INDEX.htm

Cohors V Gallorum
http://www.quintagallorum.co.uk/

The Vicus
http://www.vicus.org.uk/

The Hoplite Association
http://www.hoplites.co.uk/

SUPPLIERS FEATURED

Nodge Nolan (replica Piddington knife and Roman accessories) nodge.nolan@breathe.com

Tim Noyes (specialist ancient blade maker) Heron Armoury: heronarmoury@btinternet.com

Time Tarts (Armour and *subligaculum*)
http://www.timetarts.co.uk/

Roy King (armour)
http://1454.itworkshop-nexus.net/royking/

Greaves and manica supplier
michael.hardy477@ntlworld.com

Roman military equipment reconstructed.
http://www.romanarmy.net/fabrica.htm

PLACES OF INTEREST

Roman Legionary Museum and Amphitheatre, Caerleon http://www.nmgw.ac.uk/www.php/rlm/

Museum of London (Information on London's Amphitheatre) http://www.museumoflondon.org.uk/

London's Guildhall (The site of London's Amphitheatre)
http://www.cityoflondon.gov.uk/Corporation/leisure_heritage/libraries_archives_museums_galleries/guildhall_art_gallery/amphitheatre.htm

The British Museum
http://www.thebritishmuseum.ac.uk/

Richborough Roman Fort (amphitheatre remains)
http://www.open-sandwich.co.uk/history/richborough/fort/

Flag Fen (Historical Centre, Bronze Age to Roman)
http://www.flagfen.com/

The Lunt Roman Fort and Gyrus
http://www.romans-in-britain.org.uk/ste_coventry_lunt_roman_fort.htm

HISTORICAL INTERPRETERS, EDUCATIONAL VISITS AND LECTURES

Ars Romana
ars-romana@ntlworld.com

Portals to the Past
IanThorulf@aol.com

John Waite
waite@romans14.freeserve.co.uk

Chester Roman Tours
http://www.roman-tours-chester.co.uk/tourists.htm

Nigel Mills – Roman small finds specialist
nigelmills@onetel.com

PUBLICATIONS

www.archaeology.co.uk
www.historytoday.com

ACKNOWLEDGEMENTS AND CREDITS

With thanks to: Saffron Walden Museum, Mike Bishop, Michael Hardy, Tim Noyes Julian Dendy (RMRS) Roy and Liz Friendship Taylor, Tony Wilmot (English Heritage), Nodge Nolan, Michael Hardy, and Charlotte Chipcase at Christies. Ted Batterham, Shiela Corr of History Today, Russell Thomas, Steve Rogers of *Skirmish*, Marcus Junkelmann, Matt Bunker, Graham Ashford, Misha Nedeljkovich, Joan Echtenkamp Klein, Mei Boatman, Dr Simon Thurley (English Heritage), Iain Bell, Steve & Jude Wade, Ian Weston, Sue English, John and Karen Naylor, Mark Taylor and David Hill, Simon Barnes, Paul Harston, Len Morgan, Steve Wagstaff, the staff of EUR (Rome), Gary Langford, Matt Shadrake, Chris Grocock and Sally Grainger, Derek and Maureen Clow, Graham and Judy Keene, Simone Olla, Mandy Turner and Ian Burridge, Bryan Lightbody, John Thompson and Jez Freeston.

INDEX